The American
LEONARDO

The American LEONARDO

A 20th-Century Tale of Obsession, Art and Money

JOHN BREWER

Constable • London

Constable & Robinson Ltd
3 The Lanchesters
162 Fulham Palace Road
London W6 9ER

www.constablerobinson.com

First published in the UK by Constable,
an imprint of Constable & Robinson Ltd, 2009

A copy of the British Library Cataloguing in Publication Data
is available from the British Library

ISBN: 978-1-84529-872-2

Contents

Acknowledgements

This book began life as a paper given to the Economics Department at the University of Bologna. Carlo Poni, running a seminar on the topic of trust, asked me to write a paper about trust and the art market. Though this paper has never seen the light of day (or more accurately was never published), I have to thank him for making me acquainted with the strange story of the Hahns and their version of *La Belle Ferronnière*.

This book would not have been possible without the archival materials that, when I began my researches, were all in private hands. I have to thank Frank Ruhemann for giving me access to his father's papers, as well as serving several very agreeable lunches and allowing me to share his study. Jacqueline Hahn showed me her surviving family papers as well as her photograph albums, and provided me with several long interviews that helped reconstruct the story. The van Dantzig family consented to have Mau van Dantzig's papers deposited in the library of the University of Amsterdam and Jack Chapman in Omaha Nebraska not only showed me much of his material on *La Belle*, but allowed me to examine the painting itself. In Kansas City, Ardis Glenn turned over her late husband's very considerable archive, as well as plying me with tea, cookies and sharp wit. I apologize for monopolizing her kitchen table for so long (reading the papers, not eating the cookies!) The Ruhemann archive is now being deposited at the Hamilton Kerr Institute, which is part of the Fitzwilliam Museum at the University of Cambridge; the van Dantzig papers are now with the Netherlands Institute for Art History.

One of my greatest debts is to John Wyver, the head of the production company, Illuminations. He made a documentary about the 1929 trial of *Hahn versus Duveen* in New York, and it was through him that I was able to contact Jacqueline Hahn. He has supported the project throughout, and we have shared many lunches discussing the art world in general and Duveen and the Hahns in particular. I have to thank my former student, friend and libertarian extraordinaire, Arthur Legger, for helping me track down the van Dantzig family, arranging the deposit of their archive, and translating much of the Dutch material, as well as sharing some excellent Dutch and Belgian beers. Gary and Loekie Schwartz were wonderful hosts in Amsterdam; Gary was kind enough to read drafts and spot a few howlers. Flaminia Genari Santori read drafts, offered advice (not always heeded) and gave of her enormous expertise on the twentieth-century art world. Other friends and colleagues who helped the project in many different ways include Cindy Weinstein, Matt Hunter, Malcolm Baker, David Bomford, Shelley Bennett, Andrew Wheatcroft, Simon Schama, Roy Ritchie, Karen Lang, Martin Kemp, Stephen Melville, Michael-Ann Holly, Frank Trentmann, Dick Kingsett, Meryle Secrest, Danny Miller and Arsineh Zagarian.

I would also like to thank the staff of the National Gallery Library, the Tate Gallery Library, the Huntington Library, the Getty

Acknowledgements

Research Institute, the Clark Institute library in Williamstown, Massachusetts, the British Library, the library of the University of Amsterdam, the Missouri Valley Special Collections in the Kansas City Public Library, the library and archive of the Nelson–Atkins Museum and the Dr Kenneth J. LaBudde Department of Special Collections at the University of Missouri, Kansas City.

Once again special thanks is due to my agent, Gill Coleridge, for her perseverance in getting this book published and her patience at reading its many incarnations and drafts. Thanks also to Leo Hollis for making working with an editor such pleasure. And, most of all, many thanks to Stella, Grace and Lorenzo, for their patience, forbearance and support.

This book is for two people who have shared so much of the Hahn saga with me: Alan, prince of lawyers, and Marcella, queen of parties.

List of Illustrations

The Hahn *La Belle Ferronnière*. © *Jack Chapman*.

Harry and Andrée Hahn on their wedding day, 1919. *Reproduced by kind permission of Jacqueline Hahn*.

The Magasin des Modes, Dinard. *Reproduced by kind permission of Jacqueline Hahn*.

Harry and Andrée Hahn, Kansas, 1929. *Reproduced by kind permission of Jacqueline Hahn*.

Bernard Berenson. © *Topham Picturepoint/Topfoto.co.uk* 0472049.

Sir Joseph Duveen. © *Bettman/Corbis* BE053710.

The Louvre's *La Belle Ferronnière*. © *Artmedia/HIP/Topfoto* hip0210396.

Experts gather to examine the Hahn *La Belle*. *London Illustrated News*.

Press cutting of the trial, 1929. *Author's collection*.

Photograph of the Hahn *La Belle*, commissioned by Joseph Duveen. *Author's collection*.

Andrée Hahn in the courtroom, 1929. © *Topham Picturepoint/Topfoto.co.uk* 0753160.

The courtroom, New York, 1929. © *Bettman/Corbis* U469607INP.

Harry Hahn and Frank Glenn at a book signing of *The Rape of La Belle*, Kansas, 1946. *Reproduced by kind permission of Ardis Glenn*.

The Hahn *La Belle* is viewed under guard, Hollywood, 1947. *Reproduced by kind permission of Jacqueline Hahn*.

The Hahn *La Belle* on display. Hartwell Galleries, Los Angeles, 1947. *Reproduced by kind permission of Jacqueline Hahn*.

Introduction

In June 1920 a reporter on the *New York World* telephoned the famous English art dealer, Sir Joseph Duveen. What, he asked him, did he think about the painting that had just arrived in the United States and which its owners claimed to be the original version of *La Belle Ferronnière* by Leonardo da Vinci? Duveen – as bold, not to say as rash, as ever – bluntly told the reporter that the real *La Belle Ferronnière* was among the Leonardos in the Louvre, that the American picture must be a copy or a fake and that anyone who thought otherwise could not be called an art expert. Duveen's response, the condemnation of a picture he had never seen, initiated not just one of the most famous art trials of the twentieth century, but a battle over the attribution of the painting that has continued until today.

The dramatic story of the painting owned by Andrée and Harry Hahn, known to some as the 'American Leonardo', is not just about a single painting's travels and fortunes. It also raises questions about how attributions are made, what effect they have on the status and value of paintings, and how the entire system that validates and authenticates Old Master art has developed during the twentieth century. Above all, the experiences of the Hahns' painting document the unfolding history of the struggle between experts who relied on their intuitive but accumulated visual experience to identify works of art and those who wanted to use modern scientific techniques to secure attributions.

The controversy over the disputed version of Leonardo's *La Belle Ferronnière* raises a fundamental question that has haunted the art world and continues to do so: when you stand in front of a painting, how do you know if it is authentic? How can you tell who painted it? Of course, most of us can't. You rely on the expertise of curators, connoisseurs and dealers, putting your trust in their skills and good faith. When you enter the Louvre or the premises of upmarket art dealers on Bond Street or Madison Avenue, you look at paintings with the confidence that their importance and authenticity is underwritten by the people who display them. At the same time, the public wants to understand how such decisions are made, to share (albeit vicariously) in the process of attribution that enables it to enjoy the greatness of Old Masters.

Trust is a powerful bond, but when questioned can prove a rope of sand. The row over the American Leonardo was never just about the authenticity of a single picture, it was also about the authenticity and authority of the art world itself. The question was not just 'Is this a Leonardo?', but also one about the legitimacy and honesty of the system of museums, dealers and connoisseurs that make up the art establishment: 'Are they for real too?' This question has sometimes been asked even by those from within the art world. Kenneth Clark, Baron Clark of Saltwood and writer, presenter and producer of the television programme *Civilisation: A Personal View*, a man who stood at the centre of the art world and did much to propagate its values, expressed astonishment at the way his hunches and suppositions about works of art were accepted as truth. He had always felt, he confessed, a little bit of a fraud. There has always been an element of magic and mystery about the workings of the art world, a sense that they involved smoke and mirrors.

As Clark's distinguished career attests (he was not just Director of the National Gallery, London, but the leading English Leonardo scholar of his generation), one of the key qualities of a successful art expert was a keen 'eye', the ability, born of years of experience, to recognize the hand of a master like Leonardo da Vinci. However, in the early twentieth century, the critical eye of the connoisseur had to contend with an emerging array of scientific and forensic tests that (however crude in their inception) promised an objectivity and reliability in attributing works of art that strongly appealed to a public saturated in the notion that the advancement of science was the true sign of human progress. The tension between two different sorts of attribution lay at the heart of dispute over the Hahn *La Belle Ferronnière*. Lawyers and the press persistently asked the same questions. Could the 'say so' of someone like Duveen and his connoisseur experts override x-ray analysis and paint samples? Should not those who claimed to be reliable attributors of Old Masters at the very least import modern methods into their work?

The issue of 'How do we know? How can we distinguish original from copy, true from false?' seemed all the more pressing in 1920, when the Old Master boom was producing record-breaking prices, but has remained important in an art world whose growth continues to be fuelled by vast sums of money. After all, an original is worth millions, a copy only thousands, or maybe almost nothing at all. The line between a celebrated masterpiece and a copy discreetly assigned to the relative obscurity of a side gallery or museum basement is often a fine one. I was reminded of this very recently when I learnt that a picture that I had always loved and admired, *The Colossus*, also known as *The Giant*, attributed to the Spanish artist Francisco Goya, had been removed from the artist's canon of works. It had always seemed to me an utterly remarkable composition with its war-ravaged landscape and vast human figure rising above chaotic scenes in the Spanish country-side. However, experts in the Prado Museum, where the picture hangs, now say that they are not sure who painted it (the current viewpoint is that it may have been Asensio Julià, one of Goya's apprentices), but they are pretty sure it was not Goya. This reattri-bution depends largely on opinions formed by using the expert eye. *The Colossus*, the experts say, lacks real 'Goya' quality and does not fit with the rest of his paintings. As always, dissenting voices and different sorts of evidence, some of it technical and some to do with the provenance of the picture, challenge this view. In fact, the debate has been going on in museum circles for several years. Nevertheless, *The Colossus* has long been hung in one of the Goya rooms of the Prado (this may change); it has been reproduced on countless occasions as a Goya; and its strangeness appeared to me to be 'in the spirit' of Goya. As one commentator mordantly commented, he would always think of it as a Goya, even though it was a Goya no more. He seemed (and I sympathized with him) to be disappointed by the experts, cheated, in a way, of a cher-ished work of art.

The process of attribution is fluid, a sign, its practitioners would say, of its healthy ability to pursue refinement as scholarship changes and new techniques are developed. Public attitudes towards this are more ambivalent: often, museum-goers do not like to see a favourite painting like Goya's *The Colossus* downgraded, though they enjoy sharing in the excitement of a new discovery such as *The Madonna of the Pinks*, a work attributed to Raphael and acquired for London's National Gallery in 2004.

Yet, here again, the reattribution excited controversy. For years *The Madonna*, owned by the 4th Duke of Northumberland, had been seen as one of a large number of copies of a missing original by Raphael, a picture worth several thousand rather than several million pounds. However, in the early 1990s, Nicholas Penny, then curator of Renaissance art at the National Gallery and now its Director, argued that the Northumberland *Madonna* was indeed by Raphael. Much of his argument was based on his visual reassessment of the quality of the painting, but also depended upon the nature of the underdrawing revealed by infra-red reflectography. Nevertheless, the attribution proved controversial, challenged by experts in North America and Italy. The National Gallery organized a major symposium on the picture in 2002 and in 2003 a dossier of evidence in its favour, one that included new pigment analysis, was presented to the museum's trustees who went on to approve its acquisition for £22,000,000 ($35,000,000). Its critics were unimpressed: they dismissed the symposium as a device to help vindicate the picture, remained sceptical of its aesthetic qualities and challenged or reinterpreted a great deal of the scientific evidence. The preponderance of professional opinion is in favour of Penny's original judgement, made first and foremost through his experienced eye, but there are still sceptics within the art-historical and museum communities. It is not impossible (though it is improbable) that one day *The Madonna of the Pinks* will suffer the ignominy of *The Colossus*.

The debates about Goya and Raphael took place within the art and museum world, though they were widely reported in the press. Experts disagreed on individual judgements, but they did not challenge the entire mechanism of attribution: scientific evidence and the educated eye worked in tandem, though the final decision in both cases seems to have rested not so much on scientific evidence as on the opinion of the experienced connoisseur. By the twenty-first century a (sometimes uneasy) accommodation had been made between the two, in which it was recognized that scientific testing could show definitively that a painting was not by a particular artist but only an experienced connoisseur could recognize who was its creator.

However, in the 1920s, as the struggle between the Hahns and Duveen began, there was no accord between science and subjective judgement, the x-ray and the eye. Figures like Duveen and Bernard Berenson, the famous connoisseur, openly scoffed at scientific evidence or expressed deep scepticism of its worth. The Hahns and their supporters interpreted this hostility as deeply self-interested, not just because it defended the lucrative business of subjective evaluation and the 'experts' that practised it, but because they believed it to lie at the heart of a scam to foist poor art on gullible Americans. Duveen and his fellow 'experts', they claimed, were deliberately avoiding or denying scientific evidence when it did not suit their commercial ends. The resistance to scientific method was interpreted as a wilful attempt to mislead collectors, museums and the public.

The tensions between attributions made by the experienced eye and those sustained by science played themselves out in two overlapping arenas. The first was the art world itself where dealers, connoisseurs, conservators, curators and collectors vied with one another over the power to attribute works of art to particular painters, and therefore to shape both the art market and taste. The second was that of a public that has looked on with envy and awe at the extraordinary growth of what is arguably one of the great boom industries of the twentieth century. These people did not own Old Master art, but were given access to it in a growing number of public museums and knew a great deal about private collectors, thanks to a mass newspaper press that reported every spectacular acquisition and sale.

Harry and Andrée Hahn, one a mechanic from Kansas, the other a young woman of modest means from the French holiday resort of Dinard, were outsiders when they confronted the art world and tried to gain a place within it for their picture. They were shrewd enough to shape their cause into one that not only concerned itself with the authenticity of their painting, but brought into question the entire manner in which the art world worked. The story of their American Leonardo is labyrinthine and complex, a tale of intrigue, controversy and skullduggery. Shipped back and forth across the Atlantic, displayed in New York, Paris, Los Angeles and Kansas City, examined in the Louvre and in London's National Gallery, the Hahn *La Belle Ferronnière* was the focus of expert testimony taken in Paris in 1923 and the object of courtroom drama, when the case of *Hahn versus Duveen* came to trial in New York in 1929. The painting brought together crowds in the Midwest, puzzled experts from all over North America and Europe, attracted more than its fair share of dubious characters and cast its shadow over the Hahn family for almost a century. Beginning in the 1920s, when the Hahns brought *La Belle Ferronnière* to the United States

7

and sued Duveen in the New York courts for condemning the picture, the story pauses in the present, with the painting languishing in an Omaha storage vault, the subject of a contentious lawsuit that remains, like so many controversies over the picture, unresolved to this day.

The painting managed to become much more than one of those numerous, dubious pictures that crop up in the outer rooms of auction houses and are found nestled away at the back of auction catalogues. It kept clear of the penumbra populated by shady copies and palpable fakes. However, we can rightly ask, 'If it isn't a Leonardo then why does it matter?' It is important to bear in mind that, although no one has proved that the Hahn *La Belle Ferronnière* is a Leonardo, at least to the satisfaction of most art experts, it has not been shown that it is not. No one has been able to demonstrate conclusively, for example, that it does not date from the late fifteenth century. Like a great many artworks – many more than collectors and museum curators would like to admit publicly – the status of the picture is ambiguous and this has enabled it to play a continuing role in larger struggles about connoisseurship and scientific attribution. Besides, its sister picture in the Louvre, the other version of *La Belle Ferronnière*, though it has often been taken to be a Leonardo, is also a much-disputed painting. It has been rejected by many experts as a work of the master, sometimes attributed to one of his pupils and been treated by the authorities in the Louvre with a certain amount of coyness.

The case of the American Leonardo puts the question of attribution, expert views and public acceptance in high relief. It also reveals the big trends and microcosmic workings of the twentieth-century art world, enabling us to see what is often hidden and to understand what often goes unanalysed. The extraordinary value (both economic and cultural) placed on major works of art and the arenas in which this value is negotiated make such artefacts ripe for manipulation. Much of the history of the Hahn *La Belle Ferronnière* is the story of how different people, both inside and outside the art world, have attempted to use the picture to further their own ends. It also tells how the picture itself affected their lives. It's a story in four major acts: the first, fuelled by the desire for wealth, status and fame, propelled the legal challenge of the 1920s that exposed the weak public credibility of art experts and their skills, even when they continued to dominate the art market; the second, between 1945 and 1957, was characterized by a political attack on the art world by a coalition of its critics; the third, between 1957 and 1973, was the era in which experts in the art world attempted to use the painting to change the rules of the game so as to 'scientize' connoisseurship; and, in the final phase, as the picture has become more and more difficult to sell, so its use and value has shifted again, making it more a vehicle for raising and borrowing money than a disputed object on the art market.

To explain this history we have to step back and look at the art world from a broader and longer perspective. Forgeries and copies of great works of art and the experts and connoisseurs who were supposed to distinguish the real from the fake had long preceded the twentieth century. As far back as classical antiquity there had been fakers, copiers and experts, but developments in the late nineteenth century meant that the attribution – the 'expertizing' – of Old Masters became more important than ever before. The case of the Hahn *La Belle* was the product of a particular historical moment, one in which the arrival of extremely rich American collectors transformed the art market, fundamentally changing the relationship between collectors, dealers, museums and experts. It was also a time when connoisseurship first confronted the demand that it should be more scientific, rigorous and systematic, and when Leonardo da Vinci became the most famous Old Master painter in the western world. It is almost impossible to grasp the significance of the fight over the American Leonardo unless we are familiar with these developments. I therefore open my account with a wide-ranging analysis that looks at the Old Master art world in the United States and Europe at the turn of the century before launching into the narrative history of *La Belle*.

Harry and Andrée Hahn knew very little about art dealing, attribution and experts when they set out to sell their picture in 1920. They knew enough to realize that a Leonardo was worth a great deal – though they underestimated their picture's potential value – and they knew about the art boom from the French and American press which had regaled the public with stories of high prices, millionaire collectors and the flight of Europe's cultural heritage to Boston, Pittsburgh and New York. However, once plunged into the art world, they learned quickly, swiftly understanding what was at stake and how they could use the new public interest in the workings of the art market. Harry and Andrée arrived on the scene just as the art world was opening up to unprecedented public scrutiny. For centuries a coterie of experts, artists and royal and aristocratic collectors had fretted over the authenticity and attribution of great works of art. Thanks to the growth of public museums, first in Europe and then in the United States, and even more because of the development of a new market and a mass press that reported its sensational dealings, the question asked of an Old Master painting, 'How do you know what it is, how can you tell who painted it?' was no longer posed merely by a privileged cabal at the pinnacle of society, but by ordinary members of the public. The Hahns were ventriloquists for this public concern; they used their version of *La Belle Ferronnière* to call the art world to account by skilfully using public anxieties about deception and skullduggery to further the cause of the painting. Though humble, they were exceptionally bold, not least because, if their *La Belle* was indeed a copy, then their claim that she was an authentic Leonardo was a fine example of the slight-of-hand they condemned as typical of what Harry Hahn loved to call 'the art racket'.

CHAPTER 1

The American Scene

In 1919, the newlyweds Harry Hahn and his war bride Andrée arrived back in the United States. They landed in New York and then travelled to Kansas, ending their journey in Junction City, where Harry opened an automobile business. However, the young couple were interested in selling more than cars. They had, they claimed, been given as a wedding gift a painting by Leonardo da Vinci, the original version of *La Belle Ferronnière*. Soon Harry was trying to sell the picture. He made contact with dealers on the East Coast who referred him to Duveen Brothers in New York. On 19 November 1919 he wrote to the firm telling them about the picture and about a certificate of authentication provided by the French expert, Georges Sortais, a copy of which he offered to send if they were interested. The office sent a routine reply, in which they asked for Sortais's attribution and any supporting materials, along with photographs of the painting. Their response was routine, but excited Harry who referred in his reply to their 'valued letter'. However, given the presence of many copies of Leonardo's work and the source of the inquiry – a motor-car business in a small Midwestern town – it would have been surprising if the New York office would have treated the matter very seriously. Dealers like the Duveens were often offered pictures as Old Masters that they were almost immediately sure were fakes or modern copies. The story of the lost masterpiece in the attic made for good journalistic copy, but was an extremely rare event and usually involved its discovery by someone with some expertise. Harry offered an extremely sketchy back story – about the French family that he had married into suffering 'certain financial stresses' – but it seemed flimsy and implausible. Besides, his stilted description of his picture – 'truly a wonderful piece of DA VINCI work' – made it obvious to any expert that he knew next to nothing about Leonardo and his art.

Rebuffed on the East Coast, at first the Hahns had just as little luck selling their picture back in the Midwest. Andrée went to see the arts correspondent of the *Kansas City Star*, but was annoyed to find her incredulous that a Leonardo had fetched up in a town in the corn-belt. But then the Hahns met Conrad Hug, an art dealer in Kansas City. He had been born in Germany in 1870 and had emigrated to Omaha, Nebraska, when he was fourteen years old. He worked as a carpenter and picture framer, returned to Europe on a number of occasions to look at picture collections and find a bride, and moved to Kansas City in about 1900, where he eventually opened his own art store in 1914. His stock consisted chiefly of etchings, watercolours, mezzotints, and coloured prints. He was, according to one New York dealer who met him, 'a conservative German art dealer, unquestionably honest and of the old school'. He had cultural ambitions for Kansas City and saw the acquisition of the Hahns' *La Belle*, of whose authenticity he was thoroughly convinced, as a way of promoting the city and of helping establish an art gallery there. He was already helping the Hahns in February of 1920, when the Kansas City papers were reporting that he had photographs of the picture. They also claimed that the Hahn *La Belle* was probably the long lost original whose existence had been posited by Leonardo scholars discussing the version of *La Belle Ferronnière* in the Louvre.

Hug did a considerable amount of business with the Kansas City Art Institute, an art school with a small collection of pictures, to which he supplied artists' materials. He approached the Institute's president, a real-estate developer and Kansas City booster named Jesse C. Nichols, about buying the painting. The exact nature of their conversation was to remain in dispute for many years to come, but Hug believed that Nichols had agreed to buy the picture for $225,000 (then approximately £65,000) and to pledge some of his own money in order to help raise the funds to acquire the painting.

It was at this point, on 17 June 1920, that Duveen was dragged into the story when the *New York World* published an interview in which he had airily dismissed the Hahn picture as a copy or a fake. This was obviously a blow to the Hahns' efforts to sell their picture, though it was also known in Kansas City that experts in the Louvre did not view the Hahn *La Belle* as genuine. In November 1921, the Hahns served papers on Duveen in his New York office asking for damages of $500,000 (£145,000) to compensate for his 'slander of title' of their picture. The battle between the Hahns and Duveen began.

The Hahns were extraordinarily bold, for they clearly knew little about the world they had entered. They plunged themselves into an American art market that was in the throes of an extraordinary transformation, the effects of which were to be felt in almost every major American city with cultural aspirations, and which was to fascinate the newspaper-reading public for a generation.

They could have learned much from another American who had returned from Europe a number of years earlier and whose knowledge of the American art scene far surpassed not only their own but that of most American citizens. The Hahns, despite their transatlantic travels, were provincials and outsiders, but Henry James was both cosmopolitan and an insider, a novelist with close connections to major figures in the art world. When James returned to New York in 1904, he was not interested in taking advantage, like the Hahns, of the boom in Old Master art, but rather in coming to terms with a transformation that at once fascinated and repelled him. No one provides a better entrée into the world that was to dominate the Hahns' lives during the 1920s; no one makes clearer how these changes were prompted by a radical alteration in American society as a whole.

Walking across New York's Central Park to view the new Metropolitan Museum building shortly after his return, James was disturbed by the confident, noisy and prosperous families, many, though not rich, decked out in their best clothing, who played, picnicked and wandered through the park. The new United States, 'hustling, bustling', democratic and monied, troubled his sense of taste, order and decorum. We might expect that the sight of the museum would have offered some comfort to an aesthete like James, but even this new temple to culture failed at first to give him the solace he sought. For James' view of America, as recorded in his *The American Scene* (1907), not only condemned the new cities teeming with immigrants, but was also coloured by a highly ambivalent attitude towards the astonishing wealth and prodigious consumption he found. In this, his view of the Metropolitan was no exception. He was shocked by the way it conveyed to him the irresistible power of wealth. As he looked at the museum's exterior, all he could think of was 'acquisitiveness', a quality he had encountered almost everywhere on his travels. The fastidious James could smell the odour of filthy lucre. 'Acquisition – acquisition if need be on the highest terms – may, during the years to come, bask here as in a climate it has never enjoyed. There was money in the air, ever so much money', he recorded, 'And the money was to be all for the most exquisite things – for *all* the most exquisite except creation, which was to be off the scene altogether; for art, selection, criticism, for knowledge, piety, taste.'

At first such acquisitiveness, the exercise of economic power, struck James as 'detestable', but his reaction was tempered by the thought that the money was not to serve a selfish purpose but to promote 'values mainly for the mind'. Perhaps he was remembering the speech that Joseph Choate, one of the founders of the Met, had made to the millionaires who had assembled for the dedication of the new building back in 1880. He had urged them 'to convert pork into porcelain, grain and produce into priceless pottery, the rude ores of commerce into sculptured marble, and railroad shares and mining stocks ... into the glorified canvases of the world's masters'. Such, Choate implied, were the alchemical powers of donors that they could transmute the brute materials of modernity into the treasures of a distant, more tranquil past. Making such art available, said Choate, 'in its higher forms of beauty would tend directly to humanize, to educate and refine a practical and laborious people'. No doubt James shared Choate's preference for money spent on art, but he could not shake off his unease about the intrusion of the market into culture, jocularly (though it must be said, not very persuasively) reminding himself that if works of art 'happen to have also a trade-value this is pure superfluity and excess'. Nor was he as enthused as Choate about the idea of taking art and beauty to the people. At bottom, James felt forced to concede that the new grand Metropolitan 'was going to be great' (you can hear him mimic the voice of popular acclaim), but it filled him with discomfort.

Henry James' complex reactions to American wealth and its effect on art and taste were part of a debate in Europe and the United States about the place of 'culture' in the most rapidly growing capitalist economy in the world. It involved not just aesthetes and artists like James, but social commentators, academics, clerics and moralists, as well as those directly involved in the institutions and markets that shaped culture. The singular story of the fate of the Hahns and their American Leonardo may, at first sight, seem a far remove from such controversies and the huge changes that provoked them, and they were almost certainly not on the minds of Harry and Andrée when they returned to the United States in 1919. However, the dynamics of the art world – its growing expense and exclusively, its focus on dead Europe rather than living America – and of the larger economies of the United States and Europe that shaped them, had a profound effect both on how the case of the American Leonardo played itself out and on the tactics and stratagems the Hahns used to further their cause.

For reasons that will become apparent, in North America matters to do with the arts and culture became the subject of intense social competition, where status was confirmed or undermined and where the canons of social acceptance or rejection were formed. This was true of literature and the performing arts, but doubly so of the visual arts because they involved such valuable commodities. The cost of a reproducible object like a book was small, the price of a theatre or concert ticket a little greater, but the outlay on a painting of any quality was considerable. Of course a museum or art gallery provided access to valuable works of art, but this did not involve what James (and others) identified as the overwhelming desire for acquisition, for ownership and the chance to display art, to parlay it into an object that displayed the wealth and status of its owner. More than any other product of human creativity, works of art seemed to be the natural currency in the business that critics like Thorstein Veblen called, with more than a hint of disapproval, 'conspicuous consumption' (inventing the term in 1899 in his classic *The Theory of a Leisure Class*).

Between the departure of the young Henry James for Europe in 1869 and the year in which he composed his essays on *The American Scene,* the United States economy and its society underwent a remarkable transformation. The opening up of the West, the proliferation of railroads, the development of iron and steel, coal and oil, the growth of banking, new technologies like the telegraph and the telephone, and the adoption of new means of retailing catering to a mass society produced immense fortunes and irrevocably changed the way people lived. The population more than doubled (in part thanks to rapid immigration), but so too did gross domestic product per capita. More, bigger and richer, the largest economy in the world grew at an astonishing rate. 'US Worth in 1904 was $107,104,192,410 [approx. £22,000,000,000]', crowed the *New York Times,* whose enthusiasm was undimmed by the problems it had squeezing the headline into its column. James was right: the smell of money was in the air; acquisition was the name of the game.

The effects of the United States' newfound, newly produced riches were many, but what intoxicated and repelled observers, American and European alike, was the spectacle of wealth, a gaudiness and visual profusion that manifested itself not just in the dripping diamonds, furs, motor cars and over-stuffed mansions of the newly enriched tycoons of business, but in the lavish displays in department stores catering for the middle classes and the growth of a mass commodity culture catering for ordinary workers in which products were branded and marketed as much for how they looked as what they did. Love it or hate it, a new sort of materialism, a national obsession with the procurement of beautiful objects, whether paintings by Raphael or lipsticks by Elizabeth Arden, pervaded American society.

The emergence of a class of super-rich was the most conspicuous sign of the new wealth. The 'robber barons', excoriated and admired by turns for their unconstrained and sometimes illegal pursuit of wealth, made their money in railroads and local transport systems (the largest single category of wealth, apart from real estate in the *New York Times* survey), in banking and speculation, in iron, steel and oil, in retailing and in mass communications, notably the telegraph, telephone and newspapers. Many of them, including Cornelius Vanderbilt, J.P. Morgan, Ben Altman, Peter and Joseph Widener, Henry Walters, Henry O. Havemeyer, William Randolph Hearst, Henry Clay Frick, Henry Huntington, Samuel H. Kress and Andrew Mellon were to become some of the most important American collectors of Old Master art, bringing to the art market the same ruthlessness that repelled the likes of Henry James but had helped secure their enormous fortunes. These 'squillionaires', as Mary Berenson, the diarist and wife of the aesthete and connoisseur Bernard Berenson, liked to call them, were only the tip of the iceberg. In many American cities, not just on the East Coast seaboard which had well-entrenched local elites, but in the Midwest and West, a growing body of the newly wealthy, most of whom were from local business families originally of modest means, came to dominate local affairs. The wealth and size of these groups increased rapidly. In 1892, for instance, the *New York Tribune* reported that Pittsburgh – admittedly the centre of the steel and oil boom – was the home of no fewer than eighty-five millionaires.

Including not just the newly rich, but the very rich, these local elites embarked on a spending spree devoted to house building and decoration, erecting large mansions and filling them with expensive and often ornate 'things': bibelots, fancy furnishings, mirrors, antiques and sometimes pictures, though, before the 1890s, few bought Old Master art. Whether a mansion on Michigan Avenue in Chicago, a neoclassical palace on New York's 5th Avenue, a Queen Anne home on Irwin Street in Pittsburgh or a summer 'cottage' in Newport, Rhode Island, the 'house beautiful' became a display case of plutocratic pastiche. Paul Bourget, one of many novelists, both European and American, who wrote about these opulent interiors, described in his memoir, *Voyageuses*, a visit to the Newport summer home of Mrs Harris in terms that transposed American 'conspicuous consumption' into a picture of tasteless extravagance. The 'boudoir', he said, was 'a parody by excess of imitation, a caricature by way of *outrance*. Too many prints, too many pictures on the overly rich wall fabric, too many flowers and too big in too many precious vases, too many small English silver objects on tables, among too many photographs of princes and princesses, all with dedications.' Even Mrs Harris herself seemed part of the display, a mannequin for couturier fashion, 'she seemed too beautiful, with her too red mouth, her too scrubbed teeth, her overly polished hands with their abuse of rings'. Though Bourget voices (and he was far from alone) the snobbery and envy directed at the newly rich, he captures the experience of intense visual overload, the sense of sheer accumulation so often reported by visitors to these over-stuffed, over-polished and overcrowded interiors.

And where did these goods that crowded so many rooms come from? Some were from the New World, but a great many more were from the Old. The economic miracle of the Americas had had a devastating effect on the economies of Europe. The railroad boom had opened up the prairies and slashed the cost of grain. The vast fields of wheat and corn that stretched across Harry Hahn's home state and the rest of the Midwest were cropped not just to lower bread prices in the republic, but as exports that led to plummeting food prices in Europe and a collapse in agricultural rents, the chief source of large landowners' incomes. The flower of the British and European landed aristocracy, the holders of most of the continent's cultural treasures, faced mounting debts and insolvency. In 1882, the British Parliament passed the Settled Lands Act, which undermined entail (the restriction of bequest to a designated line of heirs) and made it much easier to sell off family heirlooms. In the same year the Hamilton Palace sale marked the beginning of a substantial divestment of British cultural treasure that rapidly escalated. Between 1884 and 1886, for example, the Duke of Marlborough sold off some of the finest works from Blenheim Palace, including two Raphaels (one genuine; one not) and works by Hans Holbein, Anthony van Dyck, Peter Paul Rubens and Joshua Reynolds. In France and Italy, where the laws governing cultural patrimony were in chaos, aristocrats turned to selling to Americans, especially when the dollar grew in strength against the Continental currencies.

Between the 1880s and the Wall Street Crash of 1929 Old Masters, contemporary paintings, furniture, silver, Chinese porcelain, rare books and manuscripts, altar pieces and church decoration, clocks, reliquaries, silver, carpets, armour, tiles, coins and bibelots were shipped in unprecedented numbers out of Europe and into the United States. Such immense transfers of cultural property had happened before and were to occur again, but, like the Roman plundering of Sicily, the mass accumulations of the French revolutionary and Napoleonic regimes or the later Nazi pillage of Europe, they were usually the booty of war. In this case cultural treasures were moved by Adam Smith's invisible hand rather than the force of arms. As Henry James put it in *The Outcry* (1914), the American pillage of Europe was carried out 'with huge cheque-books instead of with spears and battle-axes'.

The scale of this collecting was unparalleled. When J.P. Morgan died in 1913, his collections were valued at some $60 million (£12.4 million). Benjamin Altman who also died that year left a picture collection worth $20 million (£4.1 million). William Randolph Hearst was spending about $5 million (£1.1 million) a year at the peak of his collecting. Samuel H. Kress amassed a collection of 3,210 works of art. However, these famous, often obsessive collectors were only the most visible manifestation of a much broader phenomenon in which the United States' wealthy citizens, much like Mrs Harris of Newport Rhode Island, appropriated the cultural treasures of Europe, decorating their houses in the extravagant manner that shocked refined European art dealers like René Gimpel but did not stop them selling to their less cultivated clients.

Not all the new wealth, of course, was spent on homes. The city elites, acutely conscious that the spirit of competition was not just individual, but also ran among cities, helped build opera houses and concert halls, establish orchestras, museums and art galleries, and to lay out parks and boulevards. The 'city beautiful' movement, in part an attempt to bring order and decorum to teeming immigrant cities, created public spaces and plazas, parks and low-density residential districts, often in neighbourhoods that had once been slums. Museums and art galleries were part of this process of what today would be described as 'gentrification'. The 1870s saw the foundation of the first wave of American art museums – the Boston Museum of Fine Arts (1870), the New York Metropolitan Museum (1872), the Philadelphia Art Museum (1876) and the Chicago Art Institute (1879). By 1900 there were twenty-two public art galleries in the United States, though many were small collections like the Albright Galley in Buffalo, New York. The effect on the civic life of cities like Chicago, Toledo, Philadelphia, Cleveland and St Louis was to advertise private munificence and to place local culture in the hands of an elite who acted as the trustees, proprietors and public for the newly subsidized forms of cultural expression. Before the Civil War, the cultural life of America's cities had brought together performers and artists and enthusiastic amateurs often interested in making different forms of art; the line between amateur and professional was not finely drawn. By the end of the nineteenth century, civic culture was largely controlled by its wealthy consumers, who confined their interests to different sorts of patronage. They saw musicians, actors, artists and curators as employees of the trusts they administered. Increasingly, a distinction was made between highbrow and lowbrow culture. The former was seen as civilized and civilizing, refined yet based on a business model; the latter was viewed (at least by the likes of Henry James) as philistine and vulgar. Civic culture in general and the fine arts in particular increasingly looked past contemporary America, back towards the historic achievements of Europe.

The rage for acquisition and spending was not confined to the rich or to treasures from the past, for while the new economic forces helped turn art in commerce, they were simultaneously turning commerce into art. Central to the prosperous landscape of the new cities were the department stores that opened up across the United States, temples to commerce often sited no more than a few blocks from temples of culture. Stores like Wanamaker's in Philadelphia, Macy's, Altman's and Bergdorf Goodman in New York, Carson Pirie Scott and Marshall Fields in Chicago and Bullocks in Los Angeles were spaces dedicated to consumption whose methods of presentation mimicked and sometimes surpassed those of the museum. Their display was to entice the middle classes. The great court of Wanamaker's Philadelphia store, with its organ, classical columns and top lighting was every bit as grand as any American museum and John Wanamaker, who was a keen collector of art (though not of Old Masters), filled his stores with modern academic pictures from his collection. Taste, art and commerce were juxtaposed for their collective benefit. It is not surprising, then, that Macy's cashed in on the 1929 Hahn trial by selling replicas of the Hahn picture ('we admit it's a copy') and that when Harry Hahn was promoting his book in the 1940s, he persuaded department stores to display the family's version of *La Belle Ferronnière*. The department store spectacularized a middle-class life filled with objects, a culture of acquisition and display; its proprietors understood that 'art' and taste were an invaluable means of selling, turning goods from useful things into objects of beauty, items that were not so much needed as desired. Making consumer goods into works of art had a complex effect on the perception of 'real' artworks. On the one hand, it made them seem like any other consumer good, ripe, as Henry James saw, for acquisition; on the other, it intensified their importance as singular and unique instances of taste.

Department store owners took great pains to display their wares tastefully – indeed, their displays to some extent instructed customers how to arrange the goods they bought. They emphasized a degree of discrimination, even as they revelled in their spectacle of middle-class wealth, acquisition and ownership. The department store sought to distinguish itself from the mass market, from the plethora of 'things' – some novel, some familiar, some quite expensive, most very cheap – that flooded American society in the late nineteenth century. Cheap furniture and off-the-peg clothing, soaps and cosmetics, branded goods which, like Coca-Cola and Kelloggs, remain familiar today, processed foods, watches, telephones, sewing machines, phonographs, cameras, bicycles and eventually cars: the world had never seemed so full of material goods, so widely distributed among the entire population. Mass consumerism spoke to the wealth of the great mass of Americans (and also helped conceal the poverty of many others); it also attested to the saturation of an entire society in a pervasive materialism.

To old money, the clergy of many faiths, and to the intellectual elite of the East Coast, the new materialism, the power it brought to the new rich and the way its values seemed to pervade society, was profoundly troubling. Art, in their view, was not an object of conspicuous consumption – and, heaven forbid, a commodity – but an ethical matter, important as the expression of spiritual values that were opposed to the unfettered pursuit of monetary gain. Charles Eliot Norton, Harvard professor of art history, Dante scholar and friend of the British socialist critic John Ruskin, was perhaps the most eloquent and influential proponent of the view that art should stand against material progress rather than being a part of it. Norton looked back nostalgically to a time when 'there were no railroads with their tremendous revolutionary forces; no great manufacturing cities; no flood of immigrants; no modern democracy'. According to Henry James in his 1908 essay 'An American Scholar: Charles Eliot Norton', Norton saw his task as the civilizing of 'a young roaring and money-getting democracy, inevitably but almost exclusively occupied with "business success".' In his lectures to several generations of Harvard students, his conversations with influential protégés and acolytes (including James and Bernard Berenson), and in the pages of the *Atlantic*, the *North American Review* and the journal he co-founded, the *Nation*, Norton elaborated on his core belief that 'art, properly understood' was 'the expression of humanity', and that it should act as a bulwark against the tide of modern materialism.

His view was widely shared. Art, James Mason Hoppin, a fellow art-history professor at Yale argued, should help Americans 'in this contest against the money-making and money-worshiping spirit. It would tend to free us from this gross bondage of materialism.' The notion that the display of great works of art was uplifting for the citizenry, that it played a civilizing role in modern life, was at least as old as the French Revolution and was a much touted idea in the debate about the sudden influx into the United States of the cultural treasures of Europe, whether collected by the new super-rich or displayed in public museums. As Benson Lossing, the New York historian and wood engraver, wrote in his history of the fine arts, the fine arts 'have a powerful tendency to elevate the standard of intellect and consequently morals; and form one of the mighty levers that raise nations as well as individuals to the highest point on the scale of civilization'. However, critics like James and Norton doubted that what might be achieved in Europe was possible in the radically new America. 'Of all civilized nations,' wrote Norton in 'A Definition of Fine Arts' for *Forum* in 1889, the United States was 'the most deficient in the higher culture of the mind, and not in the culture only but also in the conditions on which this culture mainly depends'.

Norton and his followers had a profound effect on the college-educated men and women from the middle classes, many of whom began to think that an active interest in art and its history was not just a pleasure but an obligation. A growing number of institutions offered courses in art history. The first began in women's colleges (Vassar and Smith in the late 1860s); Princeton had the first art-history department, set up in 1883, and by 1912 there were ninety-five institutions teaching art history. More and more students began to make the pilgrimage to Europe to see its works of art and absorb its culture.

This dutiful concern for art and its history, this worship of 'high culture', fascinated many European commentators. Pierre de Coulevain, in his novel *Noblesse Americaine,* mocked the 'unequalled conscientiousness' with which Annie Villars, a rich

American heiress married to an impoverished French count, worked her way, Baedeker guide in hand, through the masterpieces of Rome. In similar fashion, Paul Bourget commented on the American obsession with refinement and 'culture' in *Outre-Mer: Impressions of America* (1894–5): 'It is a big word which Americans always have on their lips and on their mind, and which they apply with equal seriousness to morals and gymnastics, as in *ethical and physical culture.*' The prosperous youth of nineteenth-century America was saturated with the ideas of William Morris and Matthew Arnold, devoted to the cause of acquainting themselves with, in Arnold's famous words, 'the best that has been known and said in the world, and thus with the history of the human spirit'.

The moral earnestness of many critics and their followers did not please everyone, nor was it the only vision of art pressed upon the collecting classes. Towards the end of the century, though there was no let-up in the sacralization of culture, the evangelical spirit waned, enthusiasm for proselytizing among the masses giving way both to a more aesthetic view in which art's object was pleasure rather than edification and to the belief that it was probably best practised and conserved among those who already had education and culture. Better to be with the like-minded, or to retreat to Europe, where the task of conserving and cultivating 'high culture' was so much less strenuous and the rebarbative materialism so typical of the New World so much less well developed. It was so much better (and more pleasurable) to preach cultivation and refinement to the wealthy, to civilize them first so that they, if they wished, might, through a process of example, civilize the masses. Figures like Henry James, Edith Wharton and Bernard Berenson, all of whom had been profoundly affected by the aestheticism of

Europeans such as Walter Pater, Oscar Wilde and Théophile Gautier, urged the rich to a more refined, less vulgar taste, one that appreciated and understood that indiscriminate accumulation and decoration, whether of interior furnishing or art was an obstacle to a true appreciation of beauty. These figures travelled between the United States and Europe, and, though they were not, with the exception of Wharton, fully paid-up members of the new rich, they moved in the social circles of an international plutocracy. Unlike the New England Brahmins, professors and clerics, they had no problem with the acquisitive pleasures of the rich (in Berenson's case, such pleasures were his livelihood); they merely wanted to channel them in the right direction.

They faced a hard task. In the world inhabited by the likes of Mrs Harris of New York and Newport, Rhode Island, where, as one European visitor, Mary Berenson, commented in a letter, 'the table literally groaned under orchids, caviar, turtle soup and golden plate', a masterpiece was no different from an expensive diamond or a huge string of pearls. Discrimination barely mattered; what counted was expense. What shocked so many observers about the orgiastic extravagance of the Gilded Age was both its plenitude and its eclecticism, the random display of vast quantities of disparate things whose only shared quality was their high cost. Of course, the sources of that cost were varied. The most important was rarity, a quality that almost anyone could appreciate and that united a luxury motor car like a Bugatti, a jewel-encrusted bound copy of the *Rubaiyat of Omar Khayyam* and an early self-portrait by Rembrandt van Rijn. A second was 'history', a category more akin to pedigree or provenance: a French eighteenth-century commode was valued for its evocation of an earlier age of refinement; one owned by Marie Antoinette was almost priceless for its proximity to a queen. And a third was 'culture', a quality associated with human creativity – with art – and with taste and beauty. Mingled together these myriad collectables were, of course, objects of conspicuous consumption, but they were chiefly important as the source of a very private sort of gratification. It was this that made them accumulations rather than collections, lacking an order or taste that spoke to the public responsibilities of their owner. This is what the French dealer René Gimpel meant when he scornfully described American collectors in his private diary as showing you 'all their pictures like rich children showing off their toys'. If they were to become truly civic-minded collectors, Americans needed to escape the chaos of the nursery, the indiscriminate and rough handling of precious objects and their unmediated attachment to bright things.

The problem was apparent in the earliest collections made by the newly rich American collectors. Paintings and their display seemed to have little rationale; they were domestic decorations rather than collections. The sorts of pleasure they gave were ornamental or, in some cases, erotic. When American millionaires first began to buy in numbers, their interest was in modern academic painting, especially works from the French academy. The most popular painter represented in Pittsburgh houses in the 1880s was William-Adolphe Bouguereau. This was not just a 'provincial taste'. The French renaissance palace that William H. Vanderbilt had built on New York's 5th Avenue was home to more than 200 pictures, most of which were the work of modern academic painters like Bouguereau and the British Lawrence Alma-Tadema. The enthusiasm for academic pictures among neophyte American collectors is often attributed to their narrative content (they were 'story pictures') and to their academic realism, which made them accessible to those ignorant of art and its history. However, it was equally true that their attraction lay in the numerous, usually naked angels, cherubs, nymphs, bathers, classical goddesses and mythological figures that peopled the canvases and filled them with a repressed but nevertheless visible eroticism common in 'businessman's art'. These pictures were fine for cigar-smoking 'old boys' to nudge and wink at one another or admire the realistic rendering of a woman's thigh, but Bouguereau and Alma-Tadema, for all their classicizing gestures and references, were merely gratifying a private taste, linking their viewers to sex rather than civilization.

The shift in taste to the realistic landscapes of the Barbizon School, which remained popular into the twentieth century, was less censored, though still seen as 'decorative', while the growing interest in (especially English) aristocratic portraiture was rightly seen as a form of indulgent self-regard. As dealers found to their cost, they sold these pictures for their content, not their prowess as works of art; their subjects had to be beautiful, if they were women, and at least upstanding if they were men. Before the First World War you could have bought fifty-three of the brilliant but disturbing portraits of Goya for the cost of one painting by George Romney of a charming young woman.

The task the aesthetic critics set the plutocrat and the millionaire was to cease to be an accumulator and become a discriminating connoisseur. What mattered, as one critic put it, was not 'art of the mere decorative kind' but 'art of an ideal, imaginative kind'. As Edith Wharton explained in her first book, *The Decoration of Houses* (1901), written on a topic close to the hearts of the new rich, 'The man who wishes to possess objects of art must not only have the means to acquire them, but the skill to choose them – a skill made up of cultivation and judgement, combined with a feeling for beauty that no amount of study can give, but that study alone can quicken and render profitable'. As Thorstein Veblen recognized in *The Theory of the Leisure Class*, in a society dominated by conspicuous consumption, what came to matter most and place people at the pinnacle of society was less accumulation than what he called 'punctilious discrimination'. The dominant figure was no longer 'simply the successful, aggressive male, – the man of strength, resource, and intrepidity'; he was a connoisseur who cultivated his 'aesthetic faculty', a task that required time and application. 'Closely related to the requirement that the gentleman must consume freely and of the right kind of goods,' concluded Veblen, 'there is the requirement that he must know how to consume them in a seemly manner', thus acting in 'conformity to the norm of conspicuous leisure and conspicuous consumption'. As Frank Cowperwood, the tycoon collector in Theodore Dreiser's *The Financier* (1912), put it, 'What was a rich man without a great distinction of presence and artistic background? The really great men had it.'

The aim, then, was to connect modern wealth to 'high culture' not just through wholesale appropriation but by choosing, owning and collecting its finest examples. Old Master art was the perfect object to achieve this end. Such works had long been praised by scholars and critics like Norton as the epitome of both humanity and its spiritual values. Their virtues and merits required a certain amount of art-historical knowledge for them to be appreciated. They were chiefly collected by public museums, especially in Britain and Germany, rather than by private individuals, and they had been largely neglected by new wealth. They served as a means of social distinction and private pleasure, but their collection and display as part of 'the memory of humanity' served a higher purpose.

It cannot be sufficiently stressed that the competition for Old Masters began very late in the day. When Edward Strahan, who was the art critic for the *Nation* and *Harper's Weekly,* published his three volumes of *The Art Treasures of America* between 1879 and 1882, his main subject – and interest – was modern French painting. He explained the absence of Old Masters on his own and other's ignorance. The first American collection of Italian Old Masters, made by James Jackson Jarves, an expatriate American living in Florence, was refused by most museums and eventually acquired by Yale University in return for a loan in 1871. (Edith Wharton draws on the Jarves' well-known misfortunes in her short novel, *False Dawn.*) When James Edmund Scripps donated a collection of Old Masters to the Detroit Museum in 1889, he claimed it as a special opportunity because, 'No public gallery in this country has as yet made any considerable start in acquiring a collection of Old Masters'. As late as 1909 Berenson complained that the great collector, Ben Altman, who had summoned the expert for advice, 'hardly knew even a name' of an Italian artist.

Scripps and Berenson may have been exaggerating, but not very much. The lack of interest in Old Masters (and the subsequent enthusiasm) is clearly reflected in their prices. Jarves' collection of 119 pictures, covering Italian art from the eleventh to the seventeenth century, was acquired by Yale for $30,000 (£6,185). Only a tiny handful of artists – notably Raphael – commanded high prices. As late as 1879 the National Gallery in London bought its version of Leonardo's *Virgin of the Rocks* for a mere £9,000 ($43,650). Artists such as Titian, who were later to command fabulous prices, could be bought for a pittance. A great work like his *The Rape of Europa,* subsequently acquired by Isabella Stewart Gardner, sold for less than £300 ($1,450) in the 1850s. Until the twentieth century the main players in the Old Master art market were institutional – notably London's National Gallery and Berlin's Prussian Royal Gallery (later the Kaiser Friedrich Museum). Interest was largely confined to scholars and such groups of painters as the Pre-Raphaelites in Britain and the Nazarenes in Germany. Of course, Old Master prices increased towards the end of the century – all collectables rose on the tide of American spending – but it was only in the first two decades of the new century that prices took off. Andrea Mantegna's so-called Weber Madonna sold in 1903 for £4,000 ($19,400) but nine years later fetched £29,500 ($143,000). The *New York Times* reported in March 1907 that the Jarves collection, originally obtained by Yale for $30,000 (£6,185) had recently been valued at $260,000 (£53,600). The pattern is epitomized in the history of a single painting, Titian's *Man in a Red Cap.* In 1876 it was sold at Christie's auction house in London for £94 10s ($450). In 1906 it was bought by Sir Hugh Lane, the British dealer for £2,730 ($132,400). In 1914 it was knocked down at Christie's for £13,650 ($66,200) but Lane, who had just sold another Titian, *Portrait of Phillip II* to Mrs J. Thomas Emery of Cincinnati for £60,000 ($290,000), thought better of the picture and bought it back, selling it a year later to Henry Clay Frick for £50,000 ($242,000). Those who paid the highest prices were not in Europe but, as the Hahns well knew, in the United States. The one exception – and this was doubtless on the Hahns' minds as they thought about their *La Belle Ferronnière* – was the dramatic intervention of the Tsar of Russia, who in 1914 had paid a world-record £310,400 ($1.5 million) for Leonardo da Vinci's 'Benois Madonna' (*Madonna and Child with Flowers*), snatching it from the clutches of Joseph Duveen and his intended client, Henry Clay Frick. This was at a time when only two other works – by van Dyck and Raphael – had ever fetched more than £100,000 ($485,000).

Though in some sense the ferocious competition for Old Masters marks the culmination of conspicuous consumption among the richest Americans, it also posed many problems for them. Acquiring a taste for Old Masters was not easy, nor was it simple to discriminate between the work of a master and one from his workshop or by a minor artist or, indeed, by a forger. Rich these men may have been, but in their critical judgement they were no different from most museum-going visitors taking attributions on faith. Many of the richest millionaires in the United States were thus much less equipped to become men of taste than accumulators of vast wealth. Quite often they left the task of being 'cultured' to their wives and daughters. Isabella Stewart Gardner, the daughter of one wealthy man, the New York merchant and investor David Stewart, and the wife of another, Jack Gardner, a scion of a Boston shipping family, is only the best remembered of a number of women collectors who spent their family's money on Old Master art. Many of these women had attended colleges or spent time in schools in Europe; they had time to cultivate their taste. Most of the richest male collectors were not, however, university educated; they had been too busy making money to attend colleges with art-history classes or to swan around Europe. (J.P. Morgan, who spent six months at the University of Göttingen in Germany, was an exception.) Ben Altman was the son of a storekeeper, Frick of a distiller and the Wideners were butchers. All were men of acuity, intelligence and (often ruthless) ambition, but they had not been schooled in taste. Yet they knew, or had been told, that there was a higher value than business and profit, good and necessary as they might be, one that was embodied in culture and the artefacts that comprised its being – works of art, literature and music. Depending on who they were listening to, it might be a beauty that contrasted with the vulgarities of modern life, or a morality that questioned the materialism that underpinned it. Thus, the powerful and wealthy collector of art was engaged in two connected acts of cultivation – the cultivation of the self, so that he could appear to be a discriminating collector of objects and thus a person of taste, and the cultivation of the public, through the founding of museums and collections that would fulfil the civilizing mission that the fine arts were supposed to accomplish. The problem was one of how he (or less usually she) equipped himself for the task.

Anxiety about ignorance was compounded by anxiety about being taken for a ride. Any art boom is invariably accompanied by a proliferation of fakes and forgeries, and the turn of the century was no exception. Rich collectors were haunted by the figure of the disreputable, shady dealer and of the brilliant faker or copyist. Fakes and forgers seemed to be everywhere. There were famous forgers like the Italian sculptor, Giovanni Bastianini, who produced Renaissance masterpieces, and famous forgeries like the wax bust of *Flora* bought as a Leonardo for the Berlin Museums. Fakes and forgers populated works of fiction, including those of Henry James, Oscar Wilde and Norman Douglas, whose novel *South Wind* offered one of the most compelling portraits of the Italian forger, a figure that Bernard Berenson, in a letter to the London *Times* in 1903, assured his readers flourished in the numerous workshops in Florence where Renaissance masterpieces were manufactured for gullible collectors. When the Berensons visited America in 1904, they were told by Chicago collectors that their eagerness to acquire Italian Old Masters was tempered by their fear of being swindled by the dealers. In the same year, when the recently founded *Burlington Magazine*, based in London, fell into financial difficulties, a group of American collectors, headed by J.P. Morgan and John Johnson of Philadelphia, bailed out the periodical on the grounds that they needed it as an independent source of expertise. Throughout the Old Master boom the press was full of stories of frauds and fakes, both pictures and people. In 1910, for instance, the *New York Times* reported on the trial of the so-called Comte d'Aubly who had seduced a rich American widow and socialite, Mrs Charles Hamilton Paine, into buying a painting collection consisting entirely of fakes for her Paris mansion on the Avenue du Bois de Boulogne for $200,000 (£41,200). The count's real name was John Edward Dolbey. He had been born in London, and worked among the rich as a masseur and manicurist; through his father he was connected to Italian forgers. Adopting the guise of a count, in 1895 he rented a gallery on New York's 5th Avenue to display a collection that allegedly included a Titian (offered for $100,000 [£20,600]) and a Bartolomé Esteban Murillo (for $200,000 [£41,200]), as well as works by Guido Reni, Frans Hals, Rembrandt, J.M.W. Turner and a number of British portraitists. Among the paintings he persuaded Mrs Paine to buy was a version of Correggio's *The Sleep of Antiope* (now more correctly titled *Venus, Satyr, and Cupid*), the original

of which was in the Louvre. Dolbey moved in the highest circles
– he was the friend of William Morton Fullerton, the London *Times*
Paris correspondent and lover of Edith Wharton – and was by no
means the only con artist operating in the Parisian Franco-American
circles of the rich and titled. False titles and fake pictures often
went together.

Faced with such uncertainties and mostly ignorant of the quality
of what they knew they wanted, rich collectors turned to the top
end of the market, to the most reputable dealers they could find,
and the experts whose views commanded most confidence. The
Old Master business was dominated by a few firms: Seligmann's
and Sedelmeyer's in Paris, Agnew's, Colnaghi's and Sulley's in
London and Knoedler's in New York. Duveen Brothers didn't move
into that branch of the trade until 1901, a clear sign that the Old
Master market was undergoing rapid expansion. These were the
biggest dealerships, though there were also smaller businesses that
were known for the quality of their stock and the accuracy of their
attributions, notably Wildenstein's and Gimpel's in Paris. Soon
their profits were mushrooming. Between 1894 and 1901 the London
firm of Colnaghi sold Isabella Stewart Gardner, one of the first big
players on the Old Master market, more than $750,000 (£155,000)
worth of paintings. Even a much smaller dealer, the Frenchman
René Gimpel, made $162,279 (£33,460) during his first season in
New York in 1902–3; three years later his turnover was $700,000
(£144,000). Profits were even greater in the second decade of the
century. In May 1919, two months before the Hahns married and
acquired their Leonardo, Gimpel sold five works of art for a total
of $630,000 (£130,000) in the course of three weeks' trading.

Though the money was good, it was not easy for Old Master

firms, steeped in tradition, to cope with the internationalization of the Old Master trade, the blaze of publicity that accompanied its spectacular growth and the huge amounts of money involved. Most were family businesses and depended upon cultivating personal relations with their clients. As Geoffrey Agnew recalled in an essay celebrating his London family firm's 150th anniversary, 'picture dealing is a highly personal business and Agnew's has always been a family firm'. Traditional clients, museum directors, aristocrats – whether buyers or sellers – and a small group of discerning connoisseurs were loath to parade their business before a larger public whose views and tastes they saw as largely irrelevant to their collecting and which they may have even despised. On the whole, it was in the interests of dealers to respect their wishes. What mattered were the private transactions that took place on the dealer's premises, not the publicity they might excite.

The arrival of the new American collectors transformed the relationship between the dealers and their clients. In the past, though dealers and their experts had sometimes nurtured a client's taste, there was often little disparity between the knowledge of the gallery owners and that of the collectors. They shared a conversation about the appreciation of beautiful works of art. On the whole this was not true of the dealers and their new clients, though there were, of course, exceptions. The young Germain Seligman (originally Seligmann) vividly recalled J.P. Morgan's pleasure during the meetings that the greatest American collector of the age held with his father, who for many years was Morgan's chief dealer. The two men spent hours together in the millionaire's study discussing the merits of *objets d'art* that Jacques Seligman had selected for his consideration. Other collectors were willing pupils, eager to be taught both about taste and attribution, and to develop their own discerning eye. (It was the genius of Joseph Duveen as a dealer that he made this process of instruction so palatable, converting what might have been a schoolmasterly lesson into a hunt, pursuit or quest of the sort that appealed so strongly to the predatory instincts of his plutocratic clients.) By 1912, Wilhelm von Bode, the most powerful museum director in all of Europe, could comment in a *New York Times* interview that the dealers had become 'bearers of [European] culture', helping raise the quality of American collections by shaping the taste of those who created them.

However, many of the new collectors were, as Germain Seligman remarked in a memoir of the family firm entitled *Merchants of Art 1880–1960: Eighty Years of Professional Collecting* (1962), 'too busy or without a sufficiently deep interest to train the eye or the sensibilities'. They relied on the dealer and his experts; they expected quick results, and they dealt in huge sums of money. The nature, pace and scale of art dealing was utterly transformed. As Seligman explained:

> The collector of the first quarter of the century . . . preferred to deal with a leading firm, one whose name would add to the value and importance of an object in the same way that a title added lustre to its pedigree. Because he himself dealt in large sums and made large profits, he conceded the dealer the same privilege. Moreover, he had powerful competition from fellow collectors, and quick decisions were prompted by the danger of losing a coveted piece should he waver or bargain for too long.

In response to these new pressures, many dealerships revamped the scale of their operations, becoming international organizations.

This trend began even before the craze for Old Masters. Duveen Brothers had a branch in New York by the 1880s and an office in the Place Vendôme in Paris by 1905. Knoedler, a firm whose first proprietor, Michael Knoedler, had arrived in New York from France in 1846, moved back into Europe in the 1890s, opening premises first in Paris and then in London, but not before he had opened a branch in Pittsburgh to cater to the new Midwestern millionaires. Agnew's, a Manchester firm that had set up shop in London in 1860s, always portrayed itself as quintessentially British, but this did not prevent them starting branches in Paris in 1907 and Berlin a year later. Jacques Seligman's arrival in New York from Paris in 1905 coincided with the beginning of his close relationship with J.P. Morgan. Soon there were scouts trawling for old Masters all over Europe.

Yet there still remained the question of the authenticity of the growing number of Old Masters that flooded the market. Collectors did not just want old pictures: they wanted masterpieces whose allure rose from their expression of the genius of their creator. Nothing, therefore, was more important than the issue of attribution. Art historians and critics of the old school continued to make qualitative judgements about the different merits of pictures, but in the marketplace a weak (but properly authenticated) Raphael was far more valuable than a fine work by one of his lesser known contemporaries. Publicly, at least, the assumption was that there were three types of art on the Old Master market: originals (bearing the sole hand of the master), copies (acknowledged) and fakes (works of deception). Experts were aware of a more complex picture connected to workshop practice and collaborative or divided labour, but there was constant pressure on them to push works into a relationship to 'the original'. As the German curator and art expert Max Friedländer wryly commented in *On Art and Connoisseurship* (1945), 'Dealers and collectors are not served by suppositions; they demand a positive choice.'

This gave rise not just to the growth in the number of specialist experts, but to the practice of authenticating pictures in the form of a written certificate, attached either to the picture itself or written on a photograph of the work of art. As Seligman explained, 'art historians became a guiding authority for the collector and thus important to the dealer'. This did not always please the dealers – Gimpel dismissed many experts as 'irresponsible' – but American collectors came to insist that every purchase come with a certificate. As Seligman explained:

> The man who had no informed opinion of his own, yet could not bring himself, sometimes wisely, to rely entirely upon the word of the dealer, had recourse to the services of a third party – the professional expert, the art historian, or the consulting connoisseur. This was particularly true of the new collector of paintings to whom names were more important than the work of art and such attributions as 'anonymous artist of the 15th century' or 'school of' were anathema. Thus the consultant became indispensable to the dealer for he could usually supply a name as well as the detailed data which the client demanded.

The so-called 'cult of names' spawned a culture of expert certification.

For a dealer like René Gimpel, who prided himself (and with good reason) on his own expertise, the presence of such 'experts' was a sign that the art business was degenerating into a racket. As he grumblingly recorded in his diary in December 1928, a few months before the Hahn trial:

> The American collector is prey to the greatest swindle the world has ever seen: the certified swindle. Thirty years ago the American bought so many fake pictures that eventually he wanted authentications; expressly for him, experts were created and promoted; the dealer let the responsibility rest with all these irresponsible creatures, and the client no longer had anyone to whom he could appeal for justice.

Pointing to such collections as those of Jules Bache – he 'pays enormous prices but has a Bellini, a Botticelli, a Vermeer of Delft, three old pictures that aren't by the masters' – Gimpel claimed that 'Americans have bought within a short period $10 million's worth of pictures whose certifications are indefensible.'

No doubt Gimpel's remarks were coloured by his general view of American collections. For though he held many American museum officials in high regard, he was dismissive of most American private collectors, while experts like Bernard Berenson who earned their keep by offering attributions filled him with loathing. Though a dealer, Gimpel saw himself as a man of culture and discernment. He was the friend of Marcel Proust and Anatole France, an expert on the Northern Renaissance, the patron of many modern artists and the companion of Claude Monet. He made very handsome profits, but he was not altogether happy at how the art world was changing.

Gimpel's observations, though sometimes cruel and occasionally inaccurate, underscore the tremendous anxiety that surrounded the whole question of art expertise. Whoever held the power of attribution was a key player in any art market. Not surprisingly, this led to the popular perception of the art connoisseur as, in Friedländer's words, 'a magician and a worker of miracles'. Yet the miracle worker was also an object of suspicion. What exactly did he do to create such value? The object remained the same: the connoisseur did not alter its physical properties, did not reshape it with his labour. He simply gave it a new name. No wonder there were suspicions that, as Friedländer again put it, connoisseurs might also fall prey to 'charlatanism, the professional malady of experts'. These fears and apprehensions were to blossom during the Hahn affair.

If it took a while, and the evolution of a system of dealership and authentication, for the Old Master market to blossom and boom, the removal of the private collections of plutocrats into the public realm took even longer. Before 1913, the bulk of the European art in the hands of American millionaires such as Frick, Huntington, Altman and Morgan was not on public display. Huntington and Frick's collections did not open to the public until 1919. Most of Morgan's massive collection remained in Europe for most of his life. After his death it was shown at the Metropolitan in New York, but then dispersed. Isabella Stewart Gardner opened her collection at Fenway Court in Boston for only a few days a year; the Widener collections remained with the family until their donation to the new National Gallery in Washington in 1939. Altman's treasures were one of the few to move into the public realm before the First World War. Most of the biggest collectors wanted to enjoy their collections in private, to savour the pleasure of intimacy with their favourite objects; most, therefore, released them as posthumous bequests.

Yet in a way this did not matter. Although the public did not see the pictures, they participated vicariously in their acquisition. In this, developments in the press were vital. The late nineteenth and early twentieth centuries saw a massive increase in newspaper circulation and the development of new forms of journalism. The trend was most pronounced in the United States, where there were nearly 2,000 daily papers by 1900 and daily newspaper circulation per capita increased fourfold between 1880 and 1910, but also occurred in Britain, Germany and France. In part, these changes were the result of new technologies that sped the flow of information, such as the telegraph, the cable (an underwater cable link across the Atlantic opened in 1866) and the telephone. They also thrived on new techniques of image reproduction, notably the use of Eastman's portable light cameras and the development of photoengraving from the beginning of the new century. In the first few years of the twentieth century a popular magazine like *McClure's*, with sales of 650,000, ran illustrated series such as 'One Hundred Masterpieces of Painting', and 'Great Masters', featuring artists that included Michelangelo, Raphael, Rembrandt, Rubens, Albrecht Dürer and William Hogarth. These enabled many of its readers to see images of great works of art for the first time and to learn how they should be appreciated. Press coverage was facilitated by the growth of newspaper wire services and press syndicates (the Associated Press, the United Press Associations and the International News Service) that increased the density of news coverage. Together with the consolidation of newspaper ownership, they ensured that the small-town press provided global as well as local coverage. The *New York*

Times often led with news of the latest spectacular art sale (it published nearly 300 articles on American collecting of European Old Masters between 1900 and 1914), but these events were also reported in such local papers as the *Lynn Massachusetts Gazette*.

The new journalism thrived on sensational stories and dramatic events. Despite the efforts of *McClure's*, there was little in the press on technical matters of art expertise or attribution, unless it had a direct effect on the market. Art theft and art forgery (two matters with which, as we shall see, the works of Leonardo were closely associated) were well covered. They fitted easily into the well-worn journalistic genres of sensational crime and strange mystery. However, the abiding press interest was with the vagaries, intrigues and successes of the art market itself – its dealers, experts, prices and deals – and its role in the public efflorescence of art. The focus was on spectacular prices and rich collectors, and about the profit and loss of Europe's cultural heritage. Accounts of the market emphasized the vigorous competition among collectors and the fabulous prices they paid, and engaged in a sort of global accounting in which the number of works by major artists in the United States and the rest of the world was tallied: a *New York Times* report of 1909 stated that 'America now has 70 of the 650 known works of Rembrandt. It has 50 copies of Franz Hals, as against only 4 in Germany, and 7 of the Delft painter Vermeer's pictures.' Numerous examples of this sort of art-count can be found. When individual pictures were discussed, their date, provenance or aesthetic value were all overlooked for the story of their owner and recent history in the marketplace. Thus, some of the so-called 'gems' of the Altman collection given to the Metropolitan Museum were described in the *New York Times* as follows:

Mantegna, Madonna. This was the auction room sensation of 1912, its price being forced to $150,000 at the Weber sale in Hamburg ... The Crucifixion by Fra Giovanni Angelico da Fiesole. It is doubtful if another work by Fra Angelico will ever leave Europe, for all the known examples are in public collections ... Old Woman cutting her nails, by Rembrandt. Mr. Altman bought it at the Rudolph Kann sale in Paris in 1907, after rigorous competition with other well-known collectors.

The reason why paintings were reproduced in the press was almost always because of their recent arrival in the United States or their sale on the art market.

Of course, this type of coverage is in part explained by the great disparity between public knowledge of the market mechanism and ignorance of the finer points of Old Master attribution. (There was considerable support, even from within the Metropolitan Museum, for the suggestion made in 1908 by a correspondent to the *New York Times* that the museum display the price it had paid for its pictures on its gallery labels.) It was easy for the American public to understand artistic value as expressed in price, but much harder to understand aesthetic value itself. Readers were comfortable with the sort of explanation offered by the *New York Times* in the spring of 1914:

> the value of an otherwise desirable object depends on its rarity, and ... this rarity in the case of works of art has been increasing in recent years, not by any ordinary process but by an extraordinary process ... the number of purchasable works of art of

the most desirable kind is limited – extremely limited. This has resulted in a contest for them among the world's richest men.

Paintings were like pork bellies, subject to the laws of the market – this was easy to grasp – but they were not like pork bellies in that each work was supposedly unique, suffused with a singular power and beauty. Value depended not just on rarity but on identity. The pillaging of Europe was an exciting drama, a story that spoke to the emergence of the United States as the greatest economic power in the world, but it was often hard for rich plutocrats, much less an untutored public, to see why one old painting was worth so much more than another, or whether a work was a Titian or a Giorgione or merely a studio copy.

By the time of the First World War, Old Masters and their collection had become deeply bound up with the paradoxical and contradictory cultural dynamics of the United States. On the one hand they were the commodities, par excellence, that embodied the culture of conspicuous consumption. Scarce, sought after by an exclusive clientele of the super-rich who competed ferociously for their acquisition, they were hugely expensive, unique objects, whose collection and tasteful display put their owners in a class of their own. Having great masterpieces and a gallery in which to display them was *the* sign of plutocratic preeminence. On the other hand, what were these masterpieces supposed to represent? A set of values that were Old World not New, spiritual not material, aesthetic not commercial, and which, according to many critics, stood out against the acquisitiveness and crass materialism for which nearly all the rich plutocrats who owned masterpieces bore a heavy responsibility.

The public attitude to the Old Master boom was complex. In certain respects the publicity surrounding it was good news for the super-rich collectors. Reports of art collecting, patronage and the eventual donation of pictures to a 'public' institution certainly looked a lot better than the reports of violent strike breaking, collusion, fraud and stock manipulation that had battered the reputations of the robber barons. And no doubt every rich collector was heartened by the opinion of the German Professor Carl Justi who told the *New York Times* in 1910 that, 'No mere materialist could ever assemble the collection over which Mr. Morgan rules in New York'. However, press coverage and public debate paid little attention to the values that the art was supposed to embody, apart from the occasional gesture towards the public-spiritedness of the collectors. What really fascinated the press was the predatory and acquisitive conduct that had formerly been applied to railroads, banks and metals, but was now unleashed in its full force upon European Old Masters. The appropriation of Europe's cultural heritage became another chapter in the story of the triumphs of American business acumen and know-how, one in which all Americans could share. In this way the view of the Old Master boom was like so much of the response to the spoliations of the new rich – a heady mixture of admiration at their energy and enterprise, fear at their ruthlessness, and shock at their greed and the sheer egotism of it all. Henry James, then, seems to have been right: acquisition appeared to be the name of the game, a national pastime brought to perfection by modern millionaires.

However, the situation was more complex than this and James more implicated in it than his fastidious reaction to the Met might lead us to suppose. The Old Master boom, the cult of art history and good taste, lay at the heart of a new sort of culture that was at once cosmopolitan, aesthetic and exclusive. 'Cosmopolis', as Paul Bourget called it in his novel of that name, embraced rich collectors, literary figures, American students from the better colleges, bright young things from throughout Europe, art critics and experts, poor aristocrats and a fair smattering of charlatans and rogues like the Comte d'Aubly. Resolutely aesthetic, its chief cities were Rome, Florence, Paris, London, New York and Boston (with Chicago as an outlier), its chief currency Old Masters and knowledge about them, its chief value a profound social exclusiveness based on taste. Inclined, like James, to look askance on the American materialism that made it possible, members of this international elite were as much a part of the culture of conspicuous consumption as the philistine rich they affected to despise. Their snobbish claim not to deal in goods that were 'vulgar', to pursue only pleasures that were refined, and their repeated disparagement of the Middle of America as a cultural wasteland, made them far less popular than the plutocrats who were a recognizable, virile American type. The cosmopolitan pursuit of an aestheticized life which feted leisure, a cult of feeling that scorned social conventions about sex and marriage, and the view that one of the virtues of wealth was as an escape from work was troubling to Americans who believed in industry, thrift and family. This was the world that Veblen and other critics characterized less as 'acquisitive', though it was certainly that, than as marked by 'waste'.

Harry and Andrée Hahn were, in a rather different way, cosmopolitan: he American, she French, resident at different times on two continents. However, Junction City is not New York – not even Chicago – and Dinard not Paris. The Hahns were acutely conscious – and, at the same time, deeply resentful – of the values of the new cosmopolitanism. If they saw their picture, their *La Belle Ferronnière*, as an entrée into the world of the rich, they were also aware of the barriers they faced. They did not make a fortune and then transmute it into Old Masters; they aimed to transmute an Old Master into a fortune. This route, of course, was one followed by dealers and experts rather than collectors and it is therefore no surprise that they should come into conflict with them. When they did so, they skilfully drew on a set of distinctively American values to combat the opponents they faced. They opposed the plutocratic and elitist art world with a strong streak of native populism, exploiting the anti-monopolist rhetoric that had first been used to excoriate the robber barons against the art market and its leading figures; they opposed the intangible aestheticism of art experts with the hardheaded pursuit of 'facts' about the material properties of what was supposedly a 'spiritual' object. These arguments counted for little within the art world itself – they were antithetical to it – but the developments before the First World War, and in particular the extensive public discussion of cultural treasures in the press, meant that art was now judged not just in the private gallery but in the courtroom and the newspapers, where a much broader range of values came into play.

CHAPTER 2

The Culture of Connoisseurship

The radically different art market brought into being by American wealth in the late nineteenth and early twentieth centuries placed an enormous burden on the art of attribution. On the one hand, dealers, private collectors and public museums needed to be sure that the works of art they were acquiring were genuine masterpieces; on the other, an understanding of how these pictures expressed the genius of their creator, of what made them exemplary artefacts of human civilization, was a sign of the cultivated taste that collectors pursued, dealers brokered and experts confirmed. Connoisseurship, in other words, was crucial in giving a commodity, the work of art, a name that, like a modern brand, gave it a monetary value, but it was also the medium or currency in which the values of good taste, personal cultivation and, eventually, civic-mindedness were expressed. Everyone implicated in the new market – dealers, collectors, experts – was strongly committed to the idea of connoisseurship, for without it the new market could not have existed. As a system of fine discrimination, it produced order, structure and hierarchy, and united commercial value and taste. Yet what everyone wanted was also very difficult to obtain. Scholarly expertise could live with probabilities, nuance and qualification; but what the market demanded was certainty, the security of individual attributions. So when the Hahns, in their struggle with Joseph Duveen, attacked the unscientific and insecure nature of attributions not just of their painting but of Old Masters in general, they struck a blow against the entire modern system of selling and collecting art.

Even if the context of connoisseurship changed, the practice itself, as Bernard Berenson (an expert whom the Hahns loathed) remarked in his famous essay, 'The Rudiments of Connoisseurship', was hardly new. The idea that some sort of system of discrimination should exist that would enable viewers to identify the school, time and region from which a work of art derived, and even to specify the hand of a particular artist, was at least as old as the Renaissance itself. However, most connoisseurs before the late nineteenth century came either from the ranks of artists, because they were rightly thought to be able to identify paintings as part of their occupational expertise, or they were drawn from the large number of amateur collectors, or dealers who served them. Expertise was therefore either an aspect of being an artist or dealing in art, or it was self-taught; it was not a business on its own nor was there any formal education in connoisseurship. Credentials depended upon personal reputation. Experts who made their skills of attribution into a profession or livelihood only emerged in the late nineteenth century.

In fact, connoisseurship had undergone a radical transformation in the second half of the century. This change preceded the boom in the Old Masters market and coincided with a renewed interest in Italian art, especially the so-called primitives, works that predated such masters of the High Renaissance as Raphael, Michelangelo and Leonardo. Connoisseurship had never been confined to Italian art, but the great battles and debates about connoisseurship and attribution, which many observers referred to as 'a war', began among Italian scholars. The context of these struggles was not an international art market dominated by rich private collectors (which came later and had its own distinctive impact on connoisseurship), but an Italian concern to inventory and identify their artistic patrimony at a time when foreign museum directors and scholars, especially in Britain and Germany, were acquiring important (but comparatively inexpensive) Italian works for their collections.

The new connoisseurship was the first to claim to be scientifically rigorous and more carefully object-based. Its focus was not so much on the cultural and social context of art (though numerous such studies certainly existed), nor even the biography of the artists (a genre that never died out), as on the artworks themselves. However, this new 'science' did not involve what we would now think of as 'scientific' techniques such as pigment analysis or the use of x-rays, ultraviolet light or infra-red, all of which lay some way in the future. Rather, connoisseurship was seen as 'scientific' because it involved system and order. It aimed at the meticulous recuperation, classification and analysis of works of art so that schools, movements and history could be recorded. It relied on the scrupulous visual analysis of individual objects, whether paintings, altar pieces, frescoes or works of sculpture, that accompanied their attribution. It was a science of observation, not investigation; it still depended on the visible properties of pictures rather than unseen attributes that could be uncovered by new scientific techniques. In this it clearly differed from the sort of 'science' that the Hahns invoked in their struggle with Duveen.

This early twentieth-century science might not be 'scientific' by the standards of the Hahns, but commentators in art magazines and literary reviews congratulated art experts on advances in what they repeatedly emphasized was the 'science' of attribution. In an essay called 'Criticism and Common Sense' published in 1904 in the *Burlington Magazine*, which had just been established to develop more rigorous art criticism, its editors looked back, surveying recent progress in connoisseurship. They wrote:

> Half a century ago, all judgements upon the painting and sculp-
> ture of the past were little more than empiricism or mere pedantry.
> That can be said no longer. The labours of a host of students
> have cleared the ground at least thus far that in approaching any
> of the great masters we can judge of them through a certain
> number of works authenticated so far as mortal knowledge can
> authenticate anything.

Modern, scientific connoisseurship had brought 'order out of chaos'. 'Who', the editors asked rhetorically, 'would willingly return to the days when the whole achievement of Italian painting was attrib-uted to a few well-known names? The despised critics have rescued from obscurity a large number of personalities, some doubtless of little account, but many of profound interest, whose acquaintance we can now make through their work.' The *Burlington* admitted that the work could seem a 'dry-as-dust business', but 'discovery, attribution and classification', it concluded, were the bedrock on which modern art scholarship was built. In similar fashion, an essay in the *Edinburgh Review* commented 'Connoisseurship is a strictly modern science requiring the exercise of the closest obser-vation and subtlest analysis.'

This celebration of the new connoisseurship was fully justified. It is almost impossible to imagine that the art of the Italian primitives and Renaissance could ever have become so central to American collectors without the research and publications of a generation of scholars who scoured Italian junk shops, and hiked and rode to remote villages whose churches contained neglected, grimy and uncleaned works by Old Masters, often concealed in side chapels or stores. These connoisseurs were not just concerned with the recuperation of a neglected heritage, but also with discriminating between the detritus of a lost culture and its genuine masterpieces. Lost pictures were found and long-forgotten artists given their due, but also vague and hopelessly optimistic attributions were rigorously rejected. Thus, the corpus of works by Leonardo da Vinci, which in the mid-nineteenth century was said to number approximately ninety paintings, was whittled down by experts to the some dozen works that are accepted today as being exclusively by Leonardo's hand.

The two key figures in developing the new connoisseurship, one still remembered today, the other largely forgotten except in Italian art-historical circles, were Giovanni Morelli (1816–91) and Giovanni Battista Cavalcaselle (1819–97). Together, they mapped the art of Italy, becoming the source of the numerous travel books that guided British, German, French and American cultural tourists around Italy's cultural treasures, and they set new standards of scholarship in connoisseurship. The books for which they are most famous were first published in foreign languages: Cavalcaselle's great work, written in exile with the British journalist, Thomas Archer Crowe, was published in English in the 1850s under the title *A History of Painting in Italy from the Second to the Sixteenth Century*, and was followed by their magnum opus, *A New History of Painting in Italy*, whose three English volumes of 1864, grew into eleven in their much revised Italian edition. Morelli began publishing in the following decade in the periodical *Zeitschrift fur bildende Kunst.* All of Morelli's works, famously published under the pseudonym 'Lermolieff', a loose anagram of his name, appeared in German. Though they were ostensibly scholarly and narrow commentaries on works of Italian art in Roman collections and German museums, Morelli used them to range freely and to discuss artworks both in the peninsula and in museums all over Europe.

For all their similarities the two men had many differences and were eventually to quarrel not just over attributions, but over their general conception of how art connoisseurship and history should be practised. These rifts, in part disputes about method, were also about the politics of culture, and were to divide the connoisseurial community so deeply that they were still apparent when the Hahns came on the scene. Many of the experts who testified or wrote opinions about the Hahn *La Belle Ferronnière* in the 1920s – notably Bernard Berenson, Adolfo Venturi, Robert Langton Douglas and Wilhelm von Bode – had been involved in these battles for most of their careers. Everyone, it seemed, was an heir to either Cavalcaselle or Morelli.

The contributions of the two men were different, though in many respects complementary. Cavalcaselle's work was seen as 'scientific' because it systematized a great deal of knowledge about Italian art. Working for many years on a new edition of Giorgio Vasari's classic *Lives of the Painters* and hailed by colleagues as 'a second Vasari', he followed in the Renaissance painter's footsteps, but aimed to go beyond them. His approach was art historical, biographical, philological and archival – he and Crowe had teams of correspondents sending them information from local record depositories throughout Italy. Cavalcaselle also used the characteristics of the work of art itself, both to make attributions and to trace the history and development of individual painters. His surviving notebooks are full of (rather accomplished) sketches of individual works of art, as well as drawings of the details – hands, ears, eyes and feet – that identified their creators. Despite their differences, Morelli conceded that Cavalcasalle had an excellent eye, one that he used to survey almost the entirety of Italian art.

Morelli's contribution was somewhat different. Though he gained fame because of some of his attributions – most famously of a recumbent Venus in the Dresden Museum which he gave not to Sassoferrato but to Giorgione – he was better known for his frequent downgrading of works loosely assigned to one of the great masters and for his astringent criticism of optimistic attributions made by private collectors and public museums. Morelli saw his task as one of introducing a measure of rigour into connoisseurship to combat what he saw as the wishful thinking and crude boosterism that lay behind so many attributions. His target was not, however, the big-spending American collectors, who had yet to arrive on the scene, but art historians and museum officials in Italy and, above all, in Germany, where a long-standing interest in Italian art had been accompanied, after 1872, by an aggressive campaign to acquire Italian works for German museums.

Cavalcaselle and Morelli represented the two complementary sides of connoisseurship. Bernard Berenson, a protégé of Morelli, defined connoisseurship in his essay of 1902 (*The Study and Criticism of Italian Art*, 2nd Series) as 'the comparison of works of art with a view to determining their reciprocal relationship'. Such a procedure entailed both splitting and lumping, making distinctions through individual attributions and then gathering artists into groups. In an unpublished essay on Morelli written in 1889, Berenson put it rather differently. Connoisseurship, he said, enables us to 'learn the style of the Old Masters, to distinguish accurately one from another and to assign the many lost sheep that still stray about the walls of the galleries to their right owners'. Where the object was to establish an inventory of a state or region's cultural treasures, the emphasis was on establishing a field in which the sheep could be corralled, a task at which Cavalcaselle excelled. In the context of the museum and the market the emphasis was on the specific identity of individual sheep, and here Morelli was the master. In practice, as the careers of the two men show, these two contexts almost always overlapped and intersected.

Though the two Italian connoisseurs complemented one another, they and their followers emphasized their different approaches. Morelli made bold claims for his approach to connoisseurship, which he repeatedly asserted involved rigorous adherence to a method that was 'scientific', 'experimental' and 'observational'. In part because he wished to distinguish himself from Cavalcasalle, Morelli emphasized how much his approach was a departure from former methods of connoisseurship. 'All art historians from Vasari down to our present day,' he wrote in *Italian Painters: Critical Studies of their Works* (1892–3), 'have only made use of two tests to aid them in deciding the authorship of a work of art – intuition or so-called general impression, and documentary evidence'. The ensuring scholarship was shoddy and inaccurate and could only be emended by adopting a more scientific approach. Morelli also portrayed himself as an outsider (which he most certainly was not) attacking an orthodoxy. He was a famously bellicose critic, taking the view that 'writings on art which do not raise a storm of opposition can have little merit'. Thus, he described the 1868 Munich Pinothek gallery catalogue as 'stupid' and German art experts as 'charlatans' and 'ignorant'. Even his apologists and admirers, such as Sir Austen Henry Layard, the collector and archaeologist who discovered Nineveh and who financed the English translation of Morelli's works, admitted in his introduction to *Italian Painters* that 'He adopted . . . a bantering and somewhat sarcastic tone in his criticism on his opponents, calculated to cause offence'.

Morelli attacked everyone who did not, in his view, follow his method, but he singled out two important adversaries. The first were art historians, especially those in Italy who adopted or countenanced the more traditional and literary methods of his enemy Cavalcaselle. Art historians, he wrote, 'are the bitterest foes of the connoisseurs'. He looked forward to a time when 'the art historian will gradually disappear', adding, in a way that was sure to endear him to the profession, 'and that would be no great loss either'. Secondly, he homed in on museum directors, especially those in Germany like the powerful Wilhelm von Bode, director of the Kaiser Friedrich Museum, who had bought Italian art, scorning their tendency towards lenient and impressionistic standards of attribution. These assaults were so powerful and so bitterly resented that they divided the connoisseurial community well into the twentieth century. They set a standard of arrogance, rudeness and incivility from which the connoisseurial world has arguably never recovered.

Morelli rejected any art-historical work that did not make the object the centre of its attention, and any art history that used the artwork as a way of recovering the spirit of the times, or indeed the spirit of the artist himself. Art historians, whether in the academy or the museum, were, in his view, far too immersed in books and documents, housing art history in the library and the archive rather than working in the myriad repositories – the churches, town halls and private houses – in which art rested. At bottom, the problem with art historians was that they did not look. The proper subject of art history was the work of art itself; rigorous art history depended on the meticulous examination of large numbers of paintings. 'It is absolutely necessary,' Morelli concluded, 'for a man to be a connoisseur before he can become an art historian.'

In treating connoisseurship as 'scientific' Morelli seemed to be taking it out of the realm of humanist conjecture and into the world of scientific investigation. 'Observation and experience,' he wrote, 'are the foundation of every science'. Just 'as the botanist lives among his fresh and dried plants, the mineralogist among his stones, the geologists among his fossils ... So the art connoisseur ought to live among his photographs and, if his finances permit, among his pictures and statues.' In explaining why he so often differed from the numerous experts who had written about the attributions in German collections, Morelli claimed that his conclusions were 'based upon indisputable and practical facts, accessible to every observer, and are not merely subjective and aesthetic, dependent upon individual taste and impressions, as is usually the case in critical writings on art'.

This sort of statement should, of course, be taken with more than a grain of salt. Morelli's approach to connoisseurship undoubtedly grew out of the studies in comparative anatomy he had pursued as a young student in Munich under the tutelage of Ignatius Dollinger, one of Germany's most important biologists. These, he later recollected, taught him the importance of being 'an attentive, scrupulous and persevering observer'. However, anyone examining Cavalcaselle's sketchbooks or his written account of particular pictures would be inclined to feel that the science of painstaking observation was not simply Morelli's invention. Yet Morelli's claims should be seen for what they were, and for which they were gladly seized upon by art historians and connoisseurs: a brilliant and bold legitimation of connoisseurship as science, at a time when new social sciences were all the rage and when the inductive methods associated with botany, geology, anatomy, psychology and even astronomy promised to open up the social as well as natural world.

Morelli provoked most attention (as well as derision) by using certain small details, in particular parts of the human body, in attributing paintings. Raphael, Sandro Botticelli, Titian and Giorgione, as the illustrations to Morelli's works show, had distinctive ways of rendering ears and hands. These, Morelli pointed out, and not just overall composition or matters of style, were invaluable in making attributions. The line drawings that accompanied his text, illustrating his view that such details were vital in detecting the hand of the artist, captured the imagination of Morelli's readers and to this day are almost invariably reproduced in any discussion of his contribution to connoisseurship.

Almost as soon as it became well known, Morelli's work prompted a debate that still continues today. Was Morelli's scrupulous attention to details the sum total of his scientific technique, or was it merely one aspect of a larger method of systematic observation of the work of art? Morelli himself always insisted that examining such particulars was only one facet of his technique of attribution. He disparaged the illustrations of ears and hands, calling them 'caricatures made to engage the public', and when he was preparing the definitive edition of his works he deleted them from the proofs. He always denied that his method could be reduced to a mechanical process in which attributions were read-off, using a small detail. 'It has been asserted in Germany,' he complained, 'that I profess to recognize a painter and to estimate his work solely by the form of the hand, the finger-nails, the ear, or the toes. Whether this statement is due to malice or to ignorance I cannot say; it is scarcely necessary to state that it is incorrect.'

Whatever Morelli's own views, the response to his technique was ambiguous. Within the world of art connoisseurship, the issue of insignificant detail was disputed among the pro- and anti-Morellians. Outside it, the hands and ears of Morelli's illustrations became the most powerful evidence that connoisseurship should be seen as a true science.

The anti-Morellians among the connoisseurs portrayed him as positivistic and mechanical, belonging to what Charles Eliot Norton, Bernard Berenson's former teacher at Harvard, described as 'the ear and toe-nail school'. Wilhelm von Bode, who crossed swords with Morelli on many occasions, took a similar line in an astonishingly bitter attack on the connoisseur shortly after his death. Von Bode's otherwise rather sober report on the successes of the Berlin museums in acquiring old masterpieces, published in the English *Fortnightly Review* of 1891, turned vitriolic when its author considered what he called 'the Lermolieff mania'. Morelli, he said, 'had strung into a theory his experience as an old and lucky hand in collecting, and this theory is to make every believer in it infallible in recognizing an Old Master'. Von Bode summoned up the image of serried ranks of museum visitors marching through his museums, Morelli's works in hand (in fact, this was exactly what Berenson did several years later), thinking they 'will be able to single out unerringly the different masters, in spite of all the wretched mistakes of the directors'. And what enabled them to do this? 'A catalogue of ears, noses and fingers, the former property of Sandro, Mantegna, Titian & Co.', produced by a man von Bode dismissed as a 'quack doctor'.

This alarming picture of democratic and mechanical connoisseurship, rendering 'the directors' largely obsolete, horrified von Bode, who was no democrat, but would also have appalled the fastidious Morelli. As defenders of the connoisseur were quick to point out in such journals as the *Burlington Magazine*, the *Atlantic Monthly* and the *Quarterly Review*, 'those purely mechanical tests which are so frequently and so closely associated with his name form but a comparatively small part of his system' and were easily abused. 'In the hands of those whose faculties of comparison are themselves mainly mechanical, they degrade art criticism to the level of chirography'. The study of handwriting and the study of art were hardly the same thing.

However, von Bode's caricature of Morelli's impact on an artgoing public contained a certain truth; a naive understanding of the connoisseur's method held out the prospect of certainty and the possibility that anyone, armed with the right technical information, could make a true attribution. Such was the appeal of 'scientific' connoisseurship to a public outside those with detailed knowledge of connoisseurial expertise. Indeed some Morellians hinted that his method was a *passepartout* that gave almost anyone the key to attribution. Constance Jocelyn Ffoulkes, the English translator of Morelli, described his method as the means 'whereby beginners may hope to attain to a certain amount of proficiency in distinguishing one master from another', concluding, 'This road is open to all'. Lady Elizabeth Eastlake, in a fulsome tribute to Morelli called 'Patriot and Critic' (published in the *Quarterly Review*), imagined a time when, thanks to his method, the public could 'more easily learn to know a painter's special style, and, after a time, could themselves, without the help of art critics, detect if an imposter had been foisted upon us'. This was the world towards which the Hahns aspired in the 1920s. Though they did not support Morelli's view that the trained eye was the key to scientific attribution, they wanted a transparent form of connoisseurship that would rest on tests that were reproducible and could be understood and used by a lay audience.

The appeal of Morelli's methods lay in their similarity to other forms of conjectural reasoning that used clues and traces as a mode of scientific identification. Accurate and long-continued observation, argued scientists like Thomas Huxley, was central to all historical and paleontological sciences, enabling scholars to reconstruct what could not be seen. (Huxley called the process retrospective prophecy.) The morphology of an ear, a footprint or the shape of a bone made it possible to detect the presence of someone or something from the past, whether they be Leonardo, a criminal or a woolly mammoth.

Public fascination with the power of the technique of minute observation was at its height at the beginning of the twentieth century and was most heavily concentrated on the growing science of forensics. Whether in the fictional Sherlock Holmes stories of Arthur Conan Doyle or the sensational reports of criminal proceedings in the newspapers, the use of science was seen as a way of identifying suspects. Just as Morelli apparently used the distinctive portrayal of hands, knees and ears to detect signs of authorship, so Alphonse Bertillon of the Paris prefecture of police used these same human features to perfect his system of anthropometric measurement designed to identify thieves. A whole raft of techniques such as fingerprinting and 'sciences' such as graphology were acclaimed as holding out the prospect of virtually certain identification.

Morelli's methods, or at least one of them, were a part of this new scientific interest – they were, said one of his defenders, 'thoroughly in accordance with the scientific spirit of the age' – and this gained his work publicity and acceptance outside connoisseurial circles. Mary Berenson, one of Morelli's most important public propagandists, was the first person to draw a comparison between Morelli and Sherlock Holmes; they both appeared as master detectives. Sigmund Freud, writing about Michelangelo in 1914, saw in Morelli's methods the germ of psychoanalysis, commenting on his skills in 'questioning the authorship of many pictures, showing how to distinguish copies from originals *with certainty* [my italics]'. The method of 'insisting that attention should be diverted from the general impression and main features of a picture, and ... laying stress on minor details, of things like the drawing of the fingernails, of the lobe of an ear, of halos and such unconsidered trifles,' was, thought Freud, 'closely related to the technique of psychoanalysis. It, too, is accustomed to divine secret and concealed things for despised or unnoticed features, from the rubbish-heap, as it were, of our observations.'

Freud's remarks are more telling about the reception of Morelli's ideas than a just account of his method, but they show how effective the expert's claims to have made connoisseurship into a science had become. In the last two decades of the nineteenth century Morellianism was all the rage, both within art-historical circles (despite some voluble dissenters) and in the growing public of magazine and journal readers who wanted to know about art.

Von Bode's attack on 'Lemolieff mania' was right on target, a sign of the German museum director's justifiable anxiety and frustration at Morelli's influence with fellow connoisseurs and popularity at large. The Morellians were on a roll. These were the years in which Bernard Berenson (described by Morelli himself as 'the young Lemolieff of Boston') spoke of Morelli as 'omniscient' and when his name according to Berenson's friends 'was always on his tongue'. Mary Berenson published two long essays in the *Nineteenth Century* and the *Atlantic Monthly* explaining to more general readers what the new scientific art criticism had achieved. Her comments, comparing Morelli to Charles Darwin and connoisseurship to botanical classification, demonstrate how widespread (and intellectually slipshod) the desire to scientize the connoisseur had become: 'He has often been called the Darwin of art criticism, for he was the first to set himself resolutely against the haphazard or "inspirational" theory of genius, and to prove that art follows certain fixed laws of evolution, from which the individual artists can no more escape than the individual animal can escape its genus and species'. The amateur connoisseur and Titian expert, Claude Phillips, shared her views: 'it would be as absurd,' he wrote in the *Athenaeum*, 'to return to a pre-Morellian period of criticism, as it would be to study natural science without profiting from the discoveries of Darwin'.

Even as Morelli's popularity peaked, his reputation began to change. In part, this was because the more mechanical and technical aspects of Morelli's technique, though they helped connoisseurs reassure the public that they were engaged in a rigorous science, were widely felt to be insufficient for secure attribution. Enthusiastic Morellians, like the Berensons or the group of British connoisseurs who founded the *Burlington Magazine* in London, felt the need to go beyond a strictly scientific connoisseurship. Bernard Berenson's essay of 1902 on the 'Rudiments of Connoisseurship', though it offered the most systematic analysis of pictorial forms and their relative importance in the process of attribution to date, went much further: 'It may be laid down as a principle that *the value of those tests which come nearest to being mechanical is inversely as the greatness of the artist. The greater the artist, the more weight falls on the question of quality in the consideration of a work attributed to him.*' Berenson concluded that 'the sense of Quality is indubitably the most essential equipment of a would-be connoisseur. It is the touchstone of all his laboriously collected documentary and historical evidences of all the possible morphological tests we may be able to bring to bear upon a work of art.' And he was honest enough to add that this was not a matter of science, the 'category of demonstrable things', but was the proper subject of the *art* of connoisseurship. Thus, art experts increasingly argued that Morellian 'science' was not sufficient to secure a proper attribution. It was an important aid, but what really mattered was a qualitative judgement made through visual observation by the experienced expert. The pendulum was swinging back, against a more democratically accessible science and towards the conjectural judgements of a small elite. It was a trend that the Hahns were to challenge so forcefully several years later.

By the first decade of the twentieth century there was a fully fledged culture of connoisseurship centred on Italian art. The *annus mirabilis* was 1904, when major exhibitions of early Italian art were organized in London, Paris and Siena, the *Burlington Magazine* was placed on a sound financial footing, and Bernard and Mary Berenson made their triumphant visit to the United States to promote the collecting of Italian art. In his jaunty *The Sport of Collecting* (1914), Sir William Martin Conway, mountaineer, explorer and (perhaps improbably) the first art-history professor in Britain, once again looked back on the achievements of those he called 'lovers of art':

> Pictures have been deprived of false attributions which once masqueraded as the work of greater men. Pictures have been raised from anonymity into the rank of acknowledged masterpieces by famed artists. Finally, forgotten artists of the first rank have been found anew, and equipped with a longer or shorter list of known works now acknowledged to have been painted by them.

Out of these endeavours, he concluded, 'the whole giant growth of art-dealing had arisen with its huge monetary rewards'. However, what Conway described as 'a whole new class of investigators – experts, historians, archivists and the like' had not been shaped into a new profession. The ferocious quarrels of the late nineteenth century had instead produced a culture of sects whose hostility to one another remained unabated. The Morellians, whose most conspicuous supporter was Bernard Berenson, attacked the followers of Cavalcaselle, repeatedly accusing them of not attending to the detailed forms in pictures and of neglecting their pictorial properties for forays into the archives. The followers of Cavalcaselle, of whom the most voluble was the British critic, Robert Langton Douglas (writing in the *Burlington Magazine*), castigated the Morellians for their 'unintelligent use of scientific method' and their obsession with 'the morphological peculiarities of the artist's work' rather than 'the handling of the paint'. The German connoisseurs dismissed the Morellians as 'pseudoscientific' and Morelli himself as a charlatan; they saw his method as a spurious rationalization of immediate first impressions that they believed lay at the heart of attributions.

Of course, disagreement in a discipline is necessary and flourishing debate a sure sign of rude health, but Morelli in particular was responsible for a style of criticism that, though it claimed to be principled and extremely high-minded, was often deeply subjective, based on personal qualities and enmities. The way that disagreements over particular attributions elided into accusations that impugned the taste, sensibility, integrity and morality of other connoisseurs – or even denied that they were connoisseurs at all – was a recurrent problem. So, too, was the highly unprofessional conduct of experts. For example, in an ongoing quarrel with Douglas over who had 'discovered' the Sienese painter Sassetta, Bernard Berenson threatened the editors of the *Burlington Magazine*, demanding that they exclude Douglas's work from their pages. Douglas, for his part, repeatedly dwelt on the few known errors that Berenson had made in attributions, refusing, for much of the time, to recognize his rival's stature and importance. A similar personal animus marred relations between Berenson and von Bode, each of whom could be predicted to challenge the attributions of the other. Though they were the two most important experts on Italian art in Europe, they spent years avoiding one another, and when they finally came face to face in Berlin in 1922, the meeting was an embarrassment, marred by what the Berensons took to be Bode's repeated acts of rudeness.

This sort of conduct was partly explained by the absence of the sort of protocols that restrain conflict even in professions that thrived on dispute. The first generation of art experts often had no formal training. Even those, like Conway, who later became professors of art history, did not hold degrees in the subject. Academic art history flourished in Germany, was in its infancy in Italy and had barely been born in Britain. Besides, the culture of the connoisseur was not at all academic and many connoisseurs, Berenson included, were deeply hostile to art history as it was taught in universities. They preferred to use their eyes. Training took place not in the classroom but out in the field, and depended, more often than not, on the approval of a mentor. In short, it was practical and personal. When Conway made a pilgrimage to see Morelli in Milan he was told to prove his credentials by finding a work by the fifteenth-century Lombard painter, Vincenzo Foppa. Conway spent days searching more than fifty art and junk shops before he was able triumphantly to present Morelli with one of Foppa's works. This sort of 'testing' seems to have been begun by Morelli, and it usually took the form of asking the neophyte to identify pictures in the expert's collection. The famous art historian, Adolfo Venturi, never forgot the humiliation of Morelli's interrogation of him as a young man. Berenson, who underwent a similar test, regularly took his guests at his house, I Tatti, through a similar ordeal. In May 1907, Roger Fry, the Bloomsbury denizen and founder of the *Burlington Magazine*, was on a buying trip in Italy with J.P. Morgan. Dining at I Tatti he was annoyed by Berenson's persistent questioning. Berenson, he wrote to his wife, was 'quite absurd wanting to catch me out over his pictures. So I said, "I'm very tired and I'm not even going to try to think of the

attribution so will you kindly tell me what *you* think of them".'
Fry thought himself the equal of Berenson and could get away with
his refusal (though it clearly angered his host), but aspiring connoisseurs, if they wanted recognition, had to play the game which is
still practised in connoisseurial circles today.

Such tests were designed to show that the connoisseur had cultivated his 'eye' by examining as many works of art as possible.
Douglas and Berenson did not agree on much, but they both saw
travel and the study of pictures as vital to the formation of a
discerning connoisseur. Douglas wrote, 'I am confident that the
only way to progress in connoisseurship is by seeing fine pictures,
of all schools – every week, every day if possible. This is the only
way to train the eye.' And he was as good as his word, describing
himself in his *Leonardo da Vinci: His Life and Pictures* (1940)
as, 'tramping long distances on dusty Italian roads, sleeping sometimes in a railway waiting room in order to save the cost of a
bed, lodging in primitive *locande* in small country towns, with the
object of studying a few remote altarpieces in country churches,
or to see a picture in a provincial gallery'. Berenson and his wife
were no different. They spent much of the early part of their
marriage travelling throughout Italy (though they did so with more
style than the impecunious Douglas, using a motor car and staying
in the best hotels). Mary Berenson vividly recorded the pleasure
of the hunt to find pictures. It 'gave us such a joy I cannot hope
to describe,' she recalled in her unpublished memoirs, 'to steal up
to [paintings] in some shadowy church where the hot sunlight lay
in a shining pool on the floor by the open door, to creep around
the devout worshippers and to catch a glimpse of what was a
glimmering on the altar, to whisper to each other in breathless

excitement some name like "Falconetto" or "Giolfino" or what not.'

Because connoisseurship depended upon direct experience – seeing the work of art itself – it was a highly personal matter that could hardly be taught. Art history, of a sort, could be learnt in the classroom, but connoisseurship could not. This explained why connoisseurship seemed like a socially exclusive or privileged art. Only a few had the time and means to devote themselves wholeheartedly to what every expert from Morelli onwards emphasized was an exacting task. In fact, most of the important connoisseurs, like Berenson and Douglas, were not, at least when they first set out on their studies, rich men and, whatever may have happened to them once the art market flourished, they had not begun careers to make money but because they loved Italian art.

Yet, from the outset, there was a certain snobbery that surrounded connoisseurship, which helps explain the deep antipathies it provoked. The attraction of Old Master art, whether to rich American collectors or humbler cognoscenti, was, as we have seen, associated with values that were aesthetic and spiritual rather than those of everyday modern life. The connoisseur, as a sort of broker into the transcendental, did not just need the technical qualities of the tutored eye, but also the sensibility that made him (rarely her) especially sensitive to the qualities of the work of art. As W.G. Constable, the first director of the Courtauld Institute in London, the original research institute in Britain devoted exclusively to the history of art, explained in his *Art History and Connoisseurship: Their Scope and Method* (1938):

it is the peculiar difficulty and the peculiar glory of the art historian's task that . . . He has to bring to his work not just the same
intellectual curiosity, the same powers of discernment, the same
powers of weighing evidence as the political, and economic historian; but he has also to cultivate and train his emotional power
to comprehend what the artist has sought to express in terms of
material.

Judgements about pictures were not just cerebral matters but spoke
to the qualities and personality of the expert; skilled connoisseurship was a form of self election into the band of the great and the
good. It was this, I think, that made disputes among connoisseurs
so personal and ferocious; what was at stake was in some sense a
matter of character. Maintaining a reputation was especially important for those independent connoisseurs who could not fall back
on a professorial stipend or a museum salary, for their credibility
was their livelihood. However, we should not exaggerate the importance of money: the sort of enmities and viciousness that shocked
many observers of the art world preceded the Old Master boom
and the huge inflation of prices.

Figures within the art world tried, largely unsuccessfully, to
contain the conflict or, at least, moderate its tone. The editors of
the *Burlington Magazine*, as befitted the leaders of a journal whose
task was to represent more than one point of view, urged moder-
ation. 'There is no reason why the differences should be so acute,
nor why such bitterness should be imported into the discussion,
as is sometimes the case', they complained in 1904. 'A different
point of view even on important matters need not imply personal
enmity [in fact it almost always did], and we suspect that when

artistic and archaeological discussion becomes bitter and personal the fault lies rather with the friends and partisans of the critics than with the critics themselves.' The editors are clearly alluding to the rival supporters of Morelli and Cavalcaselle, whose ferocious personal allegiance to their mentors was, as they recognized, very difficult to overcome: 'To the thorough-going partisan his leader is an almost infallible prophet, to doubt whose message is heresy; and should the leader yield a point to the argument of another he is looked upon as guilty of weak concession; his party eggs him on to contradict for the sake of contradicting, and to fight when there is nothing to fight about.' Resignedly accepting the sectarian nature of the connoisseurial community, the editors concluded that 'only in theological controversy, perhaps, could such a parallel be found'.

Such hostilities did not enhance the public credibility of connoisseurship and its practitioners. Carl Snyder, an American journalist employed to solicit expert contributions to a series of (ludicrously expensive) volumes entitled *Noteworthy Paintings in American Private Collections*, spent much of 1903–4 in Europe talking to connoisseurs in London, Florence, Paris and Berlin. Though he was eventually to come to view art experts as 'the nicest lot of people I've met in a good while', he remained profoundly sceptical about connoisseurship, describing 'the whole stilkritic game' as 'the most utter rot that I know of outside of the same thing in biblical exegesis'. Yet what most struck him were the enmities. In Berlin he wrote to his colleagues in the United States, 'How absurd it is to talk of "expert" – what one praises to the skies, another sneers at as "a palpable forgery" . . . And the stories they tell about each other. Bode on Berenson . . . and so on ad infinitum – if I care to listen

– all crooks.' Snyder was to acquire what was probably a greater understanding and sympathy for connoisseurship than almost anyone outside the business, but his early impressions were of a quarrelsome, snobbish and contentious group practising an art that seemed at best obscure and at worst spurious.

For all the quarrels among the experts, in the first decade of the new century they were on a roll. Having in large part created the plutocratic interest in Italian art, many of them were quick to press home their advantage. The career of Robert Langton Douglas, who testified for Duveen against the Hahns in Paris and again at the trial in New York, well illustrates the fortunes of those connoisseurs who rose on the tide of American munificence. A Scottish cleric who was minister of the Protestant Church in Leghorn (Livorno) and who also worked in Genoa where he started a football team, Douglas had no formal training in art history (he had a poor second-class degree in History from Oxford) and was a self-taught connoisseur with a special passion for Sienese art. He published a monograph on Fra Angelico in 1900 and two years later a successful history of Siena, which his arch-enemy, Berenson, damned with faint praise in a review in the *Nation* as a 'good work in subjects finesse of taste and delicacy of taste are not needed'. For many years he worked on a revised English edition of Crowe and Cavalcaselle's *History of Italian Art,* peppering the text with lengthy footnotes in which he added or corrected attributions. By 1904 he was in financial difficulties – throughout his life he was addicted to extravagant living and at the time he had two families and a mistress. For a while, he contemplated living in Italy and supplementing his meagre income by private dealing 'as well as helping other tradesmen sell their wares'. He also thought about taking 'the post of privy adviser to some firm of art dealers', but he decided that what he called this 'furtive picture jobbing' was not 'an honest occupation for an art historian'. It was not right, he concluded in an unpublished typescript, 'for an art critic to pose as an impartial judge, when he is, in reality, a paid advocate'. And so he set himself up openly as a dealer. Carl Snyder, during his tour to recruit experts, was impressed by Douglas's candour. 'I have actually found an apparently honest man – Langton Douglas,' he wrote to New York, 'he is a dealer, though an art critic; and frankly says so. No Berenson business about him.'

For some twenty years Douglas made a steady living out of his business. J.P. Morgan and John Johnson of Philadelphia were among his clients; he bought pictures for the Metropolitan Museum in New York, the Detroit Institute of Arts, the museum in Worcester Massachusetts and for von Bode in Berlin. He collaborated with such dealers as Duveen Brothers and Colnaghi's, and in 1916 was appointed director of the Irish National Gallery. This public office he treated rather cavalierly: he was often absent, sold pictures from his own stock to the museum and was forced to resign in 1922. In the 1920s his high living caught up with him – he was supporting a third wife and a mysterious woman who claimed to be his illegitimate daughter – and he fell on hard times. When he died, he was given a civic funeral and buried in Siena, the city whose art he had helped to make so treasured.

Douglas's response to the art boom was characteristically flamboyant and unsubtle. The approach of Bernard Berenson, the expert who profited more than any other from the American interest, was rather more designing. Berenson, born in Lithuania, raised in a Jewish family in Boston and a brilliant student at Harvard, came to Europe in 1887, funded by a group of rich and cultured Bostonians including his future patron, Isabella Stewart Gardner. Four years later, and after meeting Morelli, Berenson was 'sitting one morning towards the end of May at a rickety table outside a café in the lower town of Bergamo' when he decided to dedicate 'his entire activity, his entire life to connoisseurship'. 'We,' he told his Italian companion in his 'Sketch for a Self Portrait', 'are the first to have no idea, no ambition, no expectation, no thought of reward. We shall give ourselves up to learning.'

Berenson's achievements as a connoisseur in the 1890s were without parallel. Travelling constantly, working with his married lover and future wife, Mary Costelloe, who played a vital role in drafting his publications, he produced a series of books on Italian painting which combined tart aesthetic judgement, a theory of 'tactile values' to explain the effect of works of art on the viewer, and extensive and detailed lists of attributions. *Venetian Painters of the Renaissance* (1894), *Lorenzo Lotto* (1894), *Florentine Painters of the Renaissance* (1896), *Central Italian Painters* (1897), followed in the next decade by his masterpiece, *Drawings of the Florentine Painters* (1903) and *The North Italian Painters* (1907), placed him in a class of his own. As the London *Times* commented in 1897 after the appearance of *Central Italian Painters*, 'no one living or dead, not even Cavalcaselle or Morelli himself, has seen or noted so much'.

Such scholarship did not prevent Berenson from acting in the art market. In the 1890s he made about $15,000 (£3,100) a year in commissions, some from the New England copper magnate Theodore Davis, but chiefly from Isabella Stewart Gardner, who had precociously and prodigiously begun to spend on Old Masters in the middle of the decade. However, as the new century dawned,

Berenson was plagued by financial anxieties. His relationship with Mrs Gardner, who was buying less and less, had soured, as had his relations with Theodore Davis. As he told his collaborator, Otto Gutekunst, the brilliant connoisseur who was a director of Colnaghi's, Mrs Gardner was buying 'less and less', so that he 'must be connected with someone who *has* a market'. His marriage to the now widowed Mary, the establishment at his house at I Tatti, his support for his own family members back in the United States, his wife's concerns about her two children and their financial future, as well as her enthusiasm for spending, all pressured the Berensons to make more money.

Their solution was to turn to the United States. In 1903–4 Bernard and Mary Berenson embarked on a tour – through New York, Boston, Chicago, Detroit, Cleveland, Buffalo, Pittsburgh, Philadelphia, Baltimore and Washington – whose purpose was to propagate an interest in (and therefore market for) Italian Old Masters and to repair the family finances. The strategy was twofold: Bernard would schmooze with rich collectors for whom he might become a buyer and Mary would deliver public lectures on the beauties of Italian art and the wonders of the new art criticism. The trip was an outstanding success: Berenson was lionized as the great expert; he was taken into collections and asked what to keep and what to throw away; in Chicago he was treated as a saviour who could rescue collectors from predatory dealers. Mary's lectures – nearly twenty in all, delivered at such illustrious institutions as Smith College, Yale, Harvard, the Art Institute in Chicago and to ladies' clubs in a number of cities like Albany, New York – were received with rapture. Her talks were enormously important in shaping public perceptions of Old Master art, moving between technical matters, such as 'The New Art Criticism' and 'How to Tell a Forgery' to aesthetic and moral themes like 'How to Enjoy an Old Master' and 'Art Collections in America and their influence on National Taste'. Berenson had, of course, acted as a buyer in the marketplace before, but after 1904 he and his wife (who had greater relish for the picture trade than her husband) moved more and more into the art market. As Mary wrote to her family from Boston at the end of their American visit, the 'trip may turn out to be the beginning of a fortune'. Earlier, astonished at the wealth on display in Newport, Rhode Island, she had expressed the wish that 'a small share of this river of gold will flow into our pockets'.

Four years later the Berensons were back in the United States, selling pictures, meeting with J.P. Morgan and cataloguing works in the Johnson and Widener collections. Once again Mary was lecturing, this time for a fee. The Berensons were even invited to the White House where they were introduced to Theodore Roosevelt. Over the next four years Bernard became slowly ever-more enmeshed in art dealing. In 1909 the repeal of the 20 per cent tariff on paintings from abroad pushed up prices and stimulated business. A year earlier, Berenson had been offered a retainer of $25,000 (£5,150) a year to work solely for one dealer, but had turned it down as too much of a compromise of his integrity. Yet the money and the business flowed in. During the period 1909–11, Berenson spent a good deal of time in Paris and London, working with such dealers as Sulley in England and Wildenstein in France. In 1910 he landed his own major private collector, Henry Walters of Baltimore, who gave Berenson a budget of $75,000 (£15,500) a year to buy Italian pictures for him. By the winter of 1909 Berenson confessed to his original patron, Isabella Stewart Gardner, 'I am making a great deal of money'; major improvements to the villa at I Tatti proceeded apace; the Berensons bought a second motor car.

Throughout this time the Duveens, who had decided that the fashion for Italian art was sure to grow, drew Berenson closer and closer to them, so that his business affairs became increasingly entangled in theirs. By the autumn of 1912 Bernard had signed an agreement with the Duveen firm which gave him 25 per cent on the net profit on pictures he secured for them. Less than two years later auditors revealed that Duveen owed Berenson £37,000 ($180,000) plus 5 per cent interest. In 1920 the agreement was amended to include £5,000 ($24,250) semi-annually against earnings. Connoisseurship made Berenson wealthy. In the first six months of 1928 Duveen paid him £30,000 ($145,500); before the 1929 market crash he had some $300,000 (£62,000) invested in the American stock market. Like so many others, the couple had to retrench after the Crash and into the Depression, but Berenson continued to make money right up until the final quarrel and break-up with Duveen in 1937 over the attribution of the 'Allendale Nativity' (*The Adoration of the Shepherds*), a work that Berenson believed to be a late Titian and which he refused to attribute, as Duveen wanted, to Giorgione.

Bernard Berenson was merely at the tip of a very large iceberg. He made more money than any other expert, had greater cachet and was more learned – at least in his chosen field – than any other, but he was only one among many who worked in the certification business. It became a commonplace that independent scholars, the growing number of art historians in universities and even some museum officials (though most were officially precluded from offering written opinions for money) were ready and willing to provide certificates for all sorts of pictures, some genuine, many dubious and quite a few just palpable fakes. The rewards and the pressures were great. A university professor could double his income with a couple of attributions, an independent scholar live well for a year. The dealer René Gimpel believed that Americans bought over $10 million-worth (£2.1 million) of 'pictures whose certifications are indefensible'. There can be no question that dubious pictures were hyped as masterpieces, poor works sold to ignorant collectors and heavily restored paintings described as pristine originals. The art market developed a food chain in which less eligible and more dubious works, unconsumed at the top and rejected by the grandest collectors, most reputable experts and most powerful dealers, were snapped up by less knowledgeable buyers, expertized by less knowledgeable connoisseurs and peddled by less regarded dealers. This was a path that the Hahn *La Belle Ferronnière* was later to follow. At the same time, press interest in the art market meant that scandals, fakes and errors, all of which made for excellent, often sensational copy, were given more than their fair share of column inches. These tended to eclipse the remarkable but less melodramatic achievements of the art world: the steady accretion of great public collections, the increasing sophistication of art-historical scholarship and the continuing acquisition of masterpieces in private collections.

The pressure of the art market and its dealers was remorseless, their pursuit of a safe 'good thing' unremitting. One of the investors in the lavish publication project, *Noteworthy Paintings*, exasperated at the independent and unwelcome opinions expressed by experts hired to boost the pictures it was promoting, put it bluntly: 'We are not offering a chance to these experts and so-called experts who do know or pretend to know about art a place where they can air their own particular notions ... When they'll do the right thing for us we'll be delighted; when they don't we won't allow them to spoil our work.' The Duveens' attitude towards Berenson was not much better. As Mary Berenson commented in a letter of 1913:

> They are continually at him to make him say pictures are different from what he thinks, and are very cross with him for not giving way and 'just letting us have your authority for calling this a Cossa instead of school of Jura' or 'allowing us to take it that you will approve us calling this by the master's hand as it is so close' etc. etc.

Paying so much money to Berenson, the Duveens wanted results. In 1917 they asked him for a written opinion on no fewer than 250 paintings, always hoping, as Mary Berenson put it, that 'their geese are swans'. This sort of inexorable pressure made the Hahns' accusations that experts were in thrall to voracious dealers like Duveen seem plausible.

The expert's position – even if he were Bernard Berenson – was perilous. In 1913 Berenson, after seeing a photograph, wrongly attributed a picture, supplied to Duveen by his old rival, Robert Langton Douglas, as a Giovanni Bellini. He wrote to Louis Duveen, 'All of us [experts], we are half a dozen at the utmost, know well enough how likely such things are to happen. The vulgar, however, expect us experts to be infallible, and if this mistake of mine got abroad it might be damaging to you.' Of course, what Berenson meant was that exposure would damage him, and he was concerned both about Duveen Brothers' confidence in his judgement and that they keep his error hidden. As Joseph Duveen had reminded him a year earlier, 'one mistake with a single client could be fatal'.

Berenson's dislike of business was well-known. As he told Mary, 'I cannot tell you what loathing that part of my past and present inspires me with . . . how much my life is scarred and fouled by that connection'. When the antique dealer Bauer responded to Berenson's compliment, 'A man as scholarly as yourself shouldn't be a dealer, it's horrible to be a dealer', by remarking, 'Between you and me there's no great difference; I'm an intellectual dealer and you're a dealing intellectual', Berenson was appalled and never forgave him. As he explained to Henry Duveen:

> If I stop my researches I shall lose my eye. If I stop my writing I shall lose my reputation and authority. Whispers already are getting harsher and louder that for money I am sacrificing my gifts and my higher calling . . . Not that I object to making money but I want to make it with scrupulous honesty and absolutely above board . . . it would be fatal to cheapen me to the rank of a disguised salesman . . . I practice it [business] only as a means to an end. The end is not to enlarge my business and to pile up money but to enlarge my mind and pile up understanding.

There is something distasteful about Berenson whingeing all the way to the bank, acting holier-than-thou while growing ever richer, and his very public hand-wringing has always attracted a great deal of criticism. As the nephew of René Gimpel told his uncle: 'You've seen how the snob plays at being disinterested in the eyes of the world; well, you should see his letter asking for money, the baldness of it.' The cars, luxurious hotel suites, holidays in St Moritz, the glittering array of friends that included aristocrats and intellectuals like Henry James, Edith Wharton and Paul Bourget, and the ever-growing villa I Tatti with its manicured grounds, private collections and splendid library made it difficult for other experts, less wealthy, less talented and less well connected, to sympathize with his dilemma. However, Berenson's predicament was real enough. Even hypocrites can feel guilty and there is no doubt that Berenson was tortured by the competing desires and ambitions that dominated his life. (Though, like many husbands, he was inclined to blame his wife for his weakness for the accumulation of riches.) His deep involvement in the art market had a profound effect on his career as a scholar. The earlier productiveness, the outpouring of monographs and articles, never gave out entirely, but after he entered the market he never published a work that matched his corpus before 1907. He continued throughout his life to work on the lists that accompanied his earlier publications and repeatedly revised them when new editions appeared, correcting old attributions and adding new ones. (The appearance of these lists always made Joseph Duveen very nervous as he was worried that they might damage his business and he was always uneasy about Berenson changing his mind.) Excluding all pictures in the hands of dealers, the lists were a refuge where he could engage in scholarly study and dispassionate analysis, the place that Berenson, at the cafe table in Bergamo, had sworn to inhabit for the rest of his days.

Berenson's career trajectory – one that moved from scholarship into the marketplace – plotted the changing context of scientific connoisseurship. Between 1894, when he published his *Venetian Painters*, and 1907, when the fourth of his volumes on Italian painters appeared, Berenson did more than any other expert to carry on and refine the work of Cavalcaselle and Morelli. The lists he produced (and then repeatedly revised) remain the bedrock of attributions on which the study of Italian art is based; he succeeded, to use his own metaphor, in rescuing many lost sheep, in placing them with their rightful owners and in their proper homes. At the same time, Berenson, both in his writings and in conversation, began to speak more and more of the viewer's engagement with works of art. For if, on the one hand, he came to emphasize the notion of 'artistic personality' in his writings about particular painters, he also drew on his youthful enthusiasm for nineteenth-century aestheticism to stress the profound and moving effect of great works of art upon the viewer. As one critic, Louis Gillet, summarized Berenson's views (in *Living Age*, 1 November 1926):

> According to him, a work of art is a kind of reservoir of energy discharging itself into our nervous system, exciting us and putting us in the state of mind the artist wishes to express; for a moment we feel like Michelangelo, or to be more exact, the artist through his picture enters our body and plays on it like a musical instrument. Muscular ideas of strength, laziness, violence and voluptuousness flow through us ... we share the existence of these supermen ... we find we are in a heroic world.

This was the sort of rhetoric that Harry Hahn and his friends condemned as vapid, pseudo-philosophical twaddle designed to bamboozle naive collectors into purchasing works of dubious merit and authenticity.

The new context for scientific connoisseurship was no longer the museum and the heroic enterprise of cataloguing a lost culture but, as we saw earlier, the market and the pursuit of 'names'. When the 'fourth gospel' of Berenson's work, *North Italian Painters*, appeared in 1907, it was praised as 'a pleasant relief from the ordinary art criticism of the day which has become too microscopic' and for avoiding a 'false scientificality'. The new customers or consumers of connoisseurship, though they wanted skilled and safe attributions, wanted, not to listen to elaborate discussions of Morellian detail, but to be told about quality and genius. Morellianism was never a discourse of selling; it was a rebarbative language of art criticism. In this new environment, Berenson's way of describing connoisseurship changed. He was no longer the hillside farmer, a Contadina shepherding sheep to safety and security, but a businessman demonstrating the value of an investment. Connoisseurship, he wrote in *The Study and Criticism of Italian Art* (3rd Series, 1916), 'pays its way by assimilating the isolated work of art to its kin, thereby giving it a clear title to the treasury of admiration and interest these have accumulated'.

Berenson was not, I think, speaking ironically when he used the language of capital, acquisition and piles of riches; he was acknowledging, albeit tacitly, the changing context of his life's work. His reaction to the exercise of crude economic power was the same as that of Henry James as he contemplated the Metropolitan Museum in New York's Central Park. They both regarded it as 'detestable', but Berenson, like James, thought money less tainted if it did not serve a selfish purpose, when it was used to promote 'values mainly for the mind'. Berenson's posthumous gift of I Tatti and its collections to Harvard University as a research centre for the study of Renaissance culture was thus an act of propitiation and a tacit admission that, whether he liked it or not, he, like so many connoisseurs, had made a compact with the forces of the market.

CHAPTER 3

Locating Leonardo

Where did the work of Leonardo da Vinci feature in the boom for Old Masters that began the American twentieth century? Da Vinci, after all, was one of the holy trinity of painters, described in Giorgio Vasari's famous sixteenth-century collective biography as having the sort of divine inspiration and genius that was matched only by Raphael and Michelangelo. He was therefore one of the most desirable of 'the names' that spurred on American collectors. Yet, of the three 'Mortal gods' as Vasari called them, Leonardo was the most inaccessible and the least likely to put in an appearance in the art market. Vasari's *Lives of the Artists* makes clear why. His heroes are all very different. Michelangelo is a lone heroic genius, determined to brook no interference with his art despite years of working for the papacy, answerable to no one but himself, contemptuous of his rivals and skilled in many arts. His art is sublime and filled with grandeur. Raphael, on the other hand, was sociable, 'charming', 'graceful', 'courteous' and painstaking, an artist who worked well with others, was immensely productive and who 'surpassed everyone else in facility, skill and ability'. Always conscious of the skills of his rivals, which he sought to surpass, he was less an intellectual than a courtier. His sole weakness was that he was 'a very amorous man with a great fondness for women', an appetite that Vasari claims was partly responsible for his premature death at the age of thirty-seven.

Leonardo is in some ways the bad boy of the trio. Supremely gifted, 'marvellously endowed by heaven with beauty, grace, and talent in such abundance that he leaves other men far behind', Leonardo's great failing was that 'he was always setting himself to learn many things only to abandon them almost immediately'. As Vasari tells his readers, time and time again Leonardo failed to complete works and projects. 'Leonardo's profound and discerning mind,' Vasari writes, 'was so ambitious that this was itself an impediment; and the reason he failed was because he endeavoured to add excellence to excellence and perfection to perfection.' As a result, Vasari's account of Leonardo is much shorter than those of Michelangelo and Raphael; there is simply much less surviving work to talk about. The great works that Vasari does discuss include not only those, like the Sforza equestrian monument, that were never completed, but others, such as a portrayal of the Medusa's head, that no longer survive (though a version of this subject, executed by a Flemish artist, was long hailed as one of Leonardo's greatest works). Leonardo's masterpiece, *The Last Supper*, in the refectory of the church of Santa Maria delle Grazie in Milan, was from the outset a wreck, the victim of his inveterate experimentalism that meant that the mural was not executed in a durable medium. Vasari, of course, famously mentions the *Mona Lisa* and its 'smile so pleasing that it seemed divine rather than human', but the overall impression Vasari conveys is one of disappointment at a restless, slightly odd genius with a penchant for the grotesque who was rarely able to fulfil his promise.

As Vasari ruefully concludes, 'he accomplished far more in words than in deeds'.

Even this claim is exaggerated and Leonardo remained in relative obscurity for most of the sixteenth, seventeenth and eighteenth centuries. Despite his penchant for novelty, ingenuity and technology, Leonardo never took advantage of the printing press to disseminate his ideas. His famous *Treatise on Painting*, published in 1651, was based on an abridged version of notes taken by his pupil Francesco Melzi; his work was not engraved in his lifetime, and very little before the nineteenth century; after his death 7,000 sheets of notes and drawings were scattered about the libraries of Europe; for all his fantastical schemes and extraordinary drawings, none of the machines or battlements that we know he designed have survived.

The greatest corpus of his painting (and of his followers) – the *Mona Lisa* (also known as *La Gioconda*), *The Virgin of the Rocks*, *La Belle Ferronnière*, *The Virgin and Child with Saint Anne*, *Saint John the Baptist*, and the *Bacchus/Saint John* – ended up in the French Royal Collections. Leonardo had been an itinerant, roving figure, moving from Florence to Milan and back again, to Rome and in the last years of his life to France, where he had also taken a number of his paintings. There, appointed by Francis I, one of his greatest admirers, as his 'First Painter and Architect and Engineer to the King', Leonardo lived for three years in the village of Cloux in the Loire Valley, close to the royal palace at Amboise. According to Vasari he died in the arms of his royal patron. The story was apocryphal – Francis was not at Amboise when Leonardo died – but in telling it Vasari unwittingly contributed to the process by which Leonardo was appropriated by the French.

It was not until the late eighteenth and early nineteenth centuries that Leonardo became better known. The opening up of the French Royal Collections in the public museum of the Louvre made his small corpus of painting more visible to a larger public; Leonardo's drawings were engraved (though some were of dubious authenticity); a Frenchman produced the first Leonardo catalogue; a Milanese scientist (Giovanni Battista Venturi) published a collection of Leonardo's scientific manuscripts, for the first time making the case that Leonardo was 'first among the moderns who concerned themselves with the physical-mathematical sciences and the true method of research'; *The Last Supper* was restored (horribly) and, more importantly, was praised by the likes of Johann Wolfgang von Goethe and Stendhal, and was widely circulated in the form of an engraving.

The modern cult of Leonardo took off in the second half of the nineteenth century, fuelled by French historians and critics. For Jules Michelet, the progressive historian who first used the term 'Renaissance' to describe European culture of the post-medieval epoch, Leonardo was a central figure, 'a great Italian, the complete man, balanced, all-powerful in all things, who summarized all the past, [and] anticipated the future'. His colleague at the College de France, Edgar Quinet, took a similar view in his *Revolutions of Italy* (1848–52): 'He had about him the distinctive trait of the Italian without a country, the same immense effort to not allow himself to be enclosed by any horizon, to be limited by any special form. Citizen of the world, he would wish to place himself in the foyer of the universe, to identify with the intimate genius of creation.' (The fact that the final foyer of the universe was the court of Francis I, where Michelet first placed the Renaissance, did the reputation of Leonardo no harm in French eyes.) His portrayal as a universal genius, a polymath equally adept in science and art, an inventor and artist driven by an insatiable curiosity, a visionary who transcended the conventions of his own time, made him decisively into a modern, progressive and largely secular figure. Michelet urged his readers to go to the Louvre and contrast the medieval insipidity of Fra Angelico with the Renaissance modernism of da Vinci. Stendhal wrote in his *History of Painting in Italy* (1817) that 'Leonardo was too intelligent to submit to the religion of his century'. This French view of Leonardo as both polymath and precursor of modernity was easily accommodated in the United States. Writing in *Scribner's* magazine in 1879, Clarence Cook summarized the conventional wisdom on Leonardo. He was:

> the first man among the moderns. And it is this modernism that gives Leonardo his hold on the people who know nothing of it except it is mixed up in their beliefs. They are drawn to him in a double sense as a man far ahead of his time in his scientific tendencies, and a useful inventor, and for having painted a picture [the *Mona Lisa*] that can be accepted by people with a reasonable religion, hung up in their parlors, and given out in cheap reproductions as a prize to subscribers to their newspapers. No other of the great Italian painters has ever so completely met their views.

Others were less sardonic. The *Brooklyn Daily Eagle* described Leonardo as 'the best-balanced genius in human history. He was painter, military engineer, courtier, politician, mechanical inventor', explaining to its readers that Leonardo was an amalgam of the inventor Thomas Edison, the engineer George Washington Goethals, who built the Panama Canal, and John Singer Sargent, the famous American portraitist. He would have been perfectly at home, the paper implied, tinkering with telephones, designing bridges or capturing the beauty of a young American socialite on canvas. Though a Renaissance genius, he was also an American type, at ease with modernity. He seemed eminently well cast as the fore-father of the engineers, designers and businessmen who were trans-forming the United States into the world's greatest industrial power. The fact that Leonardo's biography – or an edited version of it – was easily understandable to the modern reader, who was encour-aged to identify with it, made Leonardo's work all the more attrac-tive to a larger public.

However, there was another Leonardo shaped by the French critics, one that was to appeal far more to the aesthetes of the circles inhabited by Bernard Berenson, Henry James and Edith Wharton than to the American millionaires who could readily under-stand the appeal of Leonardo's robust modernity, with its rather masculine image of the inventor, scientist and polymath. The aesthetes and decadents of the second half of the nineteenth century saw a different Leonardo, not an enterprising engineer but a myste-rious, sexually ambiguous, fantastic genius, a dreamer who was 'smitten with the love of the impossible', more sorcerer than scien-tist, not so much a miraculous depicter of nature as someone who could penetrate its inner secrets. Their inspiration came from the writings of Théophile Gautier, poet, dramatist, critic, journalist and failed painter, and reached their apogee in the famous essay on Leonardo written by the Oxford don and aesthete, Walter Pater. What drew them towards Leonardo was his mystery and inscrutability, a quality most notable in Leonardo's female figures and portraits. These, above all the *Mona Lisa,* were praised for capturing what was sometimes called 'the eternal feminine', something the critics regarded as seductive, mysterious, ineffable and irresistible. Gautier, drawing on Vasari, emphasized Mona Lisa's inscrutable smile in the *Guide to the Louvre for the Amateur:* 'the arc of her lips appears to be about to erupt into divine sarcasm, heavenly irony, angelic derision; some inner pleasure whose secret we cannot fathom makes these lips turn into an inexplicable curve.' Pater's hugely influential essay on Leonardo, which was included in his *Studies in the History of the Renaissance* (1873) and induced Bernard Berenson to spend 'hours of long summer days' staring at the *Mona Lisa*, went even further. In two overwrought and lyrical paragraphs that were to be cited and repeated for many years to come, he created the enduring image of La Gioconda as an unfathomable embodiment of womankind:

> The presence that rose so strangely beside the waters, is expressive of what in the ways of a thousand years men have come to desire. Hers is the head upon which all 'the ends of the world are come', and the eyelids are a little weary. It is a beauty wrought out from within upon the flesh, the deposit, little cell by cell, of strange thoughts and fantastic reveries and exquisite passions.

The *Mona Lisa* was not just a great painting, the object of the art historian's tasteful appreciation. Much more, it was a mystery and puzzle, a statement about femininity and womanhood, a subject on which almost every citizen, man or woman, felt entitled to an opinion. What loomed large in this version of the painting were questions of 'human interest'. Who was the Mona Lisa? Was she the wife or lover of someone rich and famous? What was her relationship to the painter? Crucially, these questions appealed to a larger public; they did not require any specialist art-historical knowledge.

Before the mid-nineteenth century Leonardo's best known works were his wall-painting of *The Last Supper* in Milan and a painting *Medusa's Head* (famously celebrated in a poem by Percy Bysshe Shelley) in the Uffizi Gallery in Florence. Both *The Last Supper* and *Medusa's Head* (now believed to be a Flemish work dating from the early seventeenth century) were widely known through high-quality engravings that circulated throughout Europe; the *Mona Lisa* had yet to become the most famous painting in the world. Yet, in the hands of the likes of Gautier, Pater, Algernon Swinburne and Oscar Wilde, men well capable of falling in love with a work of art, La Gioconda became an archetype of female beauty. Inscrutable, dominant, a femme fatale with a bewitching smile, she was a match for the Salomes, Cleopatras and Delilahs that populated the paintings in Europe's nineteenth-century salons. The obsession of literary critics and commentators with the painting meant that by the late nineteenth century Leonardo had become best known as the creator of the *Mona Lisa,* a portrait of an enigmatic woman that was rapidly becoming the most famous painting in the world. As a Baedeker guide put it in 1900, the *Mona Lisa* is 'the most celebrated female portrait in the world, the sphinx-like smile of which had exercised the wits of generations of poets and artists and still fascinates in spite of the darkened condition of the canvas'. Fascination with the painting enhanced a fascination with Leonardo. In the early twentieth century the artist was the subject of a bestselling fictional biography, Dmitri Merezhkovski's *The Resurrection of the Gods*, a number of successful plays and, most famously, Sigmund Freud's psychoanalysis in his essay 'Leonardo Da Vinci and a memory of his Childhood' of 1910.

So when Bernard Berenson wrote about Leonardo in his authoritative *Florentine Painters* (1896), he was voicing not just an art-historical opinion but a public cliché:

> Who like Leonardo has portrayed the timidity, the newness to experience, the delicacy and refinement of maidenhood; or the enchantress intuitions, the inexhaustible fascination of the woman in her years of mastery? Look at his many sketches for Madonnas, look at Donna Laura Minghetti's 'Profile of a Maiden' or at the *Belle Jocande* [*Mona Lisa*], and see whether elsewhere you find their equals.

However, as Berenson's remarks unwittingly reveal, Leonardo had another sort of visibility, for the artist's work had a particular association with forgery.

In 1896 Berenson assumed that Donna Laura Minghetti's *Profile of a Maiden* was one of Leonardo's masterpieces, but the work became a notorious fake. The father of modern connoisseurship, Giovanni Morelli, bequeathed this picture from his private collection to Donna Laura Minghetti, the beautiful wife of a close friend who had also been the prime minister of Italy. Like the Hahns' *La Belle Ferronnière* some years later, the Minghetti portrait was taken to the Louvre and also examined by experts in London. Bernard Berenson authenticated the work and in 1898 it was sold to one of the first American collectors he worked with, Theodore Davis. When he heard that Davis had bought the picture, Berenson wrote to his mentor, Isabella Stewart Gardner, distancing himself from the painting. He admitted to her that he adored the picture, 'but its authenticity is not even to me certain'. It had been too touched up and altered. He was glad, he said, to see a possible Leonardo in the United States, even though it was a 'wreck of a Leonardo, and thoroughly modernized to boot'. The picture continued to haunt him. In 1904 he published a letter in the *Nation* to quash rumours that he had been paid a huge fee for the sale of the picture. By the second decade of the twentieth century it had been exposed as a fake, executed by a nineteenth-century Italian sculptor and restorer of pictures, Angiolo Tricca. The discovery discomforted Berenson and gave ammunition to his enemies who mocked his injudicious public assertion (made in an article to the London *Times*) that the good connoisseur would never be fooled by a forger. Thereafter, Berenson dropped all mention of the picture, but the case remained prominent in the growing literature that voiced misgivings about the number of fakes on the market.

Nor was this the only instance of a fake Leonardo. In 1909 Berenson's rival and enemy, Wilhelm von Bode, the most important figure in the European museum world, purchased for the Kaiser Friedrich Museum a 'Leonardo' wax bust of *Flora* for the sum of $40,000 (£8,250). Letters appeared in the British press claiming the *Flora* as the work of a London sculptor named Richard Lucas. The sculptor's son claimed that his father had left fragments of the London *Times* of 1872 in the base of the bust. The Leonardo was brought to London and the fragments found; the work was declared a fake. The story was so well known that when the *New*

York Times published comments on von Bode's views of American collections, he was described as 'Dr. Bode, of the Leonardo wax bust fame'. (Interestingly enough, it was later shown that Lucas had only restored the figure, which was then reattributed to Leonardo.)

The issue of forgery was made all the more complex by the existence of many copies of works by Leonardo. These had sometimes been made officially, as in the case of the Leonardos in the French Royal Collections, where copies were made for royal residences and court officials, and more frequently as sellable images in the age before the age of the camera and mechanical reproduction. Sometimes these copies were claimed to be originals and therefore became fakes. Just before the Hahns put their version of *La Belle Ferronnière* on the market, there had been a flurry of claims about Leonardo, all the result of an event that ensured that his *Mona Lisa* really had become the best-known painting in the world.

On 21 August 1911, a Monday when the museum was closed, a young Italian painter-decorator working in the Louvre, Vincenzo Peruggia, cut the *Mona Lisa* from its frame, hid it under his coat and smuggled the picture from the building. The outcry was immediate and the press had a field day. The Parisian newspapers bemoaned the loss of a national treasure and filled their pages for several weeks with every anecdote and story about the painting. The *Petit Parisien*, the French capital's bestselling daily, carried banner headlines; the illustrated magazine, *L'Illustration*, had a full-page colour reproduction of the *Mona Lisa*, as well as a picture of the empty wall where it had once hung. The *London Illustrated News* also published a double-spread colour version of the painting. The theft was front page news in the *New York Times* and other American papers. Soon the robbery was the subject of songs, cabarets and even a film. Though the media frenzy died down within a few weeks, it was reignited when Peruggia and the painting were apprehended in Florence in November 1913. Safely recovered, the *Mona Lisa* was shown before huge crowds in the Uffizi, then in Rome and finally in Milan (where the picture was seen by an estimated 60,000 people), before being returned to Paris on the last day of the year. The painting was then put on special display in Paris prior to its return to the Louvre.

The international press coverage of the theft and recovery of the *Mona Lisa* meant that many who had never really studied art or visited the Louvre became familiar with the painting and its creator. The story encouraged the public to think of Leonardo's painting as if it were a person. The French press – though this was mirrored elsewhere – almost always referred to the picture as 'she'. The *Mona Lisa* was not so much stolen as kidnapped.

One of the effects of the picture's two-year absence from the Louvre was to foster a number of claims that the artwork returned to Paris was not in fact the original Leonardo, but a copy. Soon, there were all sorts of stories circulating about the painting. The *Mona Lisa* and Leonardo became the object of many claims, most of them highly implausible, many of them fantastic. In 1914 the *New York Times* reported that the well-known British art critic, P.G. Konody, had speculated that Leonardo might have painted two versions of the *Mona Lisa*, a suggestion that initiated a spate of *Mona Lisa* sightings in different countries. In 1915, for example, John R. Eyre claimed to have found a better version of the *Mona Lisa* than the painting in the Louvre; it was in the possession of his stepson in Isleworth, West London. This was one of the earliest claims that the true Leonardo was to be found elsewhere.

It may be that these various attempts to recycle his works were a consequence of the almost total absence of new works by Leonardo on the art market. In this, he was unlike Raphael who had been far more productive as a painter. In 1910 J.P. Morgan paid a world record price of £100,000 ($485,000) for the Raphael Colonna altarpiece and, not to be outdone, Peter Widener bought the smaller of the two 'Panshanger Raphael Madonnas' for £116,500 ($565,000) three years later. However, in the boom before the First World War, sales of works by Raphael's great rivals, Michelangelo and Leonardo, were limited to drawings. The one great exception was the sensational sale of Leonardo's 'Benois Madonna'. Duveen had intended this for the Frick Collection but had been outwitted by the seller, who accepted an offer (and world record price) of £310,000 ($1.5 million) from the Tsar of Russia in 1914. As Louis Levy, Joseph Duveen's lawyer, was later to remark, finding a Leonardo on the open market was a bit like discovering a new planet. It was not until 1967 that the first undisputed Leonardo painting was acquired by an American buyer, when Paul Mellon purchased the artist's earliest surviving portrait, *Ginevra de' Benci*, from the Prince of Liechtenstein and gave it to the National Gallery in Washington.

So, as the Hahns set out to sell their version of Leonardo's *La Belle Ferronnière*, they could be sure that their painting would excite interest not just in the showrooms of dealers but, with appropriate publicity, among the public at large. To have a painting that claimed to be a Raphael was almost as desirable as one that appeared to be a Leonardo, but any work by Leonardo had the advantage that it came with a name that was immediately recognizable outside the art world. To have a Leonardo female portrait that was not a

Madonna and that seemed to have 'the same haunting, unfathomable expression' as the *Mona Lisa* – it was always a claim of the Hahns that their picture had much more of a 'Leonardo smile' than the version of *La Belle Ferronnière* in the Louvre – was also to have a painting that lent itself to a variety of stories that went beyond the purely art historical.

On the other hand, the dramatic events that surrounded the *Mona Lisa* before the First World War had thrown up a number of charlatans and fantasists ready to latch on to the Leonardo name. (This was why, when Peruggia went to London in 1912 and offered Joseph Duveen the *Mona Lisa*, he was treated as deluded and shown off the premises.) Duveen's rather cavalier dismissal of the Hahn *La Belle* as an obvious copy, an act that was to cost him dear, has to be seen in the light of the large number of so-called Leonardos in circulation in the period around the First World War. (Duveen was able to obtain at least two other *La Belle Ferronnières* when he was preparing for the trial with the Hahns in 1929.)

Besides, as Leonardo rose in popular esteem, so his star began to wane among the art-historical intelligentsia. The cult of Leonardo, despite its roots in Vasari, was literary as well as populist, its relation to the new forms of scientific art criticism tangential at best. Roberto Longhi, the highly influential Italian art historian and connoisseur, launched a full-scale attack on Leonardo and the *Mona Lisa* in 1914, making it clear that Leonardo's popular appeal should not lead to his over-valuation by serious scholars. Berenson, repelled by what his biographer calls the 'outpouring of sentimental idolatry' provoked by the theft of the *Mona Lisa*, backed away from his youthful enthusiasm for Leonardo, his admiration of Pater's assessment of the artist and his most famous works. By 1916, in an essay on Leonardo in his *Study and Criticism of Italian Art*, uncharacteristically addressed to 'the general reader', he had almost wholly turned against the artist. He sharply criticized *The Last Supper* ('a pack of vehement, gesticulating noisy foreigners') and the *Mona Lisa* ('an incubus') and lambasted the 'Benois Madonna' (the most expensive picture in the world) as 'a young woman with a bald forehead, and puffed cheek, a toothless smile, blear eyes, and furrowed throat ... the uncanny anile apparition plays with a child who looks like a hollow mask fixed on inflated limbs and body'. He deprecated much Leonardo criticism as excessively literary ('What an enchanted adept died in me when I ceased listening and reading and began to see and taste!') and claimed that the artist was responsible for the decline of Tuscan art. Leonardo's invention of *contrapposto* (turning the body on its own axis), wrote Berenson, had the immediate effect of killing Florentine art: 'No Tuscan painter or sculptor, born after Leonardo's death, produced a single work with the faintest claim to general interest.'

Interestingly, Berenson blamed his loyalty to Morelli rather than his debt to Pater for his continued adherence to Leonardo. 'Morellianism,' he wrote, 'surgical, pitiless, iconoclastic even as it seemed, was yet inspired by the Romantic ideal of genius and founded on the axiom that the greatest artist from cradle to grave never derogated from his greatness ... It was in defence of this that we Morellians fought for authenticity with the uncompromising zeal of Legitimists.' But pursuit of this cause had some ill consequences:

It was indeed, a brave fight and worthy, although it fortified the snob collector's blind confidence in mere names, and led him to accumulate unpalatable but authentic daubs by Rembrandt and other prolific geniuses, but the very method of establishing authenticity by tests so delicate, so subtle, and so complicated, has led us on, little by little, to conclusions the exact opposite of the axiom with which we started out.

Strict connoisseurship, he concluded, had to recognize that great masters sometimes produced 'poor things'. Quality should not be slavishly subordinate to 'names'.

However, Berenson allowed one exception to his caustic criticism. His 'whole heart went out to the portrait of the girl known as "La Belle Ferronnière". I was on my own level again, in my own world, in the presence of this fascinating but yet simple countenance with its look of fresh wonder.' Yet, here the Morellian attributor returned. He may have loved the painting but admitted that, 'I resented this beautiful thing because I could not name its author'. He was uncertain about its attribution. As he concluded, in words that prefigure the bitter contest between Duveen and the Hahns that was to begin just four years later: 'But whose in all the world if not his, and if his, in no matter how limited a sense, in what moment of his career could he have created her?' Berenson always insisted that the great connoisseur would admit to errors, doubts and changes of mind, but the case of the Hahn *La Belle*, driven as it was by the remorseless demand for incisive certainty, made such a course of action, as he and his fellow connoisseurs were to discover, hazardous in the extreme.

CHAPTER 4

Dealers and Clients

In the first two decades of the twentieth century the world of Old Masters was dominated by plutocratic collectors from the United States and by European connoisseurs and dealers. Centred on New York, Paris and London, it was part of a cosmopolitan society that combined the progressive energy of modern American capitalism with the stable culture and tradition (art, aristocracy and 'culture') of Old Europe. Its doyens bore a marked resemblance to the characters that inhabited Henry James' novels: snobbish impoverished aristocrats, like Prince Amerigo, or financiers and art collectors, like Adam Verver, in *The Golden Bowl*. Metaphors of collecting and acquisition were common throughout the fiction of the period, though nowhere more explicit than in James' very last novel, *The Outcry* of 1914. The title alludes to the public opposition to the acquisition by an American collector, Breckenridge Bender (loosely modelled on J.P. Morgan), of works of art in British aristocratic collections. Lord Theign and Lady Sandgate, stalwart members of Europe's *ancien régime*, struggle between the private temptation of taking the plutocrat's inflated offers for their masterpieces, bending to the power of modern riches which will also relieve them of financial embarrassment, and their more traditional obligation, as custodians of the national heritage, of keeping great works of art in Britain. The plot is complicated by the actions of a young Morellian connoisseur, Hugh Crimble, redolent of Roger Fry, engaged in 'playing football with the old benighted traditions and attributions you everywhere meet', who reattributes one of the Italian Old Masters in Lord Theign's collection. Improbably but not impossibly, and in large part because of the efforts of Crimble and the woman he loves, Lord Theign's lovely daughter, Theign and Sandgate's paintings end up not in New York but in the National Gallery in London. *The Outcry* is not a great novel – it was originally a play that never made it to the stage – but in placing Old Masters at the heart of the social exchange between Old World snobbery and New World money it perfectly captures the nature of the world that James' French friend and novelist, Paul Bourget, called 'Cosmopolis'.

It is almost impossible to imagine Harry and Andrée Hahn as characters in one of James' fictions and it is equally difficult to see them as part of the cosmopolitan society of the early twentieth-century art world. They belong not to that strand of American fiction that casts its eye over the inner sanctum of the rich and famous but to the more socially capacious vision of writers like Theodore Dreiser and Sinclair Lewis. Andrée Hahn seems like a French version of Caroline Meeber, the eponymous heroine of Dreiser's *Sister Carrie*, a small-town girl bent on escaping the narrow confines of provincial life and using her not inconsiderable charms for social advancement. Harry was a character straight out of Lewis's *Babbit*, a Midwestern businessman and booster, an habitué of Rotary Clubs and Masonic meetings. However, the couple remain an allusive target for the historian, not just because of their humble origins, but also because they and the press told conflicting stories about their past. What we know about them comes either from retrospective accounts from the Hahns themselves and from Louise de Montaut, the woman who 'gave' Andrée the painting of *La Belle Ferronnière* as a wedding gift, or from detectives hired by Joseph Duveen to investigate the family and the picture. The former were designed to defend the Hahns and their picture, the latter to blacken the family's reputation. Both contain their fair share of fiction.

Harry Hahn was a man who liked to talk and tell stories. His daughter describes him as a bon viveur, a man of great personal charm but also a bit of 'a braggart' who liked 'to talk about himself'. He was born in a small town in Kansas on 14 June 1896. Unfortunately, what he said about himself was often inconsistent and sometimes untrue. Speaking late in life to a chapter of the PEO, a women's education organization, in the small town of Ellsworth north of Wichita, he told them that he was born in the town of Leavenworth, some thirty miles north of Kansas City, and that by the time he was ten both his parents were dead; he was brought up, he said, by 'an uncle and aunt', Dr and Mrs Henry Mayer. It is no surprise to find that his claims do not accord with the information on his marriage certificate which records his place of birth as Junction City, Kansas. This was the town in the middle of the state to which he brought his bride in 1920 and where for a while he had an automobile business. At all events, it seems plausible that Hahn was born in a small Kansas town. Leavenworth and Junction City, though they differed in size – the former had a population of 19,000, the latter of about 5,600 – were quite similar. They both had large military bases nearby, and their plants and small businesses manufactured products for the railroad industries and processed agricultural goods. Leavenworth had a greater variety of businesses and a large penitentiary – one in twenty inhabitants was a prisoner – but both were communities dominated by the army, their local churches and a tight-knit business community.

Harry told his audience of PEO members that, after graduating from high school, he worked for an equipment company in Kansas City on the Missouri side of the river. On an earlier occasion he had told the *Wichita Beacon* that in 1917 he volunteered to serve in the US army and was assigned to the 96th Bombardment Squadron, based first in Texas and then in France where it provided air support for the French 8th and the American 1st armies. Here he seems to have worked as a motor mechanic rather than as a flier. Once he found himself in the limelight because of his wife's painting, he liked to refer to himself as Captain Hahn, though the uniform he wore at his marriage a few months before his discharge is not that of an officer but of a humble sergeant. Later newspaper reports sometimes referred to him as both an aviator and a member of General John J. Pershing's general staff, and claimed that he had been decorated by both the French and American military author-ities, having won the Legion of Honour and the War Cross, decor-ations not normally awarded for engine maintenance. It is difficult to imagine that these 'facts' came from anyone but Harry himself.

Information about Andrée Hahn is a little more secure than the mystery that surrounds the earliest years of her husband. When the trial of the Hahns' case ended in 1929 and a retrial seemed immanent, Sir Joseph Duveen decided to get tough and dig out any family dirt that could blacken her character. He was particu-larly concerned about the newspapers' repeated claims that Andrée was an aristocrat. She was variously described in the American and French press as 'the daughter of the Marquis de Lardoux', the niece of the Marquis de Chambure and of the Comtesse de Pontbriand. There was, as Duveen knew, no Marquis de Lardoux, though Ladoux was Andrée's maiden name; Andrée was not related to the Chambure family (they published denials in the press of any family connection), but she was the niece of the Comtesse de Pontbriand, for the first husband of her aunt Anna was an impecunious aristocrat, the Comte de Pontbriand – known in the family as the count of no account. By 1919, however, Anna was no longer married to the count and was with her third husband, a dealer in antiques.

Duveen hired a new criminal lawyer and employed a number of detectives to dig up dirt about the Hahns and their relations. Some of this information is suppositious and unreliable, intent on blackening his opponents (there were unsubstantiated rumours of prostitution and a bastard child), but the investigators also unearthed a good deal of concrete information, especially about Andrée's family, much of it corroborated by Jacqueline, her daughter.

According to the detectives, Andrée was born on 19 August 1896 at Argentan, a village in Normandy, south of Caen. (She celebrated her birthday on 17 August and claimed to be born in 1897.) Her father, Adrien, was a small jeweller in La Haye Pesnel, some miles east of Dinard and St Malo; her mother came from Vendôme in Loire-et-Cher. The marriage was not a success and at a young age Andrée left her parents and was taken into the care of Josephine Massot, who ran a millinery shop in the main street of Dinard, not far from the harbour. The premises on the rue Levavasseur were owned by Andrée's grandfather, a man of some substance

who was a process server (*huissier*) and owned a number of properties in the town. Andrée went to the local municipal school and,
according to her daughter, was also educated across the Channel
in Greenwich, where she learned to speak English. The shop was
quite a large establishment; Andrée and her 'godmother' lived on
the floor above the piles of hats and dresses; the third floor contained
rooms that were rented out in the holiday season. Jacqueline Hahn
recalls that Josephine Massot employed seventeen workers in the
millinery shop. Whether Andrée worked in the shop is not clear –
her daughter denies that she ever worked in her entire life – but
it is difficult to imagine that she did not help out her godmother
once she had left school in 1910. Here she settled, surrounded by
relatives, most notably her grandfather, but also her aunt, Anna,
who visited from Paris where she worked for an antique dealer on
the Boulevard des Batignolles.

Dinard had originally been a fishing village but by the late nineteenth century had become a fashionable resort town; its resident
population, augmented by an annual influx of summer visitors,
was 4,787 in 1913. Its development owed much to the wealthy
British and American visitors who had built villas overlooking the
Atlantic on the cliffs around the town (more than 400 survive as
listed buildings) and to the English-speaking community of former
army officers and retired colonial civil servants who worshipped
in the town's Anglican church – there were often over 250 commun-
icants at Christmas and Easter – and patronized its cafes, pastry
shops and clubs. Before the First World War, the town had two
casinos – the High Life, completed in 1900 with a large theatre
and ballroom, a restaurant and billiard and gaming rooms, and Le
Grand Casino, open for '*representations populaires*'. In addition,

the resort boasted a large number of hotels, with names such as Hotel Windsor, Anglo-Norman and Hotel de Provence et l'Angleterre that betray the British influence. Visitors could use a golf club, a tennis club, a lending library called 'Le Book Club', and a race-course where summer meetings were held. Much of the British clientele was wealthy. Dinard was visited by Edward VII when he was Prince of Wales, and his brother the Duke of Connaught and the Duke's wife were regular worshippers at the English church, whose parish registers record gentlefolk and their servants and chauffeurs (the middle class is largely absent). It is, therefore, not surprising that Andrée was apparently sent to Greenwich to learn English, a skill that was extremely useful in dealing with the British and Americans who gave the town what one French guidebook described as its 'worldly' (*mondaine*) atmosphere.

Most of Dinard's inhabitants worked in the hotels, casinos, cafes and restaurants that catered to its visitors and to those who had retired there. Andrée's street, the rue Levavasseur, included not only her godmother's '*magasin des modes et fantasies*' at number twenty, but four hotels as well as an annex to the Grand Casino. In addition, four agencies in the street rented out furnished rooms, apartments and villas, several premises provided horses and carriages for visitors, and there were three banks. No doubt the town was lively in the summer season, with its balls, concerts, regattas, theatrical performances and crowds of tourists, but in the winter it became a sleepy provincial town, its grandest hotels like the luxurious 200-room Crystal shuttered up against the winter cold, the smaller premises slashing their rates in the hope of keeping a little custom. A number of small proprietors and hoteliers had other businesses on the Côte d'Azur where they spent the winter, returning to Dinard for the summer season. One can't help but compare the childhood of Andrée in Dinard with that of Federico Fellini in Rimini – an ordinary life enlivened by the sleek, well-heeled and sometimes extremely rich visitors and tourists that passed through the town.

The seasonal rhythms of the seaside resort were shattered by the First World War. In 1914 the town was inundated with refugees from Mons and Charleroi, civilians who had been driven from their homes because of fighting to the east and who were accommodated in its hotels, boarding houses and villas; after the terrible French casualties of the first year of the war, its hotels and casinos were converted into temporary hospitals manned by volunteer nurses to treat wounded soldiers. Though far from the front, the life of the town was profoundly affected by the war. It also almost certainly brought Harry into Andrée's life. His postings in France were all in the eastern part of the country, close to the front, far from Dinard on the Brittany coast. Perhaps he was visiting a wounded comrade; just as probably he was seeking excitement during leave. At all events, less than two years after Harry's arrival in France, he married Andrée on 12 July 1919, shortly before he was discharged from the army. A poor boy from Kansas may not have been much of a catch, but as an American he offered an escape from the humdrum life of a small French town. Harry was always a braggart and he probably plied Andrée with stories of the wonders of the New World. It is also not difficult to imagine why he would have been drawn to a handsome young woman with the additional attraction that she spoke good, if sharply accented English. (There is no evidence that Harry knew any French when they first met.) The couple had similar tastes. Neither liked the dull life and both, according to Jacqueline, loved company and the excitement of parties. Andrée was vivacious, Harry a skilled raconteur. They enjoyed being the centre of attention. Yet none of this is apparent in their wedding photograph, which shows a nervous young couple. Harry holds a pair of dark gloves in his hand, Andrée rests her hand on his arm and they lean rather stiffly towards one another. The groom looks anxiously towards the camera, Andrée's face and smile are more open, but she also seems apprehensive. It was difficult to imagine that these rather diffident twenty-three-year-olds were about to shake up the art world.

Yet appearances can be deceptive. Harry may have been something of a moonfaced small-town boy, but he was a man who thrived on adventure and enjoyed taking risks, the bigger the better. Charming, feckless, constantly short of money (which he borrowed from everyone, including his own daughter) and eager to enjoy the good life, Harry was one of life's chancers. He was also often profligate with the truth, raising his military rank and claiming at different times to have introduced petrol pumps into France and to have entertained the Queen of Romania, the King of Spain and the Aga Khan at what he described as his 'exclusive restaurant', the so-called Celtic or Rally Bar which he and his wife set up after their marriage on the premises of the *'magasin des modes'* on the rue Levavasseur. Harry was a dreamer and schemer, someone for whom the ordinary life held out few attractions. For him the American Leonardo was an opportunity to enjoy a certain notoriety, to put himself about on the public stage – he especially liked to address the numerous business associations and women's clubs that were scattered across the middle of the country – and to bask in the limelight.

Andrée was a rather different character, someone who added firmness and resolution to Harry's flights of fancy. Strikingly attractive with her bobbed hair, high cheekbones and cloche hats (courtesy of the family business), she made a profound impression when she appeared at the trial in New York and carried herself as a woman of dignity and consequence. *Time* magazine described her as bringing to her husband 'a natural dowry of dark hair and eyes, Gallic chic'. (Her performance on that occasion must have been extraordinarily difficult – the young French provincial facing not just the trial lawyers but the entire American press – yet she acquitted herself with aplomb.) It was always her concern to be a lady: she never seems to have worked, even at times when the family's finances were precarious. Her abiding concern, revealed repeatedly in her correspondence about her painting, was in the social advancement of herself and, even more importantly, her family – the daughter, Jacqueline, she bore on her first trip to Kansas, and her son, Harry Junior, who was born some years later in Dinard. For Andrée, the American Leonardo was not about publicity or fame, and certainly not about art – she showed no real interest (and far less than Harry) about the painting as an art object. She saw it simply as a means to family fortune, though the resistance she met to her claims for its authenticity also rankled her pride. However, where Harry was mercurial, sometimes showing an obsession with the picture, at others seeming to view it almost with indifference, Andrée was doggedly persistent, determined to persevere against all the odds. Typically, after the trial in 1929 had ended with a hung jury, she had sworn that, if necessary, she was ready to fight Sir Joseph Duveen for another nine years to vindicate her picture and see justice done.

Harry and Andrée made a formidable team, their strengths (and weaknesses) complementing each other. Yet any outside observer must have thought that the young couple stood little chance against their adversary, the man they had decided to fight because he obstructed their ambition to sell their *La Belle Ferronnière*. When Joseph Duveen was asked about the Hahn painting by the *New York World*, he was already a figure of notoriety and not just in the art world. In 1919 he was fifty years old, the son of one of the most successful decorative arts dealers in London and the chief partner of a family firm determined to dominate the rapidly expanding American market for Old Master art. Dapperly dressed, always ensconced in the best hotels and often to be found in the headlines of the world press, Joseph Duveen was the great showman of the art market, the self-proclaimed most spectacular art dealer of all time. Known as a bon viveur, impeccably dressed in perfectly tailored suits, never without a cigar in hand, he had a reputation as a hard-nosed negotiator who would nickel-and-dime an old friend, but then impulsively shower him with lavish gifts. In the years before the First World War Joseph Duveen had perfected the manner that was to be his trademark for the rest of his career: an ostensible contempt for money that drove his partners to despair; a willingness to take risks – the more vertiginous the better; a relish for conspiracy and undercover activities; and a determination to live on a par with the richest men in Europe and the United States, matching their extravagance but exceeding them in taste. Duveen was a showman, clowning it in England, according to Kenneth Clark, but lording it over clients in the United States. Anecdotes about his stupendous deals and flamboyant largesse flourished not just in the showrooms and corridors of dealers and galleries, but in newspapers and magazines. Never one to hide either his talents or his foibles, Joseph Duveen was the chief propagator of his own legend.

Duveen was fond of portraying himself not merely as the greatest art dealer in the world, but as someone who monopolized the trade in the greatest Old Masters. He wanted the sort of control over the art world that such clients as J.P. Morgan and John D. Rockefeller had over finance and oil. As his brother-in-law, the French dealer René Gimpel, remarked, 'Joseph Duveen does business as he would wage war, tyrannically.' And when his collaborators and clients were angry or alienated by him, they reinforced the Duveen myth of absolute power. Otto Gutekunst, Agnew's finest connoisseur who worked closely with Berenson, called Duveen 'the "Anti-Christ" Octopus'. Robert Langton Douglas, who testified on Duveen's behalf at the Hahn trial in 1929, nevertheless wrote to a friend several years earlier complaining about what he called 'The Great Art Trust'. Douglas didn't mention Duveen by name, but it was clear whom he meant. (He was in the midst of a quarrel with Duveen about some acquisitions at the New York Metropolitan Museum.) Monopoly, said Douglas, was bad for the trade. A collector, he wrote:

does not want to have to go to a Trust, and to take what the Trust hands out to him ... I am, as you know, a lover of liberty; and in commercial life, I believe in an open market and honest rivalry. But there are whole classes of people who want neither. They want to dominate, to crush, and, secretly, if not openly, to tyrannize over others.

Berenson, after his split with Duveen, delivered a similar verdict: 'Duveen stood at the center of a vast circular nexus of corruption that reached down from the lowliest employee of the British Museum, right up to the King.'

However, we should beware of taking Joseph Duveen's hyperbolic claims or the bitter comments of his rivals and enemies at face value. Many of the great collections and artworks had been sold before Joe Duveen moved into paintings in 1901. Most of Isabella Stewart Gardner's magnificent collection was purchased through the London dealership of Colnaghi; for most of his collecting career Henry Clay Frick used Agnew's to acquire his pictures. Knoedler's was the most powerful dealer in New York and remained so for most of Joseph Duveen's career. It was the broker for the huge acquisition of paintings from the Hermitage by Andrew Mellon. Besides, the new scale of financial operations pushed the dealers into mutual cooperation. They had, of course, always traded with one another, but increasingly they worked together to acquire collections or used their rivals as intermediaries in international sales. In 1907 Nathan Wildenstein and René Gimpel, the Parisian dealers who had an option to buy the collection of Rodolphe Kann, widely seen as one of the greatest collections to come on the market (it contained no fewer than ten Rembrandts), struck a deal with the Duveen Brothers to acquire it for $4.2 million (£866,000). The collection was then broken up and sold to different collectors for an enormous profit. In 1920, just after the Hahn painting had arrived in the United States, a consortium of five dealers, including Duveen Brothers, pooled their resources in an unsuccessful attempt to get (the shamelessly philistine) Henry Ford to purchase some of the best works in their collective inventory.

Duveen may not have been a monopolist, and there were times when he had to cooperate with his rivals, but he quickly became the dominant figure in the Old Masters market. As the head of Agnew's ruefully admitted, he drove his London rivals out of much of the American market. Fifty-five of the 115 pictures, apart from American portraits, that Andrew Mellon bequeathed to the National Gallery in Washington were acquired through Duveen. The huge Kress collection of more than 700 works donated to the same gallery included 150 purchases from Duveen Brothers. The Huntingtons – Arabella and her third husband Henry – bought many of their finest pictures from the same dealer. Duveen concentrated on the pinnacle of the market, the richest collectors, and on the finest (and most expensive) pictures. This also brought him the most publicity. In the early years, the American press paid almost as much attention to Jacques Seligman, the Parisian dealer who had J.P. Morgan as his most important client, but by the time the Hahns appeared on the scene, Duveen dominated the major art stories.

Of all the Old Master dealers, Duveen Brothers was the firm that took the greatest advantage of changes in the art market, and it did so largely because of the initiative and inimitable skills of Joseph Duveen. This is usually taken to mean Duveen's consummate ability to infect his clients with a passionate desire and enthusiasm for acquiring pictures, and certainly this lay at the heart of the firm's business. The mordant Andrew Mellon, one of Duveen's best clients in the 1930s, parried an outburst of praise for one of his pictures with the sardonic remark, 'Duveen, my pictures never look so marvellous as when you are here!' Kenneth Clark, the art historian and director of London's National Gallery, remarked in his 1974 memoir, *Another Part of the Wood*, that 'when he was present everyone behaved as if they had had a couple of drinks'. Mary, wife of the famous connoisseur Bernard Berenson, compared his presence to drinking champagne. Berenson himself, more unkindly, said it was more like slopping down gin. Duveen talked up pictures and their virtues as if his life depended on it. However, even as he inflamed his clients' desires, he also made them think that much of what they wanted was unattainable. As the wife of the newspaper baron William Randolph Hearst complained, in an interview with S.N. Behrman, Duveen's first biographer, 'the fact is you couldn't buy anything from Duveen! Everything was either in reserve for someone else or he had promised it to his wife or for some reason he wasn't ready to sell it yet.' This drove the new super-rich, so used to satisfying their every desire, to distraction. It also helped push up prices.

Duveen also reshaped the traditional concern of art dealers to cultivate personal relationships with their clients. In the past, when collectors and dealers had shared a genteel interest and knowledge in art, the focus of their fraternization had been the artworks them-selves. Duveen did not neglect this but he realized that, in dealing with new wealth on a scale not seen before, it was important that he pander to clients' every whim – ensuring they had their favourite cigars, hotel suite and yacht berth – in order to smother them in luxury. He also recognized that he himself had to adopt the airs and values of his millionaire clientele.

Yet Duveen never thought of his audience as confined to his rich clientele. Of all art dealers he was the one who best understood the value of the press and publicity. Unlike most of his rivals, who were often publicity shy, he was a publicity hound. When he telephoned

Duveen on 17 June 1920, the reporter from the *New York World* knew that he would not get a curt 'no comment', but a statement that would make lively copy. Duveen cultivated the press as he cultivated clients: he had excellent relations with the *New York Times* (which consistently took his side in the *La Belle Ferronnière* affair); he wined and treated critics in a way that today would be considered outrageous; he exploited his connections with William Randolph Hearst, who owned twenty-two dailies and eleven Sunday papers, as well as two wire services; and he and his staff regularly tried to plant stories in the press. The company used Burrelle's cutting service to monitor all aspects of the art market and kept books of cuttings on many of its clients. Duveen understood that the art boom of the period had changed the art market irrevocably and that publicity was one key element in that transformation. His enormously rich clients, so much in the public eye both because of their wealth and business dealings, wanted their activities as collectors and future philanthropists, as men of 'culture', in the public eye. Duveen, vain and attention-seeking, was only too ready to oblige.

Yet Duveen's flamboyance as a salesman, his repeated treatment of hyperbole as a form of understatement, concealed the ruthless business practices that were as much a part of Duveen Brothers' success as the lavish parties, extravagant entertainment and personal bonhomie for which Joseph Duveen and the firm were famous. Duveen Brothers was a thoroughly modern enterprise in an age of booming capitalism, whose business tactics and organization mirrored those of the clients it served. Duveen was a man of unremitting industry and he expected the same of his employees. In 1920 René Gimpel recorded a typical conversation between Sir Joseph and one of his employees who had remarked, 'It's one o'clock and I want to go to lunch.' 'Sir,' Duveen responded, 'when I was young, I ate only on Sundays.' Art or, at least, its sale was a passion verging on obsession. Mary Berenson recalled Duveen's boredom at almost every topic, when she visited him in 1913: 'we talked politely on various topics for the first half hour – and then I broached the selling of pictures, and a loud sigh of satisfaction went up to the ceiling, and we settled into a thoroughly congenial topic'.

Rather than engaging in the piecemeal purchase of Old Masters, Duveen specialized in buying large collections by private treaty and then breaking them up, selling the high spots to his best clients. In all, Duveen bought eight large collections, paying around $25 million (£5.2 million). Individual items from such collections were not like paintings sold at auction, where their prices were known. They could be sold for what Duveen believed they ought to be worth. Such big deals required large amounts of capital. Here Duveen's relations with bankers, many of whom were his clients, were crucial. No other dealer had an arrangement guaranteeing overdrafts up to $6 million (£1.2 million); no one had better access to the house of Morgan and its funds. The firm was even able to absorb a fine of $1.25 million (£258,000) levied by the United States customs for evading import duties in 1909, thanks to a timely loan from a consortium of bankers.

The firm was not just an art dealership, but also dealt in loans. In effect, Duveen acted as a financial intermediary between the banks and his clients, offering them long-term credit in order to meet the firm's high prices. As Duveen wrote, 'We have no other course but to make dates of payment for periods with our clients, and then keep milking them, otherwise the game cannot be carried out.' Every method and means of payment (instalment plans, bonds, shares and land) was used to keep up the bull market in paintings.

This was part of a larger strategy that made Old Master art not just a cultural good (i.e. priceless), but a form of investment whose worth could be manipulated like a stock or share on the market. Of course, Duveen never spoke of art in these terms to his clients, but his business practices were those that they could recognize, share and admire. Once Duveen had acquired a stable of major clients, he used the rivalry among the most prominent new American collectors, the steel baron Henry Clay Frick, the department store millionaire Ben Altman, and the railway-owning Huntingtons to push up prices. He also traded up the works they bought. Thus the Jean-Honoré Fragonard panels called *Roman d'amour et de la jeunesse*, bought by J.P. Morgan from Agnew's in 1898 for $350,000 (£72,000) were purchased by Duveen from the Morgan estate and sold in 1913 to Frick for $1.25 million (£258,000). Duveen sold Rembrandt's *Aristotle Contemplating the Bust of Homer* no fewer than three times: first to Arabella Huntington in 1907, then to Alfred W. Erickson, who paid $750,000 (£155,000) but had to return it (for $500,000) in the aftermath of the 1929 Crash, and finally back to Erickson again in 1936, when the buyer's fortunes had mended. No picture sold by Duveen was ever allowed to decline in price.

The calm, classical facades and dignified, frock-coated attendants that fronted Duveen's galleries concealed a hive of frantic industry that worked with the constant pressure of time. Whether he was in New York, London, Paris or Vittel (where he annually went to recuperate and take the waters), Joseph Duveen was at the centre, receiving daily bulletins, cables and telegrams from all his offices. The telephone and the transatlantic cable meant that Duveen operated in real time. He was notoriously impatient, demanding that anything he wanted or needed to know was provided instantly. The massive Duveen information machine contained a library of 14,000 art books (many with detailed annotations by the Duveen staff), runs of sales catalogues, biographies of experts, dealers and collectors, albums of press clippings (six volumes survive covering the case of *La Belle Ferronnière*), files on exhibitions, art prices, the changing reputation of different painters, lists of museums and galleries from all over the world, indexes to art periodicals, scouts and runners books with updated information on pictures and their availability, opinions of different scholars on disputed paintings, ledgers and accounts of transactions, and file upon file of typewritten copies of letters and telegrams. No event that might be of use to the Duveen machine went unrecorded. If a British aristocratic couple with some fine Reynolds and Romney portraits were quarrelling and looked on the verge of divorce, Duveen's scouts would let him know about it. A newly wealthy businessman would be surprised to receive a flattering letter from Duveen, tipped off by one of his many informers and spies, suggesting a visit to his gallery. Every movement of his richest clients was recorded; information was often passed on by their butlers and maids who were secretly on the Duveen payroll.

René Gimpel, art dealer and brother-in-law of Duveen, knew that the secret to Duveen's success was not just his 'taste' and 'boldness', but 'his gift for organization'. In New York in May 1923, a few months before the Hahn *La Belle* returned to Paris, Duveen told him how he had been collecting all the articles of 'the best art critic in England', Humphry Ward. 'Now,' recorded Gimpel,

'Joe has had all his articles copied in triplicate, for his three branches, with an index, and when he wants to buy a picture or an object, he looks to see if Humphry Ward mentioned it and what he said.' Duveen was currently engaged in a similar task, putting together all his correspondence from Bernard Berenson over the previous fifteen years. 'The expert,' said Gimpel, 'speaks in them of all the fine Italian pictures from all the great European collections.' Filled with the importance of such a treasure-trove of art-historical knowledge, Gimpel suggested that Joseph should 'bequeath them to the British Museum, together with his firms business correspondence'. Duveen was appalled. 'It's too secret,' he protested. He definitely did not want his dealings, whether shady or above board, or with Berenson or any other expert, available to the nosey scholar or a prurient public. Duveen always wanted to control what was known about him, even beyond the grave. At his insistence, many of the firm's communications were transmitted in code.

Duveen's yearning for publicity and his willingness to be outspoken goes some way to explain why he was so frequently involved in litigation. He fought in the courts with family relatives, with other dealers, with clients, as well as on behalf of collectors. In 1915, for instance, Duveen was sued by the dealer Edgar Gorer for loudly insisting that a K'ang-hsi vase that was being sold to Frick was a fake. Gorer, claiming that Duveen had ruined his business, wanted $575,000 (£119,000) in damages, but was killed on a transatlantic crossing when the *Lusitania* was torpedoed, just as the case was about to begin. Two years later, Duveen became embroiled in *Huntington versus Lewis and Simmons*, a case prompted by his dismissal of the attribution of a double portrait to the British artist, George Romney. Henry Huntington had bought the picture from a London dealer. Duveen, displeased that the millionaire had traded with a rival, persuaded him to sue the vendor and lent him his lawyer, Louis Levy, to prosecute the case. Though in no sense impartial, Duveen was right. Documents in the Royal Academy archives, including a preliminary sketch of the picture, showed that the painting was the work of Romney's friend and admirer, Ozias Humphrey. What seemed like a malicious judgement, designed to undermine a rival, was fully vindicated. The case became something of a personal triumph for Duveen.

Even as the Hahns were pursuing their action against him for the 'slander of title' of their painting of *La Belle Ferronnière*, Duveen was defending himself against another litigant seeking damages. In May 1923, George Joseph Demotte, a Belgian-born, rather shady dealer in medieval sculpture and statuary, sued Duveen for slander, claiming compensation to the sum of $500,000 (£103,000). In his usual bravura manner, Duveen had dismissed a sixteenth-century champlevé object, sold by Demotte to a collector, as a modern work. Like his view of the Hahns' painting, this was a snap judgement that threw Duveen's colleagues into a panic. However, just as Duveen's experts were arriving in Paris to compare the two versions of *La Belle Ferronnière*, Demotte was killed in a hunting accident in the French countryside. Not for the first time, one of Duveen's opponents died an untimely death.

It is often said that Duveen ended up in court because he was more unscrupulous than other dealers and because he liked the publicity that came with the court proceedings. However, dealers' memoirs, such as those of René Gimpel, show that the profession was riddled with sharp practices of every sort; Duveen was unique only in boasting about them publicly. More often than not Duveen was sued not just because he was outspoken and could be a bully (though he was both), but because, as the Hahns knew, he was wealthy and any action against him was sure to place his opponents in the public eye. Duveen's flamboyance and indiscretion made him a soft target. His lawyer, Louis Levy, repeatedly urged him to silence, to avoid stirring up more trouble. Sometimes Duveen heeded him; more often he did not. There is some evidence that *Hahn versus Duveen* cured the latter of any enthusiasm for litigation. It was said that towards the end of the case, and even before he settled with the Hahns, Duveen had been ready to give up, but had been urged on by his lawyers and by allies in the art world who were worried that a Hahn victory would strangle the art market by scaring dealers and connoisseurs, making them reluctant to give their opinions on the authenticity of works of art. After his dispute with the Hahns was settled out of court, Duveen continued to be sued – most notably by his rich and unscrupulous protégé, Carl Hamilton – but he seems to have decided that his public prominence was best served by approving press coverage of his charitable and philanthropic work rather than the potentially adverse criticism that could emerge during a trial.

Duveen was a big shark in the turbulent waters of the art market, a creature who knew better than most how to ride the wave of American prosperity and to scare his rivals with a predatory show of force. In comparison, Andrée and Harry Hahn were small fry indeed, completely without resources in the art world. Yet they also shared some character traits with their much more powerful enemy. Sir Joseph and Harry were both brilliant talkers, men who made others laugh and gawp at their temerity. They both had the sort of self confidence that allowed them to embellish and embroider the truth about themselves and others. They were both salesmen whose major product was themselves, though they each believed that what they were peddling amounted to more. They enjoyed risks, the more vertiginous the better, and they loved being in the public eye. Andrée was only like Duveen in her steely determination to have her way, come what may.

It is difficult to know what Duveen thought about the young couple who challenged him. Did he have a certain sneaking admiration for them? Did he perhaps collude with them, helping them bring the case? There are hints of this, but no decisive evidence. Did he, perhaps, think that a big predator like himself would swallow them up with ease? If he did, he made a major mistake, for he was about to discover that the Hahns were capable of fighting him to a stalemate which, if we make allowance for the disadvantages under which they laboured, can only be considered a victory for the Midwestern engineer and his French bride.

CHAPTER 5

The Trials of La Belle Ferronnière

The saga of how a young couple acquired a painting attributed to Leonardo, brought it to the United States, and then challenged – and nearly bested – the most powerful art dealer in the world is a complex and shadowy tale, made all the more difficult to unravel because of the efforts of the main actors to manipulate the story to their own ends. There is much in the story to excite incredulity, but, as Harry Hahn in particular realized, this was as much a help as a hindrance, provided it was used to excite public curiosity and interest. He knew that there was a great deal of mileage in stories that seemed both strange and true, and from its inception the Hahns' story seemed improbable. How did they acquire a Leonardo? How did a Renaissance masterpiece (if such it was) fetch up on the shores of the Atlantic in a small resort town and find its way into the hands of such unlikely owners? The Hahns always maintained that the picture had been given to them as a wedding gift by Andrée's aristocratic aunt, Louise de Montaut. Though there is some reason to question whether the painting was a present or Louise a true aristocrat, or that Andrée was Louise de Montaut's blood relative, there can be no question that the woman she addressed as 'tante' was the source of the picture. The only obvious question was why anyone would want to give away one of the most valuable paintings in the world.

In a story that contains many larger than life characters, Louise de Montaut stands with the best of them. She lived on the fringes of the French aristocracy, a woman of independent though not substantial means (what she called 'a sufficiency') with a small flat in Paris and a large appetite for travel. A feisty, fussy, self-opinionated, snobbish woman, she was always ready to invoke the high moral standards of French respectability, but also more than willing to flout convention when it was in her interest to do so. According to Jacqueline Hahn, Louise was an eccentric, tall woman with a high-pitched voice who wore capes and carried her handbag in front of her on a strap rather like a village postman. (Her local representative in the National Assembly described her as an 'original'.) Born in 1867 in the fashionable 16th arrondissement of Paris, she led the life of a merry spinster, travelling extensively in Europe (including more than fifteen trips to Italy), the Middle East, North Africa and North America in the decade before the outbreak of the First World War, making many friends on her journeys. As she remarked with some satisfaction, after twenty years of travelling her address book was completely full. She took a special delight in helping women less fortunate than herself, rescuing a French woman taken ill in North America, and acting as a godmother (*marraine)* and mentor to a number of children who were the progeny of poorer friends. Fiercely patriotic, she volunteered as a nurse during the First World War and was decorated for services to her country.

During her earlier travels Louise had met a friend who had invited her to spend time in Dinard, which she had first visited in 1896 and found charming. At the house of her friend she met Mme Massot, Andrée's godmother. Louise found her new acquaintance lively and attractive. They spent some time together – Mme Massot even stayed with her in Paris – and Louise returned on several occasions to Dinard to visit her friend. Through Massot, Louise also became acquainted with Andrée's aunt, Anna, who was married to an antique dealer in Paris. Louise, as was her wont, took a shine to the young girl in Josephine Massot's care and came to call Andrée her 'god-daughter' (*filleule)*. As she later explained, this was not a baptismal relationship; Andrée was her '*filleule de guerre*'. In 1919 Louise visited Dinard (though whether for the wedding we do not know) and, according to her later testimony, decided to give the young couple *La Belle Ferronnière* as a wedding present. She responded to questions about her preference for giving the painting away rather than selling it at a profit with typically aristocratic hauteur: 'Sir, I never wanted to sell my belongings, especially the things from my people; I prefer to eat a humble meal in the silver dishes of my relatives, than to have a banquet served from dishes that were from the store.' She confessed that she thought it a good thing to give the painting to a young woman she held in the very highest regard and to her groom who had helped save France. Though this story repeatedly excited incredulity – who in their right mind would knowingly give away a genuine Leonardo? – and was used to argue that Louise de Montaut knew her painting to be a copy of little real value, Andrée's 'aunt' insisted both that the picture was genuine and that she intended it as a wedding gift. She was first told when she was six, she said, that it was by Leonardo, and she had never asked for money for the painting. Indeed, she claimed that she had contemplated donating the picture to a local museum before she had decided to give it to the Hahns as a wedding gift.

Louise's relationship to *La Belle Ferronnière* was closely bound up with her complex family history, a subject she was in the habit of digressing on at some length. The story that was told about the painting was that it had been removed from the royal collections during the French revolution and sold by August Cheval de Saint-Hubert, a revolutionary official, to General Louis Tourton in 1796. (Certainly a picture that precisely follows the description of the Hahn *La Belle* was sold at auction in 1847 as one of six pictures from the collection of General Tourton.) Louise's grandmother told her that she had been given the picture by one of the descendants of the Tourton family which had adopted her. It seems more likely, however, that Louise's grandfather, Antoine Vincent, bought the picture in 1847. A surviving copy of the sale catalogue is endorsed '*Tableaux à Mr Vincent vendu après la Collection du Compte de Betz provenant du General Tourton, Leonard de Vinci et Claude Lorrain*'. However the Vincents acquired the painting, Louise's grandmother gave the picture to Louise's sickly younger sister. Louise, in turn, took *La Belle* from her sister as she was dying, in order, she said, to keep it out of the hands of her relatives, and entrusted it to her uncle for safe keeping. She subsequently claimed that her sister had bequeathed the painting to her in 1915. Whether or not she actively sought to sell the painting (something she always denied), it was displayed in the smart apartment of the Marquis de Chambure in the avenue Friedland in Paris. (This was known in the picture trade as 'planting', putting a picture in luxurious surroundings in order to ease a sale.) Louise's relationship with the marquis is unclear. She claimed to be his cousin but called him '*oncle*'. Duveen's detectives, ever cynical, implied that she might be his mistress. At all events, he left Louise an annuity of 3,000 francs in his will when he died in 1921. In the apartment, *La Belle* was seen by a number of potential buyers and was expertized by a government official, Georges Sortais, as a genuine Leonardo in 1916. An expert who worked at the Paris dealers, Trotti, recalled that 'the picture was offered to him before the war by a lady living in the district near L'Etoile', and then again by 'three maiden ladies' but he was not interested in what he described as 'rubbish'. In 1918 the painting was left at the Louvre for examination, though not offered to the gallery for sale. It was examined by Jean Guiffrey, the head conservator at the Louvre, who considered it 'an old copy of no artistic value'. He remembered the picture as it had been at the Louvre when Paris was under bombardment from the Germans and he feared the owners might make extravagant claims if the painting was destroyed or damaged.

Later inquiries made on Duveen's behalf uncovered more about the painting. He was told by a Monsieur Carton, 'an elderly gentleman' of about 70 who appeared to be a 'rentier' with independent means, that a Monsieur Chambure, a poor army officer, had thirty years previously tried to sell the picture as a Leonardo to the Paris dealers, Sedelmeyer, but their expert had dismissed it as a copy and 'all faked up'. Fifteen years later the picture was again on the market, offered to a dealer from Cologne, who likewise refused the picture as a worthless copy. Duveen's sleuths also unearthed rumours of Louise's financial difficulties in these years and it is clear that she sold off a number of family heirlooms, including a painting by Antoine Coypel and statuettes by Clodion. However, she claimed to have refused offers on *La Belle*, including one in 1912 for half-a-million francs and another in 1916 of 550,000 francs from an American. The dealer Knoedler, she said, had wanted to examine the painting, but she would not let him see it as she did not wish to sell. In short, the history of the painting and its place in the art market was obscure and confused. Transactions were so informal, personal and secretive that even Duveen, the self-professed most powerful dealer in the world, found it hard to reconstruct the commercial history of the Hahn painting.

After she had given the painting to the Hahns, Louise de Montaut became much more enthusiastic about its sale. She professed to be glad that the painting had left France before a new law was enacted increasing the duty on the export of works of art produced before 1840 and to be glad to be rid of a painting that had caused so much fuss and bother, but she continued to follow its progress from afar. In September 1920 she was visited by Sterling Heilig, a journalist from *Paris Illustration*. He showed her an article about the picture from the *Kansas City Star* and told her that he had interviewed Georges Sortais, who had confirmed that he was fully convinced that the Hahn picture was a genuine Leonardo. Louise became very excited. She dashed across Paris, returning home to rummage through the family archives, recruiting her 'cousin' the Marquis d'Asting d'Estampes to type up copies of documents that mentioned *La Belle Ferronnière*. (At the same time, Josephine Massot was writing to her urging her to find out as much as possible about the history of the picture.) When she mentioned to Heilig that she hoped to help Andrée sell the picture in the US for $150,000 (£31,000), he professed to be shocked. He told her the picture was worth more than five million francs, and that if it were returned to France the Louvre would want to buy it. Whatever the truth of these assertions, they excited Louise greatly. She wrote a long letter to Andrée, urging her to raise her price, not lower it, and to get paid in gold. 'They didn't want it cheap without documents,' she wrote to Andrée, 'now you have the documents make them pay the price. You are in America so don't consider the change [exchange rate], get its value in dollars, anyhow, do your best and don't worry, now that everything is settled.' She added, 'If your buyers are not rich enough to buy, why not talk to the lady who bought the Titian in New York. I heard in Paris that the Museum of Chicago is very rich, and perhaps you can get your price there.' America, she pointed out 'should be glad to have La Belle Ferronnière, for the Louvre and the Museum of London want it so bad'. She concluded, 'We were expecting you pretty soon [back in France], but it is better to wait a little while than sacrifice a good sum of money, even though you are young and wouldn't need it now.'

The precise relationship been Louise de Montaut and the Hahns is difficult to fathom. In 1968, at a time when Harry Hahn was furious with Andrée and Jacqueline because he believed them to be concealing *La Belle* from him, he wrote an irate letter to his former wife in which he threatened to expose what he called 'the chicanery and irregularities of this painting swindle'. He said, 'You know very well the *true facts* about your so-called "possession and ownership" of this painting since the day it arrived in our home in Junction City in June 1920.' Then he launched into an attack on Josephine Massot and Andrée's aunt, Anna. These two women, whom he sarcastically described as respectively the proprietor of 'modes and Confections, Maison de Confiance' and a 'soul of honor', had, he claimed, swindled 'poor old Mlle. De Montaut out of her property'. 'If you don't have the facts,' he told Andrée, 'I do', including, he added, information 'about a ten-thousand francs payment I made to Mlle de Montaut as a down payment for the purchase of the painting'. He added, 'As a matter of fact I know a lot of things about this painting swindle I'll bet a good ripe camembert cheese you wish I didn't know.'

However, Louise de Montaut did not feel that she had been let down by her friends in Dinard. On the contrary, she always stuck to her story of the wedding gift and, when Duveen's agents later tried to get her to turn on Josephine Massot and the Hahns, she obdurately refused to do so. When a representative of Duveen, Noël Charrayre, visited her in the summer of 1929, she refused to answer his questions and poured scorn on his threats. She described her upbringing as one that always made her know the difference between right and wrong. To suggestions that Mlle Massot was not entirely respectable because she was a shopkeeper of *'modes et fantasies'*, she replied that an art dealer was no better and that, besides, there were no bad jobs, only bad people. Josephine Massot was 'genteel, aimiable, gracious, good, devoted' and Louise would remain her friend 'until the day she died'. When asked if she considered Andrée an adventuress, she said she loved her 'profoundly, sincerely; it made me happy to call her niece'. Andrée was, she added for good measure, 'a perfect spouse, a very good mother of a Christian family, honest, serious, sweet, industrious, amiable, attentive, complaisant'. In short, she was a paragon of virtue. Louise remained close to the family and, though dogged with ill-health, she returned to Dinard to attend the first communion of Jacqueline, Andrée's eldest child, in 1930.

Harry Hahn may have accused his wife and her relatives of

manipulating Louise de Montaut, yet, whatever the truth of the accusation, Louise herself remained ferociously loyal to Andrée, utterly convinced of the rectitude of herself and her friends. We will probably never know if she profited or hoped to profit financially from her 'gift' of *La Belle Ferronnière* to the striking young woman and her Midwestern beau. (Where, one wonders, did the young couple find the 10,000 francs that Harry alleged they paid to Louise de Montaut?) Towards the end of her life, Louise confessed to be thoroughly fed-up with the painting and the litigation it had spawned – her chief regret, she said, was the decision of Andrée to go to law, though she understood that it was a matter of honour. As she told Duveen's detectives, she was a wreck of a woman and just wanted to be left to die in peace. Perhaps Louise hoped for a comfortable sum to tide her over in her old age, perhaps her gift had not been unsolicited or unpaid for. What mattered far more to her than an admittedly much-needed *douceur* were her friends and the web of gratitude and solicitude she wove among them. She had spent her life building friendships, especially with other women. For her *La Belle Ferronnière* was less a priceless masterpiece or a ticket to financial security than a means to secure the intimacies she craved most. The words she used in closing her letters to Andrée and her family, '*je vous embrasse bien tendrement*' ('I embrace you very tenderly'), reveal what to her was the true value of this work of art.

When exactly the painting was consigned to the Hahns and when it left France is, yet again, obscure. The American press reported that Josephine Massot had smuggled the picture in a basket of washing across the enemy lines and into Belgium, so that it could evade the law prohibitively taxing the export of France's cultural patrimony. According to the *Brooklyn Star*, *La Belle* was 'taken through Belgium, to Brussels and Antwerp and was finally placed on board the steamship *Finland* of the Red Star Line and sailed for New York'. Yet this story, romantic as it may seem, makes no sense. In 1919, when the law was enacted, the war was over and there were therefore no lines to cross. If the picture did leave France in 1918, then it could not have been a wedding gift because the Hahns were not to marry until July 1919. Louise de Montaut mentioned in a letter to Andrée Hahn that she was pleased that the painting had been smuggled out of France; she had reason to be, for she was the smuggler who took it out of the country in order to evade the new duty on the export of paintings and art objects that had been enacted in April 1920. According to later newspaper reports the painting was left with a friend in Antwerp. In early June, de Montaut collected the picture and sailed from Antwerp to New York on the *Finland* (she is on the surviving passenger list), with the Leonardo in her luggage. She arrived in New York just three days before Duveen was interviewed by the reporter from the *New York World*. An experienced and enthusiastic traveller, as well as the owner of the painting, she personally arranged for its deposit in New York. Whether she actually journeyed to Junction City or whether Conrad Hug, who certainly seems to have gone to New York to meet the painting, brought it to the Midwest is unclear, though it would be surprising if she had not made the trip to Kansas to see Andrée's daughter who had been born in April.

The Hahns, then, had preceded their painting into the United States. As we have seen, in late 1919 they began trying to sell *La Belle*, contacting Duveen and probably other dealers in the East, and also working with Conrad Hug to sell the picture in Kansas City. Once they knew about Sir Joseph Duveen's pronouncement to the *New York World*, the Hahns and Hug responded by trying to win Duveen to their side and by seeking to limit the damage of the publicity against them. They were helped by a prominent Kansas City attorney and supporter of the arts, John T. Harding, who began a correspondence with Duveen's New York lawyers. He sent them a photograph of the Hahn painting, asking Duveen to restate his views. In response Duveen said he was certain that the Hahn was a copy, though he did not know who had painted it, adding 'the Louvre picture is not passed by the most eminent connoisseurs as having been painted by Leonardo da Vinci, and I may say that I am in accord with their opinion. It is suggested that the Louvre picture is very close to Leonardo da Vinci, but is not by his hand – probably it was painted by Boltraffio.' This indiscreet admission was to come to haunt Duveen in the years to come, but on the issue of the Hahn picture Duveen refused to budge.

At the same time Harding persuaded the *New York World* to publish a statement explaining the Hahns' position and why they thought Duveen 'was not sufficiently well informed concerning it to pass judgement'. Harding, according to the newspaper, said, 'I should like to make it clear that the owners have records to show that this canvas has been in the family since about 1796, and that the family has been one of prominence, both politically and financially in France, that they have owned a large and excellent collection of canvases, among which this is one.' Their decision to sell their painting he blamed on the fortunes of war. They had concluded 'that they would market this picture in the United States, inasmuch as one of the heirs had married Capt. Hahn, an American soldier.'

Harding's attempts at negotiation failed, but the material he pressed on the *New York World* marked the beginning of a publicity campaign on behalf of the Hahns that was to last over the next three years. The improbably named Hyacinthe Ringrose, the Hahns' new attorney, and Harry Hahn orchestrated the campaign, seeking out reporters and editors, and giving interviews in which they put their side of the story. They began with the widely circulated description of Helen Rice, 'a pretty and fashionably gowned young lady' who served papers on Duveen in his New York office in November 1921 asking for damages of $500,000 (£103,000) to compensate for his 'slander of title' of Andrée's picture. Almost immediately, stories began to appear in the newspapers of Andrée's aristocratic lineage and connections, sometimes accurate but most exaggerated, and of the romantic courtship by an American aviator of his French sweetheart. Details of the marriage proposal late at night on a small boat in the waters around Dinard and of Harry's wartime bravery painted a picture of young, idealistic love set in a distant romantic setting and helped the public identify with the couple. The family's desire to sell the picture in Kansas, Ringrose told the papers, was because of their 'municipal patriotism'. Andrée Hahn, French and beautiful, 'captured' by her American beau, seemed to many to be like the painting that had been 'captured' along with so many other treasures and brought to the United States. Yet, unusually, the captor was not a rich millionaire of the sort that Duveen associated with, but a humble young man from the small-town Midwest. These stories were accompanied by accounts of how the painting had been smuggled out of France, emphasizing the family's derring-do.

These 'back stories' complemented two others about the picture itself, each of which made excellent news copy. Ringrose told the press that the impress of a thumbprint could be discerned in the paint of the Hahn picture and hinted strongly that it showed the damage that it was known Leonardo had suffered to the thumb of his right hand. The press lapped this up, producing headlines such as 'Modern Science will play its part in deciding the merits of this usual lawsuit' and 'Will thumbprint made 400 years ago prove painting is Leonardo da Vinci's original?' One paper claimed that the version of *The Virgin of the Rocks* at London's National Gallery had been authenticated as a Leonardo on the basis of fingerprints in the paint. Ringrose dangled before the public the appealing prospect that an artistic conundrum would be definitively solved by the techniques of science. He and the Hahns also claimed that their picture had originally been in the Louvre, but that it had been removed, either during the French Revolution or the revolution of 1830, and replaced by a copy, which was the painting currently in the Louvre's collection. This story fed off the often repeated tale that the painting that had been returned to the Louvre in 1913 was not the original *Mona Lisa* but a copy. So potent and enduring was this story that in 1926, when the case between Hahn and Duveen was ongoing, the assertion by an American collector that he had the real *Mona Lisa* caused a panic in Paris; thousands of people rushed to the Louvre to assure themselves that 'their' *Mona Lisa* was still there. The public lapped up the Hahns' publicity; the art world was less impressed. Jean Guiffrey, the head conservator at Louvre, commented, 'You see that this history is like a romance. It is a romance similar to many others of which we have already had to interest ourselves and in which the Louvre originals are supposed to leave mysteriously without being noticed by anyone to be replaced by copies.' As he told Duveen, he much preferred what he called the romances of Rudyard Kipling; at least they were 'much more probable'.

While the Hahns worked on publicity, Duveen worked on the experts. He had already boasted that he would spend £1 million if he had to vindicate his view of the Hahn picture. Now he set out to accumulate as much expertise as he possibly could.

Within a few weeks of being served papers, he gathered a group of experts in New York to examine the Hahns' painting in Ringrose's office on 5th Avenue on 15 December 1921. These included Seymour de Ricci, a British-born, French-naturalized bibliographer and art expert who had recently catalogued the Italian pictures in the Louvre; Charles Loeser, an independently wealthy American connoisseur and collector, who had been Berenson's classmate at Harvard and who lived in Florence; Edward Forbes, director since 1909 of the Fogg Art Museum at Harvard and expert in 'methods and processes in Italian painting'; Frank Jewett Mather, art critic, professor of Art History at Princeton since 1910 and author of *History of Italian Painting*; Raymond Wyer, director of the Worcester Art Museum in Massachusetts; and Wilhelm Valentiner, the youthful protégé of von Bode, who was cataloguing the Widener collection in the Metropolitan Museum and was about to become the director of the Detroit Institute of Arts. Harry Hahn was amazed and amused: 'Eight people came including Sir Joseph Duveen, and we let them inspect it two entire days. They examined it with microscope, camera, flashlight, and on their knees. I thought one man would lose his sight.' Two of the experts reserved their judgement; the rest were not in favour of the Hahn.

Yet none of these experts were in what Duveen regarded as the big league. Their opinion counted in the art market but not as much as he would have liked. Valentiner was too young, de Ricci was an expert in manuscripts more than paintings, Loeser was a private collector and the others were part of the museum and academic world rather than the marketplace. So Duveen, with Ringrose's blessing, had a number of large photographs taken of the Hahn picture and sent them off to his favoured experts in Europe. In January 1922, their replies, a steady and inexorable tide, began flowing into the Duveen offices in London, Paris and New York. The response was universally damning. The first came from Sir Charles Holmes, former editor of the *Burlington Magazine*, director, since 1916, of the National Gallery in London and author of a recent book on Leonardo. He wrote to Duveen that he and his colleagues had carefully examined the photographs. He thought it was probably a Flemish copy. 'To suppose,' he concluded, 'it is from the hand of Leonardo da Vinci himself is nothing short of ridiculous. As we happen recently to have made particularly careful study [of] La Belle Ferronnière in Louvre we can speak on this point with absolute certainty.' A day later a crisp telegram arrived from von Bode in Berlin: 'Doubtless copy 17th Century.' A few days later, Duveen received a letter from the museum director elaborating on his verdict: 'The large photographs show plainly that the technique of the painting is later, as is also indicated by the opening of the cracks.' He concluded with an observation made by many other experts who were used to the fussy ways of the industrious copyist: 'it [the Hahn painting] indicates over-careful execution of all detail'.

Two more opinions from British experts arrived within a day of each other. Roger Fry, Bloomsbury denizen, former curator of

European painting at the Metropolitan in New York, adviser to J.P. Morgan, painter and critic, stated 'without hesitation' that the Hahn picture was a copy and that it was not Italian or contemporary to Leonardo. His views were confirmed by Sir Claude Phillips, a critic and member of the *Burlington* group, retired keeper of the Wallace Collection and expert on Titian. 'A careful comparison of the two photographs,' he wrote to Duveen, 'reveals the absolute inferiority of the version now in America in every particular. Indeed it is difficult to me to understand how there can possibly be any doubt on the point.' He also added that, though some scholars had questioned the attribution of the Louvre *La Belle* to Leonardo he, for one, had never doubted it.

From Paris came a short note from Salomon Reinach, brilliant archaeologist, founder member of the Ecole du Louvre, professor at the College de France and author of an important catalogue of medieval and Renaissance painting, confirming that the Hahn was a 'much later copy'. Robert Langton Douglas, Berenson's old enemy but an undoubted expert on Italian Renaissance art, was sceptical about the use of photographs for attributions – he had written a learned paper on the subject – but one look at those he had received from Duveen was enough to convince him: 'this photograph affords quite sufficient evidence to convince any critic who has studied the works of Leonardo da Vinci that the picture it reproduces is not by that Master, and is far inferior in quality to his generally accepted works'. He pointed to faults in the drawing of the eyes, mouth and neck. As he reminded Duveen, 'works of Leonardo and of those pupils who worked under his direction were much copied in the sixteenth [century] by Flemish, as well as by many Italian artists'. The expert was constantly dealing with excited and ill-informed members of the public who believed they had found a Leonardo masterpiece. The most valued opinion was also almost the last. Bernard Berenson was on a sightseeing trip in Egypt with his wife and his assistant Nicky Mariano. Shortly before he left Cairo for a voyage up the Nile he sent Duveen a cable that was as terse and as damning as von Bode's earlier telegram: 'American Ferronniere obvious copy of Louvre original'.

The opinions continued to come in and they were unanimous. The words most often used were 'feeble', 'weak' and 'inferior'. De Ricci, who had returned to Paris and to the Louvre, and who had therefore examined both pictures (and not merely photographs) confirmed that the Hahn painting was a copy and added that he had carefully worked through the Louvre inventories and could show that the version of *La Belle Ferronnière* in the museum had been in the Royal Collection at least since 1629 and probably since 1547. It could not, therefore, be a replacement for a picture that had been stolen. The very last opinion, delayed because of the vagaries of the Italian postal system, came from the venerable Professor Adolfo Venturi, the spiritual successor of Cavalcaselle, the author of a huge multi-volume history of Italian art, as well as two volumes on Leonardo as a painter and seven volumes on his drawings. Again, he was unimpressed: 'the proportions are changed and the fine inclination of the head is no longer seen, the delicate lengthening of the features and bust; the face is rounded and everything becomes coarser, swollen, material . . . The interpretation of the chiaroscuro is erroneous . . . and also the design of the strokes, the reflections, the high lights in the bad copy'.

Armed with a fat folder full of expert opinions, all of which vindicated his judgement, Duveen filed an answer to the Hahns' suit on 21 January 1922. He had great cause for satisfaction. He had managed to secure the unanimous support of a body of experts famous for their disagreements and quarrels. It seemed as if the Hahns' case was in tatters. And they were to suffer a further blow in late February when the Chambure family published a letter in the French newspaper *Le Figaro* denying that they were in any way related to Andrée Hahn and disclaiming any connection to the sale of the painting. In July Duveen arranged that British and French experts were deposed in London and Paris, outlining their objections to the Hahn *La Belle*. All seemed done and dusted. The focus of Duveen's inquiries shifted. He was more and more interested in the provenance and origin of the Hahn picture. He knew it was not a Leonardo; he wanted to know what it really was.

The first round in the battle seemed to have been a decisive victory for Duveen, but Ringrose and his clients were not prepared to give up and he caught Duveen's lawyers off-guard when he told them that he was going to challenge any evidence based on photographs as inadmissible and that he had every expectation of success. At this stage only de Ricci had examined both pictures 'in the flesh' and Duveen, for reasons that are not entirely clear, did not like him as a witness. Perhaps he was not prominent enough; perhaps it was because he was a 'documents' rather than 'images' man; and possibly Duveen was unnerved by his assertion that the signature of the restorer, Hacquin, who had signed the back of the Hahn painting after he had transferred it on to canvas in 1777, was in fact genuine. At all events, he needed more evidence from experts who had seen both pictures.

Duveen had been playing with the idea of setting up a commission to judge the two paintings and he now floated a scheme that involved bringing the paintings together in Paris. However, there were obstacles. The Hahns were afraid that, if the picture returned to France, it might be impounded by the authorities in lieu of the duties they did not pay when the picture was smuggled out of the country. Conrad Hug, who had, according to press reports, mortgaged his home twice to cover the rising legal costs of the case, had a verbal promise of a 25 per cent interest in the Hahn *La Belle* and refused to let the picture out of his sight. In France the Louvre, behaving as it was to do on numerous later occasions, firmly opposed any sort of formal comparison of the two pictures.

However, Duveen was not to be thwarted. The Hahns, Hug and Ringrose all wanted money to take the picture to France – Ringrose presumably was worried about his legal fees, while the Hahns and Hug had few financial resources between them. Ringrose began a tough negotiation with Duveen. He asked for $3,000 (£750) for the trip to Paris – $2,000 for himself and $1,000 for Hug. Duveen counter-offered with $2,000 (£500), but Ringrose knew that the dealer was desperate to get the painting to France, both because Duveen believed he would finally defeat the Hahns and because he knew that the 'confrontation' of the two pictures would be a great publicity coup. Ringrose would not budge; Duveen, as he predicted, caved in.

The Louvre proved less of an obstacle. At first they made public their absolute refusal to allow the comparison of the two pictures to take place. As Ed Fowles, in the Paris office of Duveens, explained to Joseph, G. d'Estournelles de Constant, director of the National Museums, was 'annoyed by the fuss made about this matter in the French papers which say that the pictures are going to be hung side by side in the Public Gallery and a Cinematograph film taken of the experts examining them. This American idea of publicity is very much against the Louvre's conservative ideas . . . They intensely dislike publicity.' But Duveen simply went over the heads of the museum authorities, using the American ambassador to get the minister in charge of the museum, Paul Léon, to order the staff to cooperate. He had merely to agree that the examination of the two works 'was not to be, in any way, public or to be used for advertisement'.

The Louvre could insist that the examination take place behind closed doors, but as Duveen knew only too well, it could not prevent publicity. This was certainly the view of Louis Levy, Duveen's attorney, who exclaimed to René Gimpel, 'What publicity for Joe. And how important he's going to seem to his American clients.' Duveen himself took a similar view. Gimpel, dining with his brother-in-law a few days before the experts' visit to the Louvre, recorded in his diary, 'He was as happy as a child, thinking that on the day of his death he'll be remembered as the man of *La Belle Ferronnière*.' (Gimpel was not impressed. 'How can anyone be so naïve!' was his final comment.) And, of course, publicity there was. When the group of experts assembled at the Louvre at 8 a.m. on Saturday 15 September 1923, a crowd of French journalists 'yelling because they weren't let in', pressed against the doors. A rumour that some American journalists had slipped in with the experts almost caused a riot. Coverage of the day's events appeared not just in the French and American papers, but in Britain as well. The *London Illustrated News* devoted a double spread to the event, complete with photographs of the experts, the two paintings and even (despite the Louvre's prohibition) of the discussion in the interior of the Louvre. The *New York Tribune* commented: 'Such a confluence of eminent authorities on art as was never seen before on land or sea filed within the sacrosanct enclosure of the Louvre this morning.'

The group that assembled in the office of Jean Guiffrey consisted of d'Estournelles de Constant, director of the National Museums; Hautecourt and Demouty, two assistant keepers of paintings; Marquet de Vasselot, keeper of the department of objets d'art; Mrs Hahn; the lawyers, Hyacinthe Ringrose and Louis Levy; and Duveen's chosen experts. Some of the connoisseurs had already given their opinion of the Hahn painting on the basis of the photographs Duveen had circulated. They included Sir Charles Holmes, Robert Langton Douglas and Roger Fry from London, and Adolfo Venturi from Rome. They were accompanied by Charles Nicolle, an expert who worked for Trotti, the Paris dealer; William Martin Conway, explorer, collector, former art history professor at Liverpool and Cambridge, and director of the Imperial War Museum; A.P. Laurie, professor of Chemistry at Heriot-Watt College and a world authority on painters' methods and materials; and Frederik Schmidt-Degener, the recently appointed director of Amsterdam's Rijksmuseum. Bernard Berenson, painfully shy of publicity, had been allowed by Duveen to give his evidence a few days earlier, after a private viewing of the Hahn painting.

After the experts had examined the two paintings, they adjourned to the main galleries to examine the other works of Leonardo and his pupils. They then moved to the United States consulate, where their evidence and cross-examination was heard before officials so that it could be used as legal testimony in an American court of law. Once again, the verdict was overwhelmingly in Duveen's favour. Only A.P. Laurie refused to make a judgement about the pictures. All the other experts affirmed not only that the Hahn was not by

Leonardo, but that they believed the version in the Louvre to be a genuine work of the master.

It had been difficult to get some of the experts to testify. Roger Fry had been reluctant to travel to Paris, but Duveen insisted. Berenson also refused at first to attend, but Duveen sent him a peremptory telegram: 'Much disappointed. In fact cannot take refusal. You will have to stand by and help us. Everyone expects your opinion on this matter . . . Do not disappoint me.' Conway probably wanted to curry favour with Duveen, as he hoped to sell a number of paintings from his collection, including one work that Duveen had controversially attributed to Giorgione. Schmidt-Degener was a recent appointee to the Rijksmuseum, an expert on Northern European not Italian art, but presumably welcomed the chance to do Duveen a favour. A.P. Laurie had been following the Hahn case for some time, and had corresponded with Duveen's London office asking for information about the painting; in the autumn of 1922 he had volunteered his services to Duveen, but the dealer was at first reluctant to use his expertise. Laurie was an independent figure, an academic and scientist; he was not beholden to Duveen who, besides, set little store by science as an aid to attribution. In fact, Laurie's evidence, as we shall see, had a damaging – in fact, near fatal – effect on Duveen's case when it was invoked at the New York trial in 1929.

All of the experts, except Holmes and Schmidt-Degener, were paid 100 guineas for their trouble. Duveen knew he couldn't pay the employees of public museums, but he made it very clear to Holmes that he would one day repay the favour. The experts took the whole affair very lightly. Roger Fry thanked Duveen for an 'exhilarating picnic for the art historians of Europe'. Holmes was reported to have burst out laughing when he first saw the Hahn picture. Though none of the connoisseurs liked the intense grilling they were subject to from Hyacinthe Ringrose, many of them were not afraid to make clear that they thought the proceedings absurd. When asked by Ringrose what he thought of the solemn proceedings at the Louvre, Sir Charles Holmes responded, 'I am afraid I thought it rather funny.' Writing to Duveen shortly afterwards, he added 'I hope that ... the preposterous Hahn bubble is now thoroughly and finally pricked.' As René Gimpel observed, from the point of view of the art world, 'the only interesting aspect of this huge hoax is that the experts all agree that the Louvre picture is by Leonardo'.

In the short run, however, it looked as if Duveen had won another round in the struggle with the Hahns; maybe he had given them a knock-out blow. The newspaper reporting was all in Duveen's favour. Some of the experts, like Adolfo Venturi, gave interviews and explained why the Hahn portrait was inferior. Levy was convinced that Duveen had triumphed. His chief concern was preventing his client from creating new problems by being indiscreet. He told Duveen in no uncertain terms not to talk to the press. 'You must be satisfied,' he wrote, 'that you have won a hundred per cent victory'. The only chance the Hahns had was to force Duveen into a error:

> Of course your adversary must feel this victory very keenly, and would like you to make some misstep which would rob you of the fruit of this victory. If you can be stung into a foolish statement or induced to say an indiscreet thing, or led into a side controversy, you would probably lose a considerable part, if not all of your prestige and benefit from the case.

For nearly a year after the Paris 'confrontation' the case languished. Skits and satires appeared in the press: A Parisian revue, *Oh the Pretty Girls*, restaged the event; two girls played the two pictures and the 'jury' found for the beauty in the Louvre. The Hahns parted company with Hyacinthe Ringrose, probably, one suspects, because of the growing expense of the case. Early in 1925, Andrée signed a new agreement with an American lawyer in Paris, Anthony Manley, in which he agreed 'diligently to pursue the prosecution of the case'; in return she conveyed 'one fourth interest in the work of art', whatever the price it eventually reached.

The Hahns were plainly in difficulties and Harry, who was their spokesman in the press, was reduced to bravura and bluster. He told a reporter from the *New York Herald* that 'he did not consider that the European experts opinion would hold much weight with the American jury', while *Art News* reported that 'Mr. Hahn says that when the case comes to trial certain testimony and revelations will be introduced which will have a lasting effect on the expertizing and selling of Old Masters both in America and abroad.' With a new set of attorneys the Hahns planned to return to New York and to bring the case to trial.

However, there were repeated delays. It was not until March 1926 that Duveen's New York offices had copies of the testimony taken in Paris in 1923 – they had not paid the huge bill for the copies, which were therefore held back by the Consulate. The Hahns' money problems grew, and for a while they were unable to proceed with the case because they had failed to pay legal expenses. In February 1928, Duveen's lawyers were suggesting that he pay the Hahns' bills because, as they put it, they did not want one of their creditors to be 'put into the position of pressing them for payment, thereby making it more probable that they would press the case further here'. But somehow the Hahns managed to pay off their outstanding bills, probably by increasing the liens on the picture, and by the end of 1928 a trial date had been set in the new year.

After months of prevarication, negotiation and bluff, the case finally came to trial in the New York Supreme Court on 6 February 1929. From the outset the trial was not merely a judicial proceeding, but a major media event. Throughout the proceedings journalists and the public clamoured to occupy the public galleries of the courtroom. Each morning there was a long queue for seats that sometimes extended out into the street. Press coverage was not confined to the major American newspapers: the story was syndicated throughout the country, reaching the pages of such small papers as the *Appleton Post-Crescent* in Wisconsin, the *Ada Evening News* of Oklahoma and the *Morning Call* of Laurel, Mississippi. In Europe the coverage was equally extensive. Papers in Britain, France, Germany and Italy all filed detailed, almost daily reports of the trial. Duveen, as always, was acutely conscious of the publicity of the proceedings, and received daily reports on the tenor and extent of the coverage.

A trial, any trial, has a peculiar dynamic of its own, one that counsels for both sides are eager to shape and determine, but Levy was in a difficult position. Duveen was determined to turn the court into a showcase for his ideas, achievements and methods. He wanted to dominate proceedings and was not interested in legal niceties. In fact, he never really understood that much of his conduct throughout the trial helped corroborate one of the chief assertions of the plaintiffs, namely that he was the controlling figure in the

Old Master art market, a sort of monopolist in art, determined to drive out or exclude competition. He failed to comprehend that what he wanted to show the world – his power and influence – was grist to his opponent's mill. True, the trial was described as a battle among experts, but Duveen was determined to take up the mantle of connoisseurship for the entire art world. He wanted to be expert in chief and he spent much of the first week of the trial giving the court a lesson in what he considered to be the art of attribution. Though most of the experts who had already given written evidence were reluctant to appear in court, he might well have called on several of them to support his case. In the event only Robert Langton Douglas gave evidence at the trial, speaking directly to the jury about how and why he had reached his conclusions. Instead, the huge quantity of expert testimony from London and Paris was read by lawyers into the written record, a tedious procedure that taxed the concentration of the jury, which frequently showed signs of boredom. Duveen vetoed Levy's suggestion that other dealers take the stand in his support on the grounds that they might steal his limelight.

The jury, notoriously, had little or no art-historical expertise. One member, Arthur S. Cooley, was described as an artist, another, George Senyard, as a poster artist, but the rest of the jury included two real estate agents, a manufacturer of women's wear and another of shirts, an upholsterer, two 'agents', a hotel clerk, an accountant and one person of no fixed occupation: fine, upstanding citizens of New York, no doubt, but not used to making art attributions. Duveen largely ignored them. He played to the press and the gallery, not to the jury, and when he wasn't on the stand he often treated the court as a minor inconvenience, conspicuously answering his mail and reading the newspaper. For Sir Joseph the trial was never simply a matter of the attribution of the Hahn *La Belle Ferronnière*; it was primarily about protecting and then propagating his vision of the art market and his place within it.

Levy built Duveen's legal defence on three tenets – that he was a competent expert entitled to give his views about the authenticity of the painting; that to challenge his professional opinion was an infringement of his freedom of expression; and that the charge against him was baseless, as there was no evidence that his views affected the potential sale of the picture. The first two issues were those of principle; the last depended on Duveen's counsel being able to demonstrate the specific claim that the Kansas City Art Institute lacked the resources and did not intend to purchase the Hahn painting.

The first four days of the trial were taken up with the cross-examination of Duveen by the Hahns' attorney, Lawrence Miller. On the second day of the trial Miller had the Hahn *La Belle* admitted as evidence; the arrival of the painting created a mêlée in the court as journalists and spectators pressed forward to see the small canvas. Miller began to interrogate Duveen about his views on the picture. As the *New York Times* reported, Miller's questioning focused on three issues: Duveen's admission that one or other of the paintings was authentic; his concession that, after the Hahn painting came into public view, he had deferred to expert opinion that the Louvre version of *La Belle* was probably executed by Leonardo's pupil, Giovanni Antonio Boltraffio; and his confession that he had condemned the Hahn painting without seeing it, because he then believed the Louvre painting to be a genuine Leonardo. The implication of Miller's line of questioning was that Duveen's claim –

'the real one is in the Louvre and therefore this must be a copy' – was spurious, because he had known that the Louvre painting was questioned by so many experts (as a putative expert he should have known that fact). Either he was not an expert because he did not know of the attribution of the Louvre painting or, more tellingly, he was lying. The latter suggestion was important to Miller's case because, as the judge explained to the jury, in order to convict Duveen of slander of title, the Hahns' attorney had to show that Sir Joseph's view of the Hahn picture was not made in good faith, but maliciously and irresponsibly, that is, to drive the Hahns and their painting out of the market.

Duveen's conduct on the witness stand was, as Miller repeatedly complained, showed he was less concerned to answer questions than to offer the court, the journalists and the reading public an account of his place in the world of art-historical expertise. The two men struggled with one another, the lawyer tenacious and terse, often sarcastic, Duveen prolix and evasive but invariably good-natured. On the first day of the trial, before the arrival of the Hahn *La Belle*, Duveen explained that his view of the Hahn painting was formed 'independently of art criticism or history. It was formed by my study of all the great pictures of the world.' He had, he reminded the court, been examining the world's great works of art for thirty-three years. He defined an expert as someone who could distinguish a genuine Old Master from a copy, saying that the latter was often lifeless and stilted when compared with the intensity of the original.

The position he took was Morellian in its approach. When asked by Miller, 'don't scholars use inventories and documents to make judgements about attribution?', he responded, 'No. Certainly not.'

Pressed by Miller, who suggested that history might be important in attributions, he expostulated, 'I do not buy pictures on history.' He added, 'An expert doesn't rely on those records [to determine] if the picture isn't right or wrong'. He was not concerned with the history of any painting or with the chemical composition of the pigments with which it was created. As he told the jury, 'the individual technique of any great painter who died centuries ago was as familiar and recognizable to him as a friend's handwriting . . . It is an artist's manner, his individuality. He cannot get out of it.' What mattered in attribution was what the *New York Times* described as 'the logical application of the experience of the eye'.

When pressed further about his skills as a connoisseur, Duveen, though he admitted that he may have made errors in his youth, claimed, 'I do not recall ever making the mistake in the authorship of a picture.' Duveen's evidence and the insouciant, pseudo-aristocratic manner in which it was presented were designed to convey to the jury and the public the sense that he had full command of the art world and the connoisseurship that sustained it. The *New York Evening Post* captured the spirit of his testimony when it headlined one article, 'Pointer in hand, Duveen gives jury $500,000 course in art'. Duveen used the same mixture of charm and irrepressible assurance that had secured him the business and respect of some of the world's richest men. This was a theatrical performance of the sort he had often put on for rich clients in the intimate setting of the Duveen Brothers' showroom, projected on to the larger stage of the court and the pages of the world press.

There is some evidence that Duveen's manner, so effective with his millionaire clientele, did not work its magic on the jury. The press noticed that during the first week of the trial only two jurors,

Arthur Cooley and George Senyard, paid serious attention to Duveen's testimony; the other jurors looked bored. However, this did not bother Duveen; his sole interest, the one he followed avidly during the trial, was in what the press was saying about him.

During the first week of the trial the *New York Times,* which had long been a firm ally of Duveen, was strongly sympathetic to his cause, its headlines reflecting his own imperious vision: 'Duveen testifies to his own expertness', 'Sir Joseph's Eye runs his Business', 'Critics see Duveen as their champion', 'Sir Joseph passes court test of skill'. These generally positive views contrast with the coverage by the rival *New York Herald Tribune* where Duveen was portrayed as less certain and more embattled: 'Duveen admits early doubt on Louvre Da Vinci', 'Hints of Frauds in Morgan art angers Duveen', 'Duveen faces new onslaughts in Art Trial'.

The *Herald Tribune* headlines capture Miller's strategy in cross-examining Duveen. Apart from hammering home his main legal points, Miller sought to crack the veneer of Duveen's effortless assurance. Over the course of the week, he had some success. On the first day of the trial he questioned the dealer about his relationship with the experts who had testified in Paris on his behalf. Duveen was forced to reveal that he 'had business relations with Mr. Berenson' and that 'a fee of 10 per cent on the purchase value of any picture is paid to the expert who pronounces on it'. (In fact, as people in the trade knew, Berenson was paid 25 per cent on the sale price of works he expertized for Duveen, an arrangement that produced much larger sums.) Nevertheless, this revelation – a breach of the oath of secrecy both men had sworn when they signed their secret contract in 1912 – caused the Berensons much heartache. Mary, who must have been reading the Italian press, sent a distraught cable to the Paris office complaining about 'this wretched *Leonardo* business'. 'It may be an excellent Ad for him, who glories in publicity,' she added, 'but it is very hard on us who loathe it.' She also feared that the revelation of Berenson's deal with Duveen might lead to an investigation by 'the tax-collector'; if that happened she wanted Duveen to foot the bill. But Miller was not interested in the Berenson's secret portfolio, except as one of what he showed were many instances in which the experts summoned to pass a disinterested judgement on the Hahn *La Belle* were on the Duveen payroll. What he wanted to expose was the system of clientage and remuneration that enabled Duveen to keep what he called 'a stranglehold on the art business'.

Later in the proceedings Duveen was visibly rattled when Miller reminded him of an incident in which he had apparently been forced to take back some porcelain sold to J.P. Morgan because it was shown to be fake. He wanted to call Bella da Costa Greene, the head of the Morgan library (and the former lover of Bernard Berenson), to his defence, but she was horrified at the prospect and said she would refuse to appear. She did not want to harm Duveen, but she also did not want to talk about the vases under oath, because she knew they were 'wrong'. Duveen was reduced to bluster, but gradually recovered his composure. He pompously assured the court, in words that were decidedly economical with the truth, that, 'No-one can say that Duveen Brothers have ever taken back a work of art because it is not genuine.'

Once it was admitted as evidence, Miller forced Duveen to go through each and every objection he had made to the Hahn portrait, hoping to catch him out. At one point he succeeded in doing so: 'In your answer to this suit you say that the painting is filled with lines and hatchings which are not in da Vinci's manner ... Show me those hatchings on the canvas.' As one paper reported, 'Sir Joseph, armed with a glass, made a minute examination of the picture. He looked up and he looked down. He hummed and hawed and finally admitted that the hatchings were not there.' (Duveen's objection filed in his response to the Hahns' suit was, of course, a pastiche of comments made by the many experts he had employed.) However, on the whole Duveen successfully combated the Hahn lawyer's questions, though the duel between the two men was gruelling. Miller described the cross-examination as an endurance test and, by the end of the week, even the unflappable Duveen was feeling the strain. One paper described him as 'increasingly nervous' and 'fidgety'. He told journalists during a lunchtime recess: 'Last night I did not get a wink of sleep. All night my mind was filled with images of pictures going round and round. How long is this sort of thing going to last, do you think?' Slowly, inexorably, Miller seemed to be gaining the initiative.

Duveen's fortunes took a turn for the better on the Monday of the second week of the trial. Asked by Miller to identify two Annunciations attributed to Leonardo – one in the Louvre, the other in the Uffizi – Duveen, after some hesitation, make the correct attributions. This tense moment marked the failure of Miller to damage Duveen's credibility as an expert and the dealer's confidence soared. He spent the rest of the day belligerently attacking the Hahn portrait, describing the hair as 'mud', the face like 'a mask' and the body like a 'balloon'.

Duveen may have successfully fought off Miller's attempt to undermine his credibility as an expert, but his adversary had succeeded in wounding him in ways that the dealer did not really understand. Levy and his legal team had fought hard, but unsuccessfully, to have Duveen's letter to the Kansas City attorney, John T. Harding, in which he conceded that most experts did not think the Louvre *La Belle* a Leonardo, excluded as evidence. If this was his and other experts' view in 1920, why did the connoisseurs questioned at the Louvre in 1923 so categorically assert that the Louvre painting was by the master? This smacked of the conspiracy and connivance that Miller was trying to persuade the jury underlay Duveen's attack on the Hahns and their painting. Duveen's response to Miller's questions was slippery, evasive and unconvincing. He denied that he had ever really thought that the Louvre *La Belle* was anything other than a Leonardo, admitting that his letter to Harding was 'an exemption to his belief' because he had 'deferred to the opinion of others'. Miller had planted the idea in the jury's mind that Duveen had not really believed in the Louvre *La Belle* in 1920 and that his defence of his action in condemning the Hahn *La Belle*, sight unseen, was nothing more than a convenient rationalization designed to conceal the dealer's malicious intent towards the Hahns and their painting. He was helped by a statement that the Louvre had issued about the time of the start of the trial to the effect that about four years earlier Berenson, Venturi and Guiffrey had examined the Louvre *La Belle*, which had also been x-rayed and subjected to scientific tests, after which the experts had concluded that the painting 'whilst undoubtedly Da Vinci school, [was] not original painting [by the] master'.

Miller also worked hard to shift the jury's perception of Duveen. At the beginning of the trial, the dealer had exuded patrician bonhomie, but on the final day of his evidence, as he sensed that the case was going his way, he became more and more outspoken.

Miller encouraged Duveen in his comprehensive and scathing casti-
gation of the Hahn *La Belle*, egging him on to disparage it even
further. Duveen did not stop to think why he was being asked to
do this, but leapt in with alacrity. Miller knew that to many of the
lay observers in the court, including the jury, it was difficult to see
the differences between the painting in the court and the large
photographic reproduction of the picture in the Louvre. As Duveen
weighed in ever-more strongly against the Hahn *La Belle* he was
made to appear conceited and arrogant, almost hectoring, in a way
that was unlikely to endear him to the jury and was prone to
convince them that some of the stories about Duveen's striving for
dominance of the art world were probably true. Throughout the
saga of the Hahn *La Belle*, Duveen's weakness was in the exces-
siveness of his responses, his penchant for overkill. The Hahns and
their lawyers learnt how to turn Duveen's strength against himself.

The dapper, blue-suited and over-confident dealer was a marked
contrast to the next witness, the Kansas City art dealer, Conrad
Hug. A short man dressed in a black suit, Hug was pale and mortally
ill – he was to die within a few months of colon cancer – a wisp
of a man whose shadowy presence was a far cry from Duveen's
flamboyance in the witness box. Miller coaxed Hug into revealing
that he had twice mortgaged his house in order to finance the case
against Duveen. (The attorney was bent on portraying him as the
little guy struggling against a giant, an impression unwittingly reinforced by Duveen's counsel who disparaged Hug's knowledge and
claimed that most of his business was in picture frames rather than
the art they contained.) Hug also told the jurors how he had been
approached by Mrs Hahn, had brokered a deal with Jesse C. Nichols,
the President of the Kansas City Art Institute and a property

tycoon, to buy the picture for $250,000 (£51,500) and had travelled to New York to collect the painting, only to be told on his return that Duveen's remarks meant that the sale was off. Judged by Hug's testimony, the dealer's comments to the *New York World* put paid to a done deal. Both the content of Hug's evidence and the earnest manner of its delivery moved many of the jurors. Journalists who spoke to them after the trial reported that his testimony 'made a profound impression of the majority of jurors'.

If the first week of the trial had been dominated by Duveen, the second saw the Hahns lay out their case. Andrée Hahn went on the stand immediately after Conrad Hug, among much press speculation about 'what sort she really is', but there was nothing very dramatic about her evidence. She told how she had obtained the painting and was asked if she had tried to sell it to others – two dealers in the court, Colin Agnew and Count Sala, were asked to stand up and identify themselves – but she claimed not to know either of them. In general, she showed herself to be (as she was) quite ignorant about the picture. Aptly enough, much of her time on the witness stand was taken up with cross-examination about a letter her husband had written to *Le Matin*, published on 8 September 1923. In it he had asserted that the Hahns had never denied the authenticity of the Louvre *La Belle* and were only claiming that their portrait was also by Leonardo. Designed to curry favour with the French public, this claim was at odds with the repeated assertions of the Hahns and their lawyers that the Louvre *La Belle* was not by Leonardo, and that it was therefore improper to compare their genuine masterpiece to it. The appropriate point of comparison, they contended, was with undisputed works by Leonardo, such as the *Mona Lisa*.

Miller's next witness was the only 'expert' to testify on the Hahns' behalf, a 'blond mild-mannered Russian with a boyish and excitable voice' named Vadim Chernoff. He explained that he had worked in Russia detecting forgeries, that he was a practising artist and that he was an expert on Old Master techniques. Part of his evidence was, according to the *New York Times*, a general account of 'fresco technique, the meaning of gesso, the use of sizing, varnish, terra verde, linseed oil turpentine and glaze', in which he explained to the jury how fifteenth-century paintings were produced; the rest was a paean to the Hahn painting, which was compared to other works by Leonardo, and a systematic disparagement of the version of *La Belle Ferronnière* in the Louvre. Under cross-examination it became clear that Chernoff's knowledge of art history did not match his expertise in artistic technique. In fact, Levy showed him to be woefully ignorant of Renaissance art. He was also able to show that Chernoff had never been consulted as an authenticator by any major museum, art dealer or major collector. This was not surprising: Chernoff was a painter, not a connoisseur.

Chernoff's enthusiastic support of the Hahns' *La Belle* was complemented by the reading to the court of the deposition of Sortais, the French government expert who had provided the certificate of authentication that in 1916 had attributed the painting to Leonardo. Sortais had been deposed in Paris – he resolutely refused to come to New York and give evidence at the trial – and his evidence added little that was new, apart from confirming his original judgement of 1916. Sortais refused to be drawn on the history of the picture: history, he responded, was interesting, but visual judgement was what mattered. However, he became extremely angry when his competence as an expert was questioned. Levy brought up a judgement against him, when he had confused paintings by Jean-Baptiste Greuze and Elizabeth Vigée-Le Brun. Sortais's response was to grow ever-more peremptory. When asked, 'Is there anybody alive whose opinion on Italian art of the fifteenth century has weight with you and whom you respect?' He replied, 'No. Not alive.' Pressed further, he was asked, 'You are the only man who ever lived whose opinion on Italian art in the fifteenth century is authentic and worthy of weight?' To which he responded, 'Yes, that is it.' Unfortunately, for the Hahns, Sortais's evidence made a poor impression.

The Hahns' case was concerned with pigments rather than aesthetics, and with history and provenance rather than appearances. As one paper reported, 'To offset the preponderance of aesthetic judgement already prepared by the Duveen art experts in Paris, a reserve of scientific and historic evidence was organized yesterday by S Lawrence Miller, counsel for Mrs. Hahn.' Using 'musty tomes and family records', Miller set out to trace the history of the Hahn *La Belle*, attempting to show that it appeared in an inventory of royal pictures made by François-Bernard Lépicié in 1752. That version of *La Belle* was described as having hands holding a piece of lace. Miller claimed that the picture had been cut down and a balustrade added some time after the inventory was taken and intended to show that the strip of white paint at the base of the Hahn picture covered the new edge of the painting. As Miller explained, he planned to make the case a question of 'whether the jury shall depend upon the subtle discrimination of an art critic's eye or on the findings of paint chemists on magnified photographs of paint surfaces, and on X-ray examinations of the paint layers below the surface where no art critic's eye can penetrate'.

However, into the third week of the trial, Duveen's lawyers dropped a bombshell, producing an affadavit in which Jesse C. Nichols directly contradicted the evidence offered on the stand by Conrad Hug. He denied that there had been any commitment on the part of the Institute to buy the Hahn picture; he pointed out that the Institute had no financial assets and was a poor institution that would not have been able to enter into such a deal. There was no agreement to buy for $250,000 (£51,500), though he conceded that he had pledged $5,000 (£1,030) of his own money if a subscription was taken up to buy the painting. Levy moved that the case be dismissed. How could the Hahns claim that Duveen's comments cost them $250,000 when there was no deal on the table? Judge William Harman Black rejected the motion but urged the lawyers on both sides to send representatives to depose and cross-examine Nichols, who was ill and therefore not able to appear in the New York court. When Nichols' evidence was produced the following week, he confirmed his account of his negotiations with Hug: there was no deal with the Art Institute and he had never said that purchase depended upon Duveen withdrawing his condemnation of the Hahns' painting. Cross-examination, however, revealed that, though strictly correct, Nichols' testimony did not mean that there was not considerable interest in acquiring the painting: 'it was established that there was plenty of money in Kansas City held by persons interested in the Institute, and that he would have been glad to raise $250,000 to buy a da Vinci painting, if convinced by experts it was genuine'.

Back in New York, the lawyers took turns in the tedious task of reading into the record the depositions of Bernard Berenson, Roger Fry, Sir Charles Holmes and Frederik Schmidt-Deniger. The press was growing tired of the case, though their interest revived when Robert Langton Douglas, the only one of Duveen's witnesses to appear in person, took the stand and began a two-day sparring match with Miller. Douglas, an extravagant man who was always short of money, had agreed with Duveen to testify provided he was paid £1,000 ($4,850), or £1,800 ($8,730) if he had to stay in New York for more than a week. He said little that was new, concurring with Duveen's other experts in his condemnation of the Hahn *La Belle* as 'fat and pudgy', as well as reiterating the technical criticisms of his colleagues. Florid, voluble, opinionated and witty, he entertained the judge and the press. What sort of impression he left on the jury as a representative connoisseur is hard to know.

As the trial proceeded the evidence became more technical. Levy called Stephen Pichetto, a restorer from the Metropolitan Museum, who testified on the basis of 'having restored tens of thousands' of paintings during the previous twenty-five years, that he was certain that the Hahn picture had never been painted on wood, as the cracks clearly indicated that it had always been on canvas. He also claimed that the eyes and the band that supported *La Belle*'s jewel on her forehead – both of which had been criticized for their execution and which Chernoff said were the work of a restorer – were part of the original painting. He could find no evidence, he said, of any restoration.

On the last two days of the trial both sides introduced x-ray evidence. The Hahns had had their painting x-rayed but had been unable to find an art historian who could interpret the radiographs; instead, they called an eminent radiologist, but he was clearly unable to explain their significance. Duveen's counsel asked that his testimony be excluded; the judge concurred.

Duveen had been extremely reluctant to introduce x-ray evidence. As he told his lawyers, 'he did not believe in it'. However, once the x-rays were produced, he agreed to call upon Alan Burroughs of the Fogg Art Museum at Harvard, a young scholar who had been building up a systematic x-ray archive. As it happened, Burroughs had already x-rayed the Louvre version of *La Belle* and, once the Louvre had given their permission, was able to compare images of the two pictures. Burroughs pointed to one major difference between them. In the x-ray of the Louvre painting, the jewel on La Belle's forehead was invisible. 'This indicated that the painter of the Louvre *Belle* had first laid down metallic flesh tints (impermeable to x-rays) then painted the jewel over them.' In the Hahn *La Belle* the artist had painted around the jewel, leaving a hole for it. This suggested that 'the Hahn *Belle* had first been carefully sketched then colored in separate sections – flesh, fabric, jewellery. This is a practice favored by copyists'. The full import of this finding was not immediately apparent to the court, but it did not favour the Hahns.

In his final summary, Duveen's counsel reiterated that there was no evidence that Duveen's opinion killed a possible sale of the Hahns' picture; indeed, there was no evidence of an impending sale. Duveen's opinion had not been given 'recklessly', but in his capacity as a frequently consulted expert. Besides, there was no evidence to show that the Hahn picture was genuine. It came 'from oblivion'. Miller, for the Hahns, reiterated his view that Duveen had conspired to drive them and their picture out of the market: 'He killed the sale of the Hahn painting when he put his foot down and crushed that little dealer in Kansas City. His influence goes all over the world.' It was almost impossible to find an expert to testify against Duveen because they were all either in his pay or under his influence. What mattered were the physical properties of the Hahn painting and these, he maintained, were entirely consistent with a work by Leonardo.

The jury was instructed by Judge Black that they were to find against Duveen if they were convinced that the Hahn painting was a genuine Leonardo. Unable to reach a verdict they asked Black if they could award the Hahns damages, even though some of them were unconvinced, beyond a reasonable doubt, that the Hahn *La Belle* was genuine. The judge demurred and urged them to reach a verdict. After fourteen hours of deliberation, the jury reported that they were unable to do so. Duveen petitioned the court to have the case dismissed, but Judge Black ruled that there was sufficient evidence to reach a verdict and ordered a retrial. In the spring of 1930 a weary Duveen reached a settlement with the Hahns, paying them $60,000 (£12,350), agreeing that the picture was old but continuing to assert his view that it was not the work of Leonardo.

Were there any victors in the case of *Hahn versus Duveen?* Certainly the Hahns had the better of the struggle: $60,000 at the outset of the Depression, approximately $600,000 by today's standards, was a great deal of money, especially when converted into French francs, but they had not secured the large sum they had demanded in damages, had outstanding legal bills and were still no closer to selling their painting. Duveen, on the other hand, had not won the victory he so ardently desired and which he felt sure should have been his. Throughout the trial he remained extremely optimistic about its outcome. There was a great deal of evidence on his side – Nichols' testimony that no deal had been struck in

Kansas, the overwhelming consensus among experts that the Hahn painting was not genuine, the x-ray testimony that pointed to the Hahn as a copy, and the support in the art press for his cause. Yet, as the papers revealed, he had very nearly lost the case. The jury had voted nine to three in favour of Andrée Hahn and her painting. How could this be, and what did it say about the state of connoisseurship? Was this the result of skilled lawyering – Miller clearly thought that he would win – or did it say something more profound about the status and strength of art expertise? Was the outcome of *Hahn versus Duveen* a one-off, or did it indicate a more profound crisis in the sort of connoisseurship that sustained the market for Old Master painting?

CHAPTER 6

The Battle of the Experts

The success of the Hahns against Sir Joseph Duveen in 1929 can partly be attributed to the skill with which their lawyers constructed their legal case. They shrewdly understood that the jurors were unlikely to be impressed by Duveen's experts and their testimony, and that, as pragmatic New Yorkers, they would demand concrete evidence rather than inference and supposition. Lawrence Miller and his colleagues did an excellent job of undermining the appearance of unanimity among the connoisseurs and in tarnishing them as effete, snobbish and un-American. In this sense the trial was a unique, peculiarly American affair, whose broader implications did not necessarily apply to the state of connoisseurship as a whole. Or did it? For Duveen, at least, the trial was an opportunity to propagate a particular view of connoisseurship, one that sought to convince the jury, the press and the general public of the central importance of the tutored eye in attributing pictures. He clearly failed with the jury, but did he win any support among a larger public?

Certainly he enjoyed some success. His old ally, the *New York Times*, was convinced of old-fashioned connoisseurship. On 11 February, the first Sunday after the trial began, it ran a major editorial explaining the mysteries of modern connoisseurship. To the layman, it said, art expertise might appear like 'charlatanism' or 'black magic', but true connoisseurial skill rested on long-term experience – a history of looking at paintings – and 'an extraordinary capacity for attention with a remarkably retentive visual memory'. Scientific evidence – x-rays and the chemical analysis of pigments, for instance – was of little value; what really mattered was a consensus of experts. The editorial conceded that expert judgement was a matter of feeling rather than analysis: 'the connoisseur also has a special gift for remembering his feelings' when he examined paintings. This had the corollary that, 'If he has quite different feelings before a new picture, he simply interprets this difference of feeling in terms of authorship, period, originality or copyism [*sic*].' But the *Times* hastened to add that this did not mean that such judgements were as subjective as readers might suppose. 'The twilight zone of expertise is narrower than most people think,' the paper argued, 'the margin of error is probably no larger than that which businessmen accept cheerfully in expertise concerning any issue of similar commercial importance.'

Quite a few supporters of Duveen, including fellow art dealers, took up the idea that connoisseurial judgement was rather like business acumen. A New York antique-furniture dealer, Adrien Wellens, relayed to Duveen a conversation he had recently had with an important banker, 'a man of untold wealth'. The plutocrat, wrote Wellens, 'asked me how I knew my pieces of American and English furniture were really old and I answered his question by asking him what he did when he took steps to be certain an issue of bonds which he offered to his clientele was worthy of their consideration and investment'. Wellens was pleased that the banker's reply 'was substantially what mine would have been', namely, 'that his judgement backed by many years of experience, a reputation which he could not afford to lose and a love of his calling which sharpened his judgement enabled him to give a decision which was as nearly right as was humanly possible'.

The analogy between art-dealing and bond-trading is a revealing one, for it shows that the dealer saw attribution as a bet on the confidence that the artwork could inspire. However, an attribution is not, of course, the same as an investment, even though the one may lead to the other. The question of whether an artist executed a picture asks for a judgement about a matter of fact, whereas a prediction about the potential value of a stock is an informed guess about investor confidence. In treating them as comparable the dealer revealed how confused issues of attribution, value and estimation had become, and how difficult they were to untangle. In the commercial environment in which Duveen and his colleagues operated, dealers and buyers were used to working with the power of opinion and were thoroughly familiar with the risks it entailed. Duveen's manipulation of Old Master prices was of a piece with the investment strategies of his rich clients and was probably a skill for which they had more than a sneaking admiration. They shared with Duveen a belief not just of art's eternal values, but of its ready transmutation into a valuable investment. It was the claim not only of Duveen but of many apologists for connoisseurship that, although individual error was possible in making attributions – anyone can make a mistake – a consensus of experts made an attribution safe and secure. Whatever the truth or value of this claim, it was easy for critics of Duveen and his colleagues to construe consensus as complicity. It was not difficult to look at the booming art market as a speculative bubble (which in part it was) in which dealers, experts and even collectors had a collective interest in promoting a bull market.

The business press, mindful that trust and confidence were the essential lubricants of the wheels of commerce, made a strong show of supporting Duveen, arguing that if he could not give his opinion about a picture, then the whole art market would grind to a halt. This was a view also shared by much of the art press which, towards the end of the trial, ran a number of alarmist editorials about the threat to art criticism and fair comment if Duveen were to lose the case. As one editorial put it, 'It would be a very bad thing for the cause of art education if competent critics were intimidated by threats of lawsuits by alleged owners' of works of art. Duveen, it added, had an obligation to give his opinion as an expert because 'at the present time there is an immense business carried on by unscrupulous dealers in the manufacture of art objects and swindling the public'. Seen in this light, Duveen was not only asserting his right to free speech, but also performing a public service:

> The collecting of genuine art objects is not merely a fad, it is a great benefit to a country like the United States which has refinement and artistic instincts, but little or no background of art history and development ... It is obviously important to make the art education of the public genuine education, based on genuine art objects, and not a false education, based on spurious articles.

To a remarkable degree, the museum world, the art market and the connoisseurs lined up in a rare show of unanimity in support of Duveen. As Philip Guedalla, the wit and author, put it in a letter to Duveen Brothers' London office, Sir Joseph had full support 'among the knowing ones of the world', but the cognoscenti showed little understanding of why so many found their position untenable. They repeatedly expressed incredulity at what the British painter Walter Sickert described as 'the historical high tide mark of ignorance and impudence', but no sense of why the art experts were not able to win the case. Duveen was no better. Throughout the trial he peppered friends with cables containing sentiments like those sent on 21 February 1929: 'case going marvellously don't worry sure to win'.

Duveen's natural optimism was probably enforced by the letters he received from the general public. Many of these approved of his views about the two *La Belle Ferronnière*s and shared his emphasis on the importance of proper connoisseurship. One anonymous New York correspondent, 'A Traveler', endorsed Duveen's 'valuable series of suggestions to the layman' which he was sure would 'be of great assistance to myself and doubtless to many others in future visits to the galleries of this and other countries'. Arthur Stephens of Little Rock, Arkansas, praised Duveen's 'valuable service ... in directing attention to the spurious works of art that are so frequently offered for sale in this country at fabulously inflated prices'. An art student, Eliza Chatfield, wrote from Seymour, Connecticut, of her fascination with the case. Margaret Scott Miller of Brooklyn offered advice about the *coiffures* of the two pictures. Some correspondents reiterated Duveen's views: John Devlin of New York wrote, 'The Hahn picture is wholly without character and is flabby and if da Vinci has ever been insulted before, this fling is the limit. The Louvre painting lives and talks, the other is not only fat but dead,' a view endorsed by a letter of support written by the architect, Harry Cunningham. Kitty Browne, the secretary of the South Carolina Motor Carriers Association in Greenville, disarmingly confessed to Duveen that 'I know very little, if anything, about fine paintings, and fear that you will consider this liberty unwarranted,' but went on to add that, 'to me the Hahn painting is so apparently a copy, I cannot but let you know that I agree with you, and why'. Another correspondent from St John, New Brunswick, wrote 'it seems strange to me how people can fail to see the enormous difference between the two pictures – the one a definite impression of a fine personality by a very great artist, the other only a vapid rendering of externals'.

However, such support could not conceal the fact that both the connoisseurs and their expertise took a severe battering during the course of the trial. From the outset the press, both in the United States and abroad, focused on what Justice Black called 'the battle of the experts'. Almost every headline used the term 'expert': 'Duveen will call Experts to his Aid'; 'Duveen experts will take the stand today'; 'Expert can't find flaw he once charged'; 'Can't be real, expert tells packed court'; 'Expert likens Hahn picture to Mona Lisa'; '*La Belle* put in peril by art expert'. Experts were the key witnesses, but art expertise itself was also on trial. Indeed, the court proceedings opened with a lengthy discussion of what an art expert or specialist was, in which Louis Levy, Duveen's counsel, drew a (positive) analogy between art-historical and medical expertise, while Miller spent much of his cross-examination challenging the right of all of Duveen's connoisseurs to call themselves 'experts'. Because all of the connoisseurs were against the Hahn picture Miller challenged not just their particular judgement, but their claim to have a general competence to make proper attributions.

Here he was helped by the version of connoisseurship presented by Duveen at the trial and by the experts in their recorded testimony. As we have seen, the case they presented resolutely rejected many sorts of evidence. They denied the value of 'scientific' evidence that spoke about the physical properties of paintings and in their testimony were quite happy to reveal a general ignorance of primers, pigments and painted surfaces. Their attitude was perfectly captured in Bernard Berenson's 1923 testimony in Paris. The flavour of the proceedings and Berenson's impatience come out clearly in the transcript that was read to the New York court:

Hyacinthe Ringrose: Can you tell me the difference between a picture painted in walnut oil and linseed oil?

Bernard Berenson: I certainly can't, and I defy you to do so, too. It is all perfect humbug.

HR: There is a picture in the Prado labelled da Vinci?

BB: Yes.

HR: Is it not by Leonardo da Vinci?

BB: No.

HR: Have you ever seen it?

BB: Yes.

HR: Is it painted on wood or canvas?

BB: On wood, to my recollection, but I may be mistaken. That is not interesting. It is not interesting on what paper Shakespeare wrote *Hamlet*.

This irascible witticism was both clever and foolish. Clever in its pithy summary of Berenson's views; foolish in its rejection of a question that an ordinary jury was bound to find important. Of course, some experts commented on the physical condition of the Hahn painting – especially on the shape of the cracks in the surface of the paint, which several witnesses said were a clear indication that the picture had never been on wood, but always on canvas – but this technical evidence was crowded out by repeated assertions about the low quality of the Hahn *La Belle*.

Shunning scientific evidence, the experts and Duveen also ignored provenance and history. Duveen himself made clear that visual judgement always overrode any other sort of evidence – from an inventory or other written description of a painting. One of his experts, Seymour de Ricci, had in fact spent a long time in the archives of the Louvre, tracing their version of *La Belle*, and trying to dig up evidence of the Hahn picture. He was convinced that he could show that the version in Paris was in the French Royal Collections as far back as the sixteenth century, and that there was no case to be made for the Hahn picture, but Duveen ignored his findings and went out of his way to exclude him as a witness. The Hahn evidence based on provenance was weak, but at least at the trial it was there.

If there was no 'science' of connoisseurship in the way that Cavalcaselle, with his penchant for documents, would have recognized, nor was there much 'science' that would have pleased Morelli. Though individual parts of the two paintings were discussed – the jewel on the band round the head, the eyes, the tapes at the sleeves – they were not discussed morphologically, or as typical or not of Leonardo, but qualitatively, and particularly as being unworthy of the skills of the master. The attack by Duveen and his experts on the Hahn painting – as grotesque, ill-executed and lifeless – and their condemnation of the figure in it as 'peasant-like', fat and German or North European in contrast to the patrician, Italian elegance of the woman in the Louvre painting reinforced the sense that what was at work in their analysis was as much social snobbery as art-historical expertise.

This spoke to another feature of the testimony offered by Duveen's experts. They refused to be tutored or trained, to work with Levy and his legal team to produce a coherent body of evidence. 'Wood shedding' – the tutoring of expert witnesses – has long been a common (though usually unacknowledged) practice of lawyers in their preparation for trials. Levy had an elaborate questionnaire prepared for all the expert witnesses. It asked them to provide information about their professional qualifications and evidence, in the form of publications and consulting by museums, dealers and collectors, of their expertise not just in Italian art but the works of Leonardo in particular. This anodyne request, analogous to asking an expert doctor about his career at medical school, his technical papers and speciality, was greeted with horror by most of the art connoisseurs. Levy was told in a terse cable that 'the questions sent would be considered insult to people of such intellectual standing and sensitive temperaments'. When Maurice Brockwell, Bernard Berenson's former assistant, saw the questions 'he looked quite frightened and almost turned pale'. Only one of Duveen's experts, the professor of Chemistry, A.P. Laurie, provided a *curriculum vitae* for the lawyers.

This response was a clear sign of how far art expertise had to go before it could be seen as properly professionalized. A connoisseur was still not far from an amateur – a lover of art – whose skills depended not on external qualifications but on the cultivation of an inner sensibility. Neither the rule-governed, arid procedures of science nor the dry-as-dust scholarly investigation of documents could explain the dismissal of an inauthentic work or capture the genius that was the connoisseur's elusive quarry. Thus Sir William Martin Conway, justifying his rejection of the Hahn picture testified, 'I simply look at the Hahn picture and the impression produced on my mind is that it is not by Leonardo.' Maurice Brockwell said, 'it is a question of psychology, not of the magnifying glass; it is the mind of the great master that we see, the spiritual content, the psychological correlations'. Bernard Berenson spoke of a 'sixth sense ... difficult to find the vocabulary to express oneself'. He also emphasized the importance of 'accumulated experience upon which your spirit acts almost unconsciously'.

It would be wrong to say that the expert's judgements fell entirely on deaf ears. Both the *American Art News* and the *New York Herald Tribune* defended Berenson's often derided remarks about the importance of a sixth sense. 'A sense of aesthetic values which has been developed through years of study and comparison,' wrote the *News*, 'is indefinable but none the less real.' In similar fashion the *Herald Tribune* took the view that 'experience in the domain of art criticism is related essentially to the imponderables', and that therefore, 'One great service the trial has rendered has been its ventilation of this fact and of another closely allied with it in the makeup of the expert – that elusive thing which the French call flair.' But the widespread circulation of a view is not the same as its widespread acceptance. As the *Herald Tribune* had to concede as it plunged in deeper on behalf of the values of connoisseurship:

'There has been mirthful comment on the passage in Mr. Berenson's deposition indicating that the art critic functioned by virtue of a mystical sixth sense, fortified by accumulated experience.' It concluded:

> Mankind is slow to admit the possession among comparatively few of its members of a faculty denied to many more of us. It may confess cheerfully enough that it 'has no ear for music', but, having eyes, it will look at pictures with anybody. It is dubious about the dogmatism of an expert who recognizes in a picture what untrained eyes cannot see. Nevertheless Berenson was right. His scholarship cannot be challenged. His knowledge of the literature on Leonardo is as great as that of any man living, if not greater. But what he relies on, first and last, when he is studying the work of the master, is native flair and a lifetime spent looking at pictures.

However, the court was not impressed with sixth senses and psychological correlations. As the press was quick to note, Judge Black, who had a lawyerly sense of hard evidence and a strong commitment to proof on the basis of facts, was withering, both in the court and in his written opinion, about Duveen's experts. He also explicitly challenged Duveen's view of the nature of expertise. He told the jury, 'there are two ways that experts in this case can help you with their opinions. One is in their study of the authentic history of a painting. The other by their study of the methods used or materials employed by the painters or schools of painting of the period in which it is claimed the pictures were painted.' Black, in other words, was pointing to the importance of the historic, documentary record about pictures and the nature of their physical properties as vital to establishing an attribution or determination 'founded on facts'. He was instructing the jury to take note of the two grounds of attribution that had been explicitly rejected by all of Duveen's experts apart from the chemist A.P. Laurie.

Black conceded that court experts were not just concerned with 'the facts' but were also useful in making inferences from them that would not be immediately apparent to jurors. He went out of his way to express his general support for expert witnesses: 'I have profound respect for critics whose conclusions rest upon facts. What they say should be carefully considered by a jury.' But then he went on to consider those experts whose claim to expertise he viewed as suppositious. 'Beware experts,' Black warned the jury. 'Because a man claims to be an expert does not make him one.' As he wrote in his opinion of the case:

> the opinions of any other kinds of experts are as 'sounding brass and tinkling cymbals'. Some of them expound their theories largely by vocal expression and gesture; others wander into a zone of speculation founded upon nothing more tangible than 'psychological correlation.' I do not say that this is as absurd as it sounds to a layman, but it is too introspective and subjective to be the basis of any opinion a jury can pin its faith upon.

Alluding to Berenson's remarks, Black added, 'There are also experts who admit that they have no formulas, rules or ability to produce any artistic thing, but who claim to have a sixth sense that enables some of them after they have seen a picture even for five minutes to definitely determine whether it is genuine or not.' Once again,

Black played the legal sceptic: 'I do not say that this faculty may not be possessed by some men, but it is not based upon enough objectiveness to convey definite meaning to a jury.' Where, Black was tartly asking, was the 'science' in 'scientific connoisseurship'?

Black was also unimpressed by the way in which so many of Duveen's experts had changed their mind over the Louvre version of *La Belle*, rejecting it as a Leonardo before the 1920s, but accepting it as a Leonardo when questioned in Paris. 'It required,' he remarked in the opinion which rejected Duveen's attempt to prevent a retrial, 'some mental agility to follow some of the experts from their positive testimony on the stand to the diametrically opposite views they had expressed in their books long before.' Here, he was tacitly acknowledging the skills of the Hahns' attorney, Miller, who had adroitly diverted attention away from the experts' unanimity about the Hahns' picture in order to emphasize their disagreement over the Louvre *La Belle*. In this he was again assisted by the conduct of the experts who cheerfully admitted to frequent disagreements and who could never resist a jibe at an old rival or enemy. Robert Langton Douglas, whose conduct on the witness stand in New York was entertaining rather than constructive, willingly confessed that 'experts fight like cats and dogs'. Asked about experts in the Louvre, he resurrected a remark that Berenson had made in his earlier testimony in Paris, saying, 'Frenchmen know nothing about painting and there are no authorities in the Louvre.' The chemist A.P. Laurie dismissed all his fellow experts by saying that he had 'no faith in literary statements of critics'. Sir Charles Holmes, asked about Bernard Berenson's views on Leonardo, responded that he did not know because Berenson was always changing his mind. Dismissing fellow experts in this way – part of a long history of acrimony and deep personal rivalry that dated back to the days of Morelli – undermined both the credibility of the experts and the value of their testimony. The old idea that connoisseurship, as an evolving practice or science, meant that reattributions and individual changes of mind were inevitable, was turned by Miller into evidence of a craven desire to appeal to Sir Joseph Duveen.

Yet the most damning evidence of Duveen's failure to persuade the jury or public of his view of connoisseurship was the testimony of the jurors after the trial was over. When asked how they had arrived at their verdicts, the nine jurors who supported the Hahns all pointed to the scientific evidence that, ironically, had been offered by one of Duveen's witnesses, the chemist A.P. Laurie. In Paris, after examining both pictures with a microscope and having failed to find what he called 'dating pigments' that would prove either of the paintings to be later works or copies, he refused to testify on the authorship of either picture as he did not 'pretend to be an expert on technique and did not want to be drawn into artistic questions'. But what he did say, which was seized upon by the Hahns' lawyers, was that the Louvre picture contained 'neither lapis lazuli, vermillion, Naples yellow or a non-fading green, which were the finest and most prized paints'. and that 'the red ochre used in the bodice is termed barn painters' paint'. He added that the greens in the Louvre picture 'are verdigris crystal which have faded'. Compared with the pigments used in the Hahn painting, the lawyers claimed, 'The paints . . . are of the most ordinary and inferior kind, and not such as would be used by a master in da Vinci's time.' While three jurors (not surprisingly, they were the most prosperous members of the jury) felt convinced that the cumulative testimony of recognized art connoisseurs had to be heeded, the remainder of the jury relied on the sort of hard scientific testimony that they and the court had always wanted.

During the trial the press had commented on how the flagging attention of the jurors had been reawakened once x-ray evidence was presented. As one paper put it, the juror 'wants something tangible to go on'. So did the press. Towards the end of the trial, as it ground on tediously with the reading of the depositions taken in 1923, the newspaper coverage was enlivened by the story of Duveen's belated attempt to get x-rays of the Louvre *La Belle* admitted as evidence. Duveen called the Louvre on the transatlantic phone – an expensive act of modern extravagance – and then capped it by chartering an aircraft to bring the x-rays from Boston where they were deposited in the Fogg Art Museum. 'X-rays, airplane, trans-Atlantic phone figure in attack on authenticity of Hahn' crowed one headline, obviously relieved to report something other than the testimony of fuddy-duddy experts. As *Time* magazine, a publication that prided itself in taking the pulse of the American people, commented:

> There is probably only one way of convincing a twentieth-century jury that a given painting is by a particular 15th Century master. That is by absolute evidence, such as a fingerprint, document or signature known to be valid. Such evidence the Duveen trial did not produce. Arguments on technique, expression, nuances of genius, only served to exhibit the latitude and variance of personal opinion.

Though he didn't realize it, Duveen's goose was cooked when, during their fifteen hours of deliberations, the jury asked for a copy of Laurie's book on the chemistry of pigmentation.

Duveen had embarked on the trial in the enthusiastic expectation that he could use the court to vindicate his firm and its practices, especially that of connoisseurship. The case resembled others in which Duveen had been involved in that it partly hung on his professional reputation, but it also differed in its emphasis not just on his probity but on the efficacy of the techniques on which his and other Old Master dealerships depended. The Hahns, or more accurately their lawyers, had, of course, made this the key issue of the trial, but it was a challenge that Duveen welcomed. He clearly thought that he could get the court to endorse the aesthetic judgements of his experts and that such approval would enhance his reputation both within the art world and outside it. When, during their arguments against a retrial, his lawyers argued that a court of law was not competent to determine the authenticity of a picture like the Hahn *La Belle* because this entailed an aesthetic judgement, Duveen in effect conceded that, in this forum at least, he could not win. Connoisseurship would continue to dominate transactions in the art market, to be the currency of the trade, but it ventured into the courts with extreme peril.

The case of *Hahn versus Duveen* shows that the pressures on traditional connoisseurship came from several directions. Connoisseurs had to respond to a general sentiment that innovations in science and technology would solve problems that had previously been intractable. They were forced to face the assumption that science and human progress marched hand in hand. More specifically, as questions of authenticity moved into the courts and the public sphere, connoisseurship had to confront the growth of forensic inquiry and the public fascination it attracted. Connoisseurship was concerned with the identification of those who had created a painting and the elimination of false suspects or imposters. Similarly, the new means of criminal detection developed in the late nineteenth and early twentieth centuries was concerned to identify perpetrators (not artists but criminals) and exclude false suspects. Whether in the fictional Sherlock Holmes stories of Conan Doyle or the sensational reports of criminal proceedings in the newspapers, the use of science was seen as a way of eliminating uncertainty. There were two strands to forensics: on the one hand, the use of 'clues' or traces to reconstruct the crime and its perpetrator – a sort of conjectural and inferential science that made detection more probable; on the other, the development of practices that were supposed to virtually eliminate interpretation, of which the most important and sensational was the development of fingerprinting, a forensic practice that became established at the very moment when the Old Master market was reaching its peak. (The first major convictions based on fingerprint evidence were made in 1905 in Britain and 1911 in the United States.) Somewhere between these two poles of conjecture and certainty were such 'sciences' as graphology – the analysis of handwriting – and the use of chemical analyses, such as those that proved substances to be poisonous.

At first sight it might seem that the emergence of a science of forensics and of legal experts would tend to reinforce the power and credibility of the art connoisseur. After all, the use of visual 'clues' to identify a great artist was akin to the use of traces of evidence to catch a perpetrator. Both involved sleuthing. Indeed, forensic techniques began to seep into the traditional practice of Old Master connoisseurship. As we have seen Morelli's use of hands, ears and feet to make attributions employed the very same human features that Alphonse Bertillon, of the prefecture of Paris police, used in his system of anthropometric measurement designed to identify thieves. However, the art connoisseur's method differed in one vital respect from the procedures used in the new science of criminal detection. Unlike the criminal detective who proceeded from accumulated evidence to a conclusion, the connoisseur made a snap judgement and then gathered corroborative evidence for his view. 'Science' supported but did not replace qualitative judgement. As the art historian Max Friedländer reminded his readers in *On Art and Connoisseurship*, Morelli pointed 'to the individual forms in order to convince the reader of the justness of his attributions; but he, like every successful expert, has formed his opinion from the "accidental" impression of the whole picture'. The authority of the art connoisseur stemmed from his personal familiarity with many great works of art and on personal intuition, not on technical expertise and the accumulation of evidence. In the end, as expert after expert at the trial attested, it was still the trained eye that mattered. The art expert was like a policeman on his beat who, as a result of years of experience, could identify criminals with whom he was familiar. His judgement would be accepted by those who trusted him, but it was altogether a different matter to prove in a court of law or to a group of strangers that he had identified the right man.

Though there was a special fascination with the power of experts in many fields in the first half of the twentieth century, there was also a great deal of public suspicion. This was especially true in the United States where a strong belief in technical knowledge as a key to economic and social progress was countermanded by a fear that the recondite and therefore largely inaccessible skills of the expert were anti-democratic. As an essay by Joseph Lee in the *Atlantic Monthly* put it, 'In the last analysis, the expert's claim is a claim to the exemption of himself, and the subjects with which he deals, from the ordinary jurisdiction of the human mind.' The 'blind faith' demanded by the expert makes intrusion into his world virtually impossible: 'any knowledge of the inner mysteries that the layman may seem to acquire is necessarily wrong and spurious. What looked like knowledge is . . . turned to dross when once you cross the threshold of the sanctuary.' This, as Lee concluded, was 'a denial of the catholicity and sovereignty of the human mind'.

The art connoisseur, a rather unusual type of expert with little or no professional grounding, was placed in a difficult position. Market pressures to give sure and safe attributions, along with the growing culture of experts in many walks of life, led to much higher expectations about a science of connoisseurship which most of its practitioners could not fulfil. At the same time, suspicion of art experts was especially pronounced because their status seemed to depend less on technical qualifications – like a physician, a lawyer or an engineer – than on a social exclusivity that allowed them privileged access to pictures. The New York trial brought this out in stark relief. Expert witnesses were becoming increasingly common in the trials of this period and so were a set of conventions about how they established their qualifications as experts before the court. However, as Judge Black made clear in his opinion of *Hahn versus Duveen*, the connoisseurs barely looked like experts at all, while their apparent snobbery made them a ready target for public criticism, for it compounded the suspicion of the anti-democratic aura that already surrounded other professional technical experts. Connoisseurs, with their hostility to much 'science', seemed to revel in their subjective views, to imply that their view was better than that of others not because of some external criteria, but because it was *their* view.

The sense among connoisseurs that treating art attribution as a science meant downgrading or re-evaluating personal acquaintance with a large number of works of art (a form of knowledge that was also only available to a select few) meant that for much of the first half of the twentieth century they remained deeply hostile to any attempt to 'scientize' attribution. Connoisseurs used some of the appurtenances of modern science – they employed photographs probably more than they should have done to make attributions – but they repeatedly and vehemently denied the value of the recent technology of x-rays and were reluctant to place much faith in chemical analysis. It is an attitude that persists today. Thomas Hoving, former director of the Metropolitan Museum in New York, in his study of art fakes, *False Impressions*, published in 1996, begins his book with a checklist of eleven vital steps towards making an attribution. The tenth reads, 'Subject the piece [of art] to a scientific examination using a wide number of methods ... Then discount everything you find'. Only listening 'to street talk' is less important.

The roots of this hostility in the first part of the twentieth century lay partly in connoisseurs' desire to protect their (lucrative) turf from the incursions of self-confessed scientists. (They were equally hostile to historians who investigated art through the written record, claiming that only the works of art themselves could reveal 'the truth' of their making.) However, the experts' defensiveness was also a consequence of their profound unease about artworks as physical objects. An Old Master may have been made up of panels or canvas and paint, but what the connoisseur looked for (and knew about) – and, equally important, what the rich collector was collecting – was something altogether more intangible: those signs of the human spirit that emanated from the hand of a great master. To treat such an artefact as a gross material object rather than an expression of genius was, quite simply, an act of desecration. In consequence, many experts were proud to admit that they knew almost nothing about the materials and techniques employed in painting, and remained hostile to the idea that such knowledge had any bearing on the task of the connoisseur. Technical expertise was left to restorers or conservators (often disparagingly referred to as 'cleaners') who, in line with a long-standing distinction between the mechanical and fine arts, between hand and head, were seen as lacking the capacity to make connoisseurial judgements.

At the same time science was intruding into art – not so much in the market-place as in the museum, especially the major museums of Europe and North America, whose foundation was one of the most important developments in the history of nineteenth-century collecting. As these institutions accumulated large representative collections of the different national 'schools' that made up the history of art, the issue of the physical condition of the objects under their care became ever-more pressing. Of course, conservators and restorers had practised their craft for just as long as connoisseurs had followed theirs (though it was a while before a conservator was a scientist rather than a painter). However, in the nineteenth century their knowledge and skills were systematized in a number of manuals written by museum officials in Italy, Britain, France and Germany. The first science laboratory in an art museum opened in Berlin in 1888, followed by Vienna, the British Museum and the Louvre. By the 1930s such facilities were becoming more common, largely thanks to the all-important League of Nations 'International Conference for the Study of Scientific Methods for Examination and Preservation of Works of Art', held in 1930 at Rome, whose deliberations, including its *Manuel de la Conservation et Restauration des Tableaux,* set international standards for art conservation. Delegates came to the conference from Austria, Belgium, France, Germany, Britain, Italy, Yugoslavia, the Netherlands, Poland, Spain, Sweden, Switzerland and the United States. They included two of Duveen's experts – A.P. Laurie from Scotland and Professor Adolfo Venturi from Rome – though only Laurie played a prominent part in the proceedings.

The vast majority of participants were from the museum world; also in attendance were professors of physics and chemistry; there was a smattering of academic art historians; no 'experts' or 'connoisseurs' who worked in the marketplace were present. The professional culture that the conference and its participants cultivated was very different from that of the traditional connoisseur. The emphasis was not on the individual skills and flair of experts, nor was there any of the tribalism that marked connoisseurship; rather, the participants aimed to set up informal and institutional means of sharing information and knowledge about artworks that were both professionally and publicly accessible. To that end, they wanted to establish shared conventions and protocols about how to analyse, describe and treat works of art. Much of the conference was taken up with technical papers, chiefly about means by which artworks could be conserved. However, the question of what place 'scientific' investigation could play in attribution was also discussed at length, and the most striking feature of those deliberations was the repeated call for open and candid cooperation between art connoisseurs and technical experts, for the two groups to work together on an equal basis. Not that the meeting supported extravagant claims for 'science'. On the contrary, participants emphasized that technical investigation could not replace the expert eye and that public perception that 'science' somehow had the answer to problems of attribution should be actively dispelled. Here, then, was a profession in the making. This was the period in which Alan Burroughs, who testified on behalf of Duveen, first pioneered the use of x-rays to examine works of art in the United States, when the value of ultraviolet light to detect flaws and fakes was first developed, and when the first professional journal devoted to scientific preservation appeared as *Technical Studies in the Field of the Fine Arts*.

The traditional connoisseurs looked askance at such developments, but the public, which had always been intimidated by the recondite skills of the art 'experts', welcomed these scientific innovations with considerable enthusiasm because they seemed to make art recognition at once more certain and more accessible. The technical knowledge needed to restore a great work of the fifteenth century could, it seemed, be applied equally to help determine whether it was the genuine work of a master.

Art booms are invariably accompanied by a surge in the number of forgeries and the early twentieth century, as we have seen, was no exception. Fakes were not confined to Old Masters; antiquities and the decorative arts as well as modern painting were all inundated with forgeries and copies. In 1924, the British Royal Academy mounted one of the first exhibits of fakes, a guide to the techniques of the forger and a warning to the collector of how they might be tricked. At a time of high anxiety about authenticity the new science seemed to offer reassurance and a greater degree of certainty in attribution.

At the same time, traditional connoisseurship suffered a series of setbacks and scandals. Three spectacular trials – not just *Hahn versus Duveen*, but the prosecution of the art dealer Otto Wacker in Berlin in 1932 for forging a series of Vincent van Gogh paintings, and the indictment of the Dutch painter Han van Meegeren in Amsterdam in 1945 for faking a series of Johannes Vermeer paintings – all exposed connoisseurs to public ridicule. In all three cases their views were revealed in court and found either weak or wanting, their qualitative judgements challenged by different sorts of scientific evidence. The New York trial was much the most important of these cases. In the other two, the main issue was forgery: were the paintings attributed to van Gogh or Vermeer genuine or faked? The judgement of several connoisseurs was shown to be erroneous and to be motivated by a good deal of wish fulfilment. For a variety of reasons, some commercial and some art-historical, they wanted the paintings to be genuine and this threw off their judgement.

The Hahn case was different. The question before the court was never one of forgery. Duveen and his lawyers never argued that the Hahn painting had been created with intent to deceive, though they did assert that it was not a genuine Leonardo. What was at issue was the nature of Duveen's judgement – was it informed by malice and self-interest? – and the value of the testimony of the experts he gathered to sustain his view. This, in turn, was bound up with the Hahns' claim that the unscientific and highly subjective nature of connoisseurial expertise made it possible to exploit and abuse the system for personal gain and aggrandizement. From this point of view, Duveen's action was a symptom of a system that was fundamentally unsound. This was why the case attracted such widespread attention, being reported in detail in the newspapers not just of North America, but Britain, France, Germany and Italy.

Nevertheless, the Wacker and van Meegeren trials were important in pointing out the limitations of traditional expertise and the growing importance of 'scientific' evidence. The press connected the Wacker and New York trials, linking the Hahn case to the efforts in Germany to use scientific evidence to convict Wacker and discredit his fakes. Of course, Wacker's more than thirty forged van Goghs were not Old Masters, but the issue of attribution, of the educated eye versus scientific investigation, remained the same. In the late 1920s and early 1930s van Gogh had become one of the most valued and admired modern painters in Germany. Two major exhibitions of his work – one of drawings in Otto Wacker's gallery, the other of paintings in the gallery of Paul Cassirer, a key figure in German modernism – were planned to celebrate the publication of the first *catalogue raisonné* of the Dutchman's work, an eleven-year labour of love by Jacob-Baart de la Faille, a self-taught art expert from the Netherlands. Together, these events would have canonized van Gogh as one of the great modern artists. Instead, the events were dominated by scandal. When all the pictures were brought together one of the directors of the Cassirer gallery, Grete Ring, rejected four of Wacker's offerings for the painting show. This began an investigation of all van Goghs paintings sold by Wacker; most were supposed to come from a collection of a member of the Russian imperial family, to have been smuggled out of Russia and into Switzerland and to have been purchased from an intermediary there. De la Faille and Julius Meier-Graefe, the well-connected critic, author of a history of modern painting and biographer of van Gogh, had (quite innocently) written certificates of authentication of the Wacker pictures. However, the dealers' inquiries uncovered a trail of false assertion, dubious documentation and probable fraud. They began legal proceedings against Wacker in December 1928, though the case did not come to trial until the spring of 1932.

During the trial itself, the testimony of the so-called van Gogh experts, notably de la Faille and Meier-Graefe, was confused and contradictory. De la Faille, after Wacker had been exposed, published a list of false van Goghs and admitted his errors, but during the trial he again changed his mind, saying he believed at least some of them to be genuine. Another expert, Hans Rosenhagen, testified that he believed the Wacker pictures to be inferior works, but nevertheless by the hand of van Gogh. H.P. Bremmer, a connoisseur relying on 'inner perception', argued that eight of the disputed pictures were fakes, but that another eight were also genuine. Not every connoisseur was taken in: Ludwig Justi, the director of the Berlin Nationalgalerie, for example, testified that all of Wacker's paintings were fakes, so too did one of his curators, Ludwig Thormaehlen. However, it was the technical experts that were most damning. A.M. de Wild, a painter, carried out pigment tests that showed the presence of a resin not present in the paint used by van Gogh; Kurt Wehlte, a restorer, used x-rays to show that the Wacker pictures were not like others attributed to van Gogh; and Helmut Ruhemann, chief conservator at the Berlin Staatliche Gemäldegalerie, showed that dirt and indentations had been artificially introduced

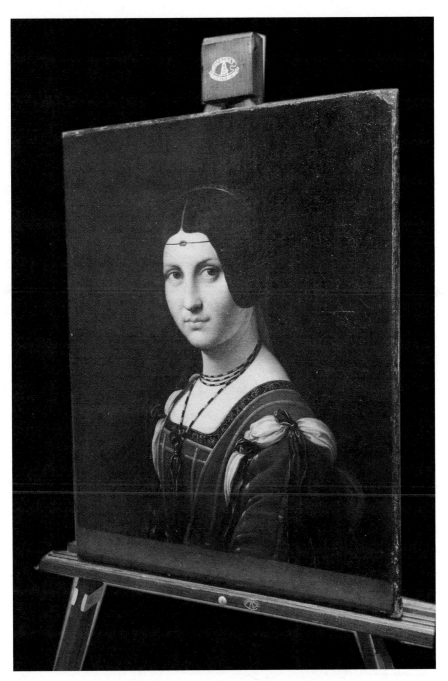

The Hahn *La Belle Ferronnière* as she appears today.

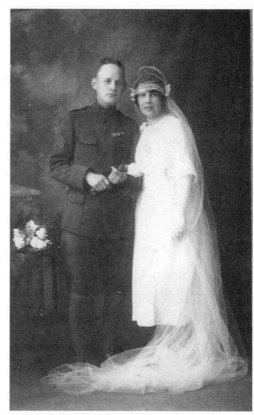

(*right*) The diffident couple: Harry and Andrée Hahn's wedding photograph, 1919.

(*below*) The Magasin des Modes, rue Levavasseur, Dinard, where Andrée grew up.

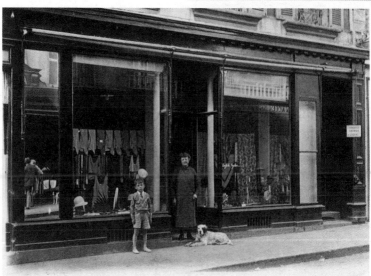

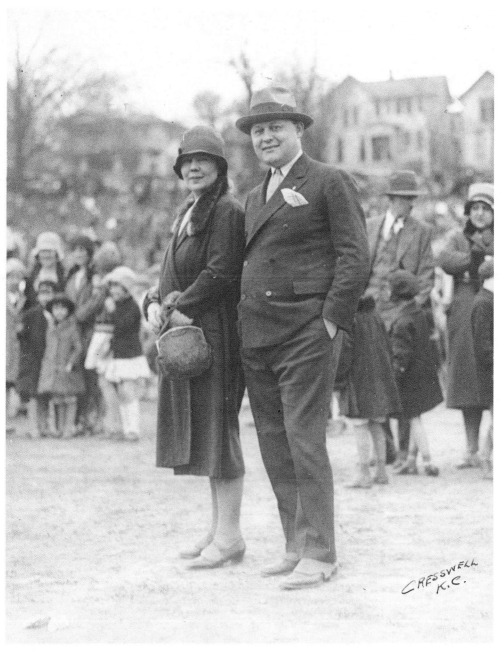

Harry and Andrée Hahn exude confidence in Kansas in the year of the trial, 1929.

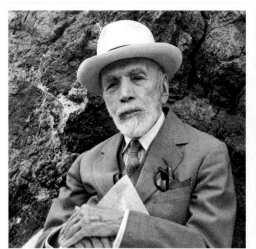
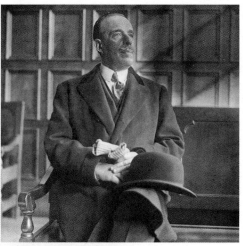
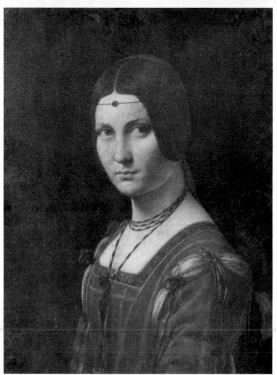

(*top left*) Bernard Berenson, master connoisseur and foe of the Hahns.

(*top right*) An ever-dapper Sir Joseph Duveen at the trial of *Hahn versus Duveen* in 1929.

(*above*) The version of *La Belle Ferronnière* in the Louvre collection.

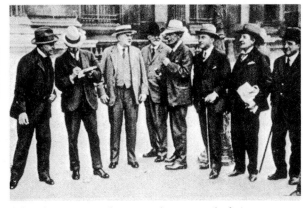

(*above*) Experts gather near the Louvre before examining the two versions of *La Belle Ferronnière*, Paris 1923.

(*left*) One of the huge number of press cuttings covering the New York trial in 1929.

(*below*) Duveen commissioned this photograph of the Hahn *La Belle*, overwritten with the opinion of Robert Langton Douglas that the painting was not the hand of Leonardo.

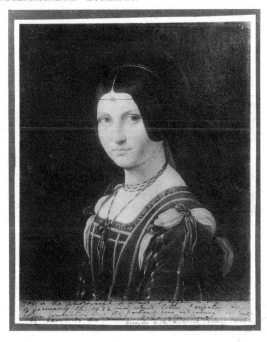

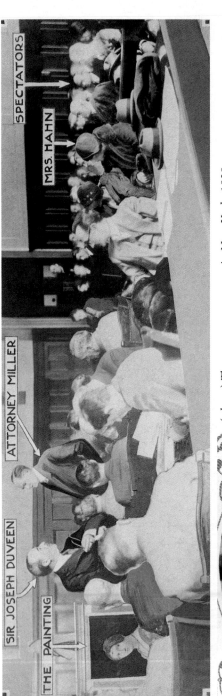

SIR JOSEPH DUVEEN ATTORNEY MILLER SPECTATORS

THE PAINTING MRS. HAHN

(*above*) The courtroom scene in New York, 1929.

(*left*) Andrée Hahn, elegantly attired in a cloche hat, as she appeared at the New York trial in 1929.

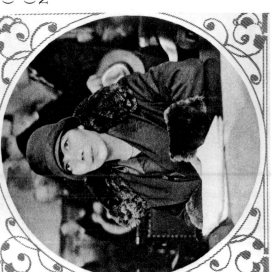

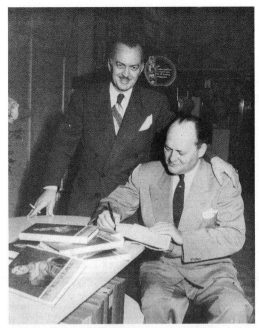

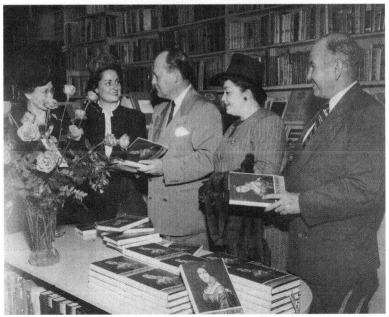

Harry Hahn and Frank Glenn enjoy a book signing of *The Rape of La Belle* at Glenn's bookshop in Kansas City, 1946.

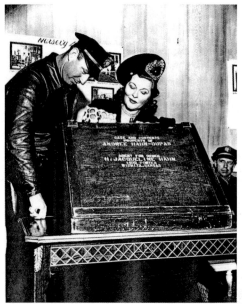

(*above and right*) The Hahn *La Belle* in its special case is viewed before guards by admirers in Hollywood, 1947.

(*below*) Frank Glenn, gossip columnist Hedda Hopper and Harry Hahn admire the Hahn *La Belle* as it was exhibited at the Hartwell Galleries, Los Angeles, 1947.

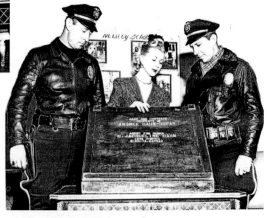

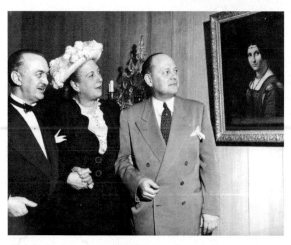

into many of the pictures. This proved that the paintings had been deliberately executed with the intent to deceive. Wacker was found guilty, imprisoned for nineteen months and forced to pay a fine of 30,000 Deutschmark.

Wacker's guilt was beyond doubt and it seems probable that the fakes were the work of either his father, who was a painter, or his brother, who was a restorer. Yet, even after his conviction, there remained confusion over van Gogh's oeuvre, which was not dispelled by de la Faille's revisions to his *catalogue raisonnée*. On a trip to the United States in the spring of 1952, Helmut Ruhemann was surprised to see one of Wacker's paintings that he had testified as being a fake displayed at the National Gallery in Washington as a genuine van Gogh.

In the short run, the Wacker trial, coming close on the heels of *Hahn versus Duveen* and subject to almost as much publicity, had the effect of bringing van Gogh before a large public that before the case knew little of the Dutchman's work. However, it also put the connoisseurs in the dock and put experts on the defensive. Grete Ring, whose experienced eye first spotted the forgeries, was careful to maintain after the trial that what really counted were traditional skills: 'Technical methods of examination are welcome when their role – as in this case – is confined to that of an auxiliary science,' she wrote. 'Precedence must always be given to intuitive, subjective human perception, aided and checked as it fortunately can be by technological means.' Her insistence is testimony to the public fragility of connoisseurship and to the widespread sense that scientific testing was more reliable than the old ways.

If Wacker's forgeries were embarrassing to some connoisseurs, they never came near provoking the mortification caused by the fakes produced by the Dutch artist Han van Meegeren. He was a prolific faker, responsible for what was probably the most notorious case of art forgery in the twentieth century, faking works by Frans Hals, Pieter de Hooch, Gerard Ter Borch and, above all, Johannes Vermeer. Like the Hahn and Wacker trials, this scandal, which ran for more than a decade between 1945 and 1955, achieved international notoriety; indeed, it prompted films and novels as well as a large body of critical commentary. The American journalist, Irving Wallace, wrote a story based on van Meegeren's adventures, 'The Man who swindled Goering', which was originally published in the *Saturday Evening Post,* but was subsequently syndicated round the world. In the Netherlands the case became something of an obsession, for van Meegeren's fakes struck at the heart of Dutch national heritage, while the case itself, like the Hahn trial in New York and the Otto Wacker case in Berlin, seemed to call into doubt the skills and professional competence of art connoisseurs and experts.

In the late 1930s and early 1940s van Meegeren, a moderately successful portraitist but violent anti-modernist who smarted at his critical rejection by fashionable Dutch art critics, made a sizeable fortune selling a series of carefully executed fakes, chiefly pastiche after the work of Vermeer and de Hooch. Eight major fakes were sold for 7,400,000 guilders, enabling van Meegeren to indulge his not inconsiderable appetite for fast living. The fakes were a great success and remained largely unquestioned in the Netherlands.

Van Meegeren's most famous Vermeer painting, *The Disciples at Emmaus,* 'discovered' in 1937, was acclaimed as a masterpiece, a picture that filled the gap between the artist's few early large

Italianate works redolent of Caravaggio and the later, serene Delft interiors. The leading Vermeer scholar in Holland, the ageing Abraham Bredius, wrote an ecstatic appraisal of the picture in the *Burlington Magazine*:

> It is a wonderful moment in the life of a lover of art when he finds himself suddenly confronted with a hitherto unknown painting by a great master, untouched, on the original canvas, and without any restoration, just as it left the painter's studio. And what a picture! Neither the beautiful signature ... nor the *pointille* on the bread that Christ is blessing, is necessary to convince us that we have here a – I am inclined to say *the* – masterpiece of Johannes Vermeer of Delft.

His opinion was endorsed by other scholars including Dr Dirk Hannema, the director of the Museum Boijmans Van Beuningen in Rotterdam, which was to acquire the painting, and Arthur van Schendel, a future director of the Rijksmuseum. The picture was the centrepiece of the exhibition *Four Centuries of Masterpieces*, opened at the Boijmans to celebrate the jubilee of Queen Wilhelmina's reign in the summer of 1938.

The enthusiastic reception of *The Disciples at Emmaus* helped van Meegeren to pass off less accomplished fakes of Vermeer. Experts and dealers looked at *The Head of Christ*, the *Last Supper, Isaac blessing Jacob,* the *Washing of Christ's Feet* and the *Adulteress* and recognized in them the hand that created *The Disciples*. Van Meegeren's first forgery had become a benchmark for Vermeer's work and for years the fakes remained undetected. However, in 1945 allied investigators found the *Adulteress* among the vast cache of pictures concealed outside Salzburg by Hermann Göring. The picture was traced back to van Meegeren whose vague and evasive account of how he had acquired the picture, together with his inability to produce any documentary proof of its purchase, led to charges that he had knowingly sold a national treasure to the enemy. He was forced to confess his forgery not by a group of art connoisseurs but by the Dutch police in pursuit of collaborators and traitors.

At first, the authorities dismissed van Meegeren's confession that he had painted the *Adulteress*. It seemed like a desperate ploy to escape conviction on the charge of collaboration. Van Meegeren bombarded his interrogators with details of all the Vermeers he had faked – where he had acquired the seventeenth-century canvases, how he had prepared his pigments, how he had aged the pictures – but he was still met with scepticism. Eventually, a member of the Allied Art Commission suggested he 'copy' a Vermeer from memory. Van Meegeren was scornful – he would never make a copy, but he would paint an original Vermeer. Watched by officials of the court, and by journalists and photographers, over the course of two months he produced his last Vermeer, a version of *The Young Christ Teaching in the Temple*. The charges of collaboration were dropped to be replaced by those of forgery, but there were still eminent experts, notably the Belgian art historian Jean Decoen and Hannema, who were convinced that *The Disciples at Emmaus* remained a genuine Vermeer.

The Dutch court established a commission of experts led by Paul Coremans, a distinguished chemist who was the head of the Royal Institute for the Study and Conservation of Belgium's Artistic

Heritage, a professor of Art History at the University of Ghent, and later founding member of the International Institute for Conservation. Coremans was the chief prosecution witness at van Meegeren's trial in 1947 and two years later published a magisterial study of the scientific evidence against the Dutchman.

The public reaction to van Meegeren, once he was exposed as a forger rather than a traitor, was remarkably positive. The fact that Göring had paid for his fake Vermeer by returning a large number of Dutch works of art to their homeland rather than in cash transformed van Meegeren from a possible Nazi sympathizer into a patriotic hero who had outwitted the Reichsmarshall. A number of intellectuals and writers lauded his genius, taking the view of the popular writer Godfried Bomans in an Amsterdam newspaper that, 'It is not the Vermeers, but the experts who authenticated them that are the fakes!' As van Meegeren's defence counsel pointed out at the trial, 'The art world is reeling, and experts are beginning to doubt the very basis of artistic attribution. This was precisely what the defendant was trying to achieve.' Even after van Meegeren's death – he collapsed shortly after he was sentenced – the case rumbled on, largely because Jean Decoen continued to challenge the evidence of the Coremans commission, reiterating his belief that *The Disciples at Emmaus* was a genuine Vermeer. Only after Coremans won a case against his detractors in 1951 was the case laid to rest.

Of course, it would be easy to maintain that, for all the adverse publicity, practices within the commercial art world remained largely unchanged, continuing to rely on the opinions of experts who were thought to have a natural ability to make attributions through their tutored eyes. And no doubt in the showrooms of the dealerships in Bond Street, on Madison Avenue and the rue de Rivoli in Paris little changed: rich collectors came and went, experts continued to issue certificates of authentication and dealers developed their connoisseurial skills. However, in the public at large there developed a postmodern scepticism *avant la lettre*, a feeling that in the art world the emperor had no clothes. This sentiment can be seen most clearly in the public attitude towards stories of forgery and forgers. Of course, forger stories that mock experts, collectors and the institutions of the art world (as opposed to the works of art themselves) are as old as art history itself. Vasari in his *Lives of the Artists* tells the story of Michelangelo's sleeping cupid, a sculpture crafted by the master, aged and buried to appear like a classical antiquity. Its discovery is used to embarrass Cardinal San Giorgio who sees it as an affirmation of his belief that modern sculptors will never match the skills of the ancients. Two hundred years later, Pierre Mignard painted a penitent Magdalene as if it were a Guido Reni. He deliberately encouraged doubts about the picture in order to secure its authentication by the great connoisseur Charles Le Brun. He then admitted the forgery, but the buyer of his picture refused to believe his confession. Mignard then revealed his signature concealed on the picture.

These forgers' stories, most of which contain a number of common elements, about the skills of artists, the ignorance and arrogance of experts and collectors, and the unmasking of erroneous attribution (quite often by the faker himself), are both a playful subversion of the art world – as much a prank as a crime – and a confirmation of the value (not seen by all) of true 'art'. Deception is a means of securing justice. Obviously, the Hahn story does not quite fit a genre that is best represented in the twentieth century in the astonishing story of van Meegeren's fakes; there is no artist/genius to hoodwink the authorities. Instead, as befits a story told in the age of mass society, it has a populist twist, one in which the protagonists are ordinary members of the public – neither rich nor especially skilled in ways of art – who use a picture condemned by almost everyone within the art establishment as a worthless copy to expose the machinations and slight of hand of the art world. The Hahns did not create a fake, like Michelangelo and Mignard, by using their skills as artists; but, in asserting the authenticity of their picture, its genuineness as a Leonardo, they did transform a copy (if such it was) into a forgery. In doing so they unveiled the snobbery and conceit, one might say the 'aristocratic' values, of the art world and undercut its claims to expertise. And in a mass society this drama could be played out before a mass public, one that every morning of the New York trial (and on many other mornings) was to be found in the headlines and columns of the newspaper press.

CHAPTER 7
The View from Kansas

Kansas City, on the junction of the Kaw and Missouri rivers and the border between the states of Missouri and Kansas, is an unlikely spot to feature in the history of a supposed painting by Leonardo da Vinci. When Nina Powell, the music and arts correspondent of the *Kansas City Star* expressed her incredulity at Andrée Hahn's remarks, made in her office in January 1920, about the presence of a Leonardo in their midst, she was voicing sentiments that would probably have been shared by most inhabitants of the city, at least those who were familiar with the artist's name. Kansas City, after all, was less known for its culture than for its rough and tumble ways – as one would expect from a city that bore the brunt of violent struggles between Abolitionists and pro-slavers before and during the American Civil War, and which became the trail-head to the Pacific West and, after the erection of the Hannibal rail bridge over the Missouri in 1869, a town with vast stockyards and many railroads. Kansas City stood on the cusp between civilization and the 'Wild West', and its disproportionate number of young men and its frontier ways (even after Frederick Jackson Turner had famously declared the frontier closed) made it one of the most wide-open towns in the United States with a nationwide reputation for vice and loose living. As one Midwest newspaper remarked, 'If you want to see some sin, forget about Paris. Go to Kansas City. With the possible exception of such renowned centers as Singapore and Port Said, Kansas City has the greatest sin industry in the world.'

However, the Hahns' Leonardo arrived in Kansas City at an opportune moment, one when the city's elite, grown rich on the burgeoning industries of 'Cow Town', was trying to transform the city and its reputation, clean-up its image, and make it a rival of the metropolises in the East. Following in the footsteps of cities that had cleared their slums and built parks, boulevards and upmarket residential neighbourhoods, they wanted to refashion their city; a vital part of that programme of change was the foundation of cultural institutions – a university, an orchestra, an opera and, above all, an art gallery and museum – that would expunge Kansas City's low-life reputation and replace it with one of progressive civility. As Harry Hahn astutely understood, the American Leonardo was extraordinarily enticing to those who wanted to civilize Kansas City; *La Belle Ferronnière* was tempting because she promised to embody and exemplify the changing character of a town, to broadcast to the nation that Kansas City was not just an ugly industrial centre with a reputation for squalor and depravity, but a leader in the march towards a more refined way of American living.

The early twentieth century saw Kansas City grow by leaps and bounds, nearly doubling in size between 1910 and 1930. Down by the river on the floodplain of the Kansas River, known as the West Bottoms, stockyards, slaughterhouses, meatpacking houses, smelting works, railroad sheds, flour mills and lumber yards employed a large number of poor Afro-Americans, many migrants from the South, together with equally impecunious immigrants from Europe – Germans, Swedes, Irish, Italians and, later, Eastern Europeans – who lived in rackety tenements, shacks and hovels cheek-and-jowl with the stench, noise and pollution of the riverside industries. Meatpacking dominated the local economy. As early as the 1890s firms like Armour and Swift were contributing to the slaughter of over 700,000 cattle and more than 2 million hogs a year, shipping over 200 million pounds of dressed beef, much of it in Pullman's new refrigerated freight cars. In the Bottoms and up to the North End the town was filled with taverns, bars, jazz clubs, gambling houses and brothels (147 of them within the city limits) which came to be protected and presided over by a ruthless Democratic political machine, run by Tom Pendergast and Italian mobsters. The 'Bosses', who rose to power in the 1920s and by the 1930s ruled the city, turned out the voters, provided jobs and handouts, controlled city contracts and building, and sheltered any business, including many that were illegal, as long as they paid their dues to the party. The lynch-pin of the Pendergast operation was the Pendergast Ready-mix concrete company whose products were used to build up the city and, reputedly, to bury its enemies.

The introduction of Prohibition in 1920 had little effect, apart from increasing the power of organized crime. Tom Pendergast ensured that it was never properly enforced in Kansas City. In downtown and its surrounding districts, especially at 18th and Vine, there were speakeasies, cheap hotels, gambling joints and jazz clubs full of hustlers, whores, grifters and con-artists. North of the city, Pendergast opened an illegal racetrack; nearby, John

Lazia, the local mob leader and Democratic precinct captain, hosted guests at the Cuban-Gardens, an upmarket club and casino. Bootlegging, gambling and politicking were central to the city's economy. As a Justice Department report concluded in 1933, 'the whole town in under the control of a racket – composed of bankers and business men working with exconvicts and gangsters'.

Legitimate business was also booming, even if the city sometimes seemed to resemble the frontier towns of old. The 1912 booklet, *Men of Affairs in Greater Kansas City*, listed more than 250 successful businessmen, not just in meatpacking but banking, insurance, newspapers, lumber, railroads and streetcars, milling and metal smelting, as well as real-estate development. This new wealthy community had begun, at the turn of the century, to move out of the city, away from the businesses that made them rich and the disreputable bars and jazz clubs that helped fill the Pendergast coffers. They built and bought mansions in the city's southern and western suburbs served by elegant boulevards and parkways. These rich men had to make deals with the Pendergast machine, though they fought its support of organized labour. They shared Pendergast's enthusiasm for civic projects like the elegant new railway station erected in 1914 – it brought work and building contracts for his supporters and helped commerce and profits – but wanted to keep their distance from the immigrant labour and Democratic politics he represented. Above all, they wanted to dispel Kansas City's tough, uncivilized image, of what one of them called this 'incredibly ugly and commonplace' town and to promote it as a rival to Chicago, Cleveland, Pittsburgh and Detroit. They enjoyed the fruits of the city's swashbuckling capitalism, but wanted to dispense with its squalor, filth and vice.

In the first two decades of the twentieth century, much of this civic improvement took the form of real-estate development and the enthusiastic support of the City Beautiful Movement. Here the key figures were the reforming, Progressive newspaper magnate, William Rockhill Nelson, proprietor of the *Kansas City Star* and scourge of the Democratic political machine, and the (much younger) property developer and Kansas City booster, Jesse Clyde Nichols, the man who was also, in 1920, the president of the Kansas City Art Institute.

Nelson dominated the city's political scene until his death in 1915, repeatedly promoting Progressive causes both locally and nationally and remaining a booster for the city, even when he was one of the most severe critics of its graft and maladministration. He was the driving force behind the establishment of the Board of Park Commissioners and their report by George Kessler of 1893 for the southward development of the city through a system of parks and boulevards, a transformation from which he directly benefited as the property developer of what became known as the Rockhill district. By the year of Nelson's death there were 90 miles of roads and boulevards and 2,000 acres of parks south of the city. The cow town had been transformed into the city beautiful. Even the machine politicians, whose support had been necessary to the success of the scheme, were proud of the result. Years later, Tom Pendergast was eager to take credit for the transformation of 'a hick town into a metropolitan city'. 'Look at our streets and our parks and public buildings,' he once boasted. 'This is a metropolis – one of the greatest in the world.'

In 1895 Nelson embarked with his family on a twenty-month 'Grand Tour' of Europe. Convinced, like so many Americans, of the civilizing power of art, he purchased nineteen copies of Old Masters in Florence, including versions of works by Diego Velasquez, Botticelli, Raphael and of Leonardo's *Mona Lisa*. On his return to Kansas City he presented them to the Kansas City Art Association and arranged for the paintings to be displayed in the town's library, along with a collection of casts and photographs. He continued to add copies until his death and, in his will, he arranged that, after the death of his wife and daughter, the *Kansas City Star* would be sold off and the proceeds used to buy works of art for the city. However, Nelson made no provision – and provided no funding – for a gallery in which to display works of art and because his bequest had to wait until his daughter's death, the funds were not released until 1926.

Funds to build an art gallery in Kansas City already existed, held by the trustees of the bequest of a wealthy widow and real-estate investor, Mary Atkins, who had left about $300,000 (£62,000) towards a building at her death in 1911. Like Nelson, Atkins had fallen in love with art in Europe. Her niece had married a Swiss language teacher and moved to Geneva. In the seven summers before she died Mary Atkins visited her niece in Europe and made a pilgrimage to major museums and collections. As one of her friends recalled, 'I could tell from the joy she felt in the Louvre and the Florentine galleries that they satisfied a real hunger.' However, Atkins' bequest was not large enough to pay for the sort of museum the great and the good of Kansas City yearned for. They had to wait for the contributions of Nelson's widow, daughter, son-in-law and lawyer to accumulate the necessary funds. They were thinking big. As Frank Rozzelle, Nelson's attorney, put it, 'I would like to see erected in Kansas City, a great art gallery, similar to, but more splendid than the Metropolitan Museum of New

York, the Corcoran in Washington, or the Carnegie Institute in Pittsburgh.'

By 1920, then, there was a radical difference between the aspirations of those who wanted a Kansas City art museum and the actual provision of art in the city. While the major cities of the East and the near Midwest (Chicago, Cleveland, Toledo and Detroit) and even St Louis had fine museum buildings with collections that were being developed with the aid of European dealers, Kansas City had a bunch of copies, casts and photographs, and some very ordinary American pictures in the collection of the local art school, the Kansas City Art Institute. In the early 1920s dealers such as René Gimpel were regularly visiting the museums and private collections in Chicago, Detroit and Toledo, praising their quality and admiring the enthusiasm for opening public galleries: 'This devotion to the cause of art is found throughout the United States, and gives an idea of the fervor that convulsed the Middle Ages, when its churches were erected.' Kansas City, as its richest citizens were aware, was failing to keep pace with its rivals. Gimpel records an anecdote that puts the city in its lowly place. Writing in his journal under the heading 'Ignorance', he recalls, 'A dealer told me that at Kansas City, where he had shown a Van Dyck, two Rubens, a Teniers, a Lawrence, a Largilliere, a Goya and several other canvases, a visitor asked him if all those pictures had been painted by the same artist.' Whether or not the anecdote was true, it speaks to the reputation of the city as an art centre.

This situation deeply distressed Jesse C. Nichols, a man who came to rival William Rockhill Nelson as one of the great boosters of Kansas City. Nichols was one of those supremely energetic, entrepreneurially canny figures that crop up in the early history of most American cities. He was known, even as a child, for his prodigious industry and ability to turn almost any activity into a profitable enterprise. In the first decade of the twentieth century he moved into real estate, inspired by a tour of European cities, a Harvard economics professor and the City Beautiful Movement. By 1910 Nichols had over 1,000 acres under his management and a $1.5 million (£310,000) operation. In the next decade he was to develop a model residential area in Kansas City, the Country Club district, and one of the first shopping malls in the United States, the Country Club Plaza. He was one of the first developers to plan neighbourhoods for car ownership and a pioneer (one among many) in using zoning laws to maintain the value of middle-class districts and to exclude people of colour.

As a civic booster and improver he was everywhere. Not just president of the Kansas City Art Institute, he was on the board of local schools and universities, a director of the Kansas City Symphony, a founding member of the City Philharmonic, a member of many local planning committees and bodies for civic improvement, and a member of the trust that was eventually to establish the Nelson–Atkins Art Museum. As his news-sheet, the *Country Club District Bulletin*, put it in 1923:

> We believe that Kansas City's splendid growth in recent years in her school facilities, Art Institute, Conservatory of Music, Horner Institute, Symphony Orchestra, Grand Opera Company, Kansas City Theatre, Golf Clubs, Parkview Riding Academy, Speedway, splendid new ballpark, or Fall festival, our various exhibitions and annual entertainment events are offering more and more for the real enjoyment of life.

For Nichols, like Nelson, the development of the 'City Beautiful' and the creation of an art museum were part of the larger aim of making Kansas City an attractive place to live for the right sorts of (white, middle-class) people. Taste, improvement and profit went hand in hand. Nichols shared with William Rockhill Nelson the view that, 'Beauty always pays in the end.'

Such were the circumstances in Kansas City which Andrée and Harry Hahn sought to exploit in 1920. The city had no art museum, it had no funds to buy pictures – though it was known that Nelson's fortune would eventually become available – and it had no real collection of pictures. Nichols had just been appointed as the head of the Kansas City Art Institute and had been recruiting new trustees to enhance its finances. He was passionately committed to the city and could envision the enormous publicity coup if Kansas City were to acquire what seemed to be the only painting by Leonardo in North America.

This might not seem to accord with Nichols' deposition, taken on 23 February 1929, and used by Joseph Duveen's lawyers, when he claimed that he had not struck a deal with the art dealer Conrad Hug to acquire the Hahns' painting in 1920. At the same time, he testified at some length to the lack of financial resources available at the Kansas City Art Institute, which had a few cheap paintings in its collection and an annual budget of between $40,000 and $60,000 (£8,250 to £12,370). However, Nichols' testimony, as his subsequent cross-examination was to reveal, was slightly disingenuous. It may have been strictly correct that a specific deal had not been struck and that the existing resources of the Institute were insufficient to buy a masterpiece, but he could not hide the fact that he had made diligent efforts to acquire the Hahns' painting.

He conceded that he was interested in 'anything that would contribute to the artistic development and beautification of the city' and that he was 'trying to get the good things and the biggest things and the best things for Kansas City'. He also admitted that he had told Hug that, if the picture were genuine and the price fair, he would try to put together a consortium of wealthy local people to buy it for the city. He had not asked for specific amounts of money, but he had asked his friends for a commitment in principle. Asked if he still had an interest in the picture, Nichols said that he admired it greatly 'as a layman', and that, if it were proved genuine, he would still be interested in acquiring it.

The questioning of Nichols by the Hahns' lawyers revealed just how much the rich citizens of Kansas City were worth (hundreds of millions of dollars) and how, when put to the test, they could raise huge funds. In 1919, Nichols and his friends had taken only two weeks to raise $2.5 million (£550,000) to fund the Liberty Memorial, a monument to the dead of the First World War which was to be erected opposite the recently opened and magnificent Beaux-Arts Union Station. There was no doubt that there was both the will and the wherewithal in Kansas City to acquire a genuine Leonardo.

However, in 1929 Nichols was not prepared to help the Hahns' case and went so far as to contradict the testimony of Conrad Hug, a man whom he worked with for many years. Duveen's lawyers regarded him as a friendly witness. What had changed? In 1920, the Hahns' Leonardo seemed like a brilliant quick fix, a way to kick-start Kansas City in the art world; by 1929 it had become a distraction, one that raised awkward questions for Nichols and his friends. The trustees of the different bequests had coalesced to develop a plan for a museum and collection on the site of William Rockhill Nelson's mansion which was demolished in 1928, designs by the local architects Wight and Wight had been approved and Nichols, as one of the three trustees administering the Nelson estate, was already travelling to Europe and the East looking to purchase works of art. The trust was awash with money at a time when the nation was plunging into Depression. As Nichols knew, he was about to become the most powerful art buyer in America. He no longer needed a stunt like the acquisition of the Hahn painting; he needed the advice of the very experts and dealers the Hahns had been fighting.

As builders worked on the new museum's neoclassical limestone facade and erected the interior pillars of Black Pyrenees marble, as gardeners planted almost 300 trees and shrubs and shaped paths and walkways in its grounds, Nichols and his colleagues moved into the art market. From the outset both they and the public were afraid of buying fakes. The local press repeatedly took the populist view that the art world was 'a racket', full of conmen and subterfuge, but also maintained that the hardheaded businessmen of Kansas City would not allow themselves to be fooled. However, Nichols knew that, though no one could drive a better bargain, he did not know about pictures. He turned to two experts at the Fogg Art Museum at Harvard, Edward Forbes and Paul Sacks, both of whom had been consulted by Duveen when *La Belle Ferronnière* had first been examined in New York in 1921. On their recommendation, he hired Harold Woodbury Parsons, a Harvard graduate who described himself as a 'marchand amateur who dapples from time to time in the amusing avocation of making the perfect marriage between a collector, a sublime work of art and a rich

American museum, for their mutual benefit – and for the benefit of yours truly'.

Together Nichols and Parsons turned to the top dealers and, above all, to Duveen. Joe Duveen, knowing full well that Nichols could become one of his most important clients, had written him an ingratiating letter after the New York trial, apologizing for imposing on him and causing him any inconvenience, and promising to be of service to him if the occasion arose. In January 1931 Nichols was shopping at Agnew's, Wildenstein's and Steinmeyer's in New York, but his real target was the purchase of two pictures, a Rembrandt of a young man and a Meindert Hobbema of a road in woods, on sale from Duveen Brothers. In a private letter Nichols described the negotiation in great detail to one of his fellow trustees. Duveen was the first to make a concession: 'in appreciation of what I had done for him in the lawsuit and a desire to get established in our museum', he would offer the two paintings at $425,000 (£88,000). Nichols shook his head 'and told him how disappointed I was not to be able to do any business with him and produced all the arguments and recalled to his mind pretty forcibly how I had turned down my fellow citizen Mr. Hug and gained the enmity of a good many people in Kansas City in upholding Sir Joseph and the cause of art'. Duveen then 'put his arms around me and said on behalf of Sir Joseph and not from the firm he wanted to present me with a marble statue by Carpo [Jean-Baptiste Carpeaux]'. Nichols refused it as a personal gift but accepted it for the museum, saying 'it expressed a wonderful feeling on his [Duveen's] part to give up the most treasured object of art that he kept at the side of his desk all these years'. Duveen now expected Nichols to accept his price, but the trustee kept bargaining. In the end it was agreed that

Duveen would take $400,000 for the two paintings 'with the statue to carry a plate stating it had been given by Sir Joseph Duveen which I said would be worth millions in selling objects of art in the middle west'. Duveen and Nichols were in business. A couple of months later, the *Kansas City Star* announced Duveen's gift and the acquisition of the Rembrandt, the collection's greatest masterpiece.

Less than three years later Duveen, now Lord Duveen of Milbank, was playing poker with a group of other art dealers from Europe and New York in a special carriage on a train speeding to Kansas City and the opening ceremony for the new museum. Knoedler, Seligman and Durand-Ruel, who lent paintings by Edouard Manet, Paul Cézanne, Pierre-Auguste Renoir and Edgar Degas, all loaned works for the special event, though for most people the presence of James Abbott McNeill Whistler's painting of his mother was the star turn of the opening. On 10 December 1933 a gala dinner for 2,000 guests was held at the Mission Hills Country Club. The next morning, the museum was officially opened and 7,950 people squeezed and pushed their way through the museum's galleries. In a speech made to the assembled crowds Nichols laid out his vision for the museum and the city. For him the new museum and the works of art it contained were part of an aspirational culture that linked beauty to achievement:

> No man need be ashamed because he feels a tug at his heart string and a tear glistens in his eye as he stands before objects of art which grip his soul . . . Every lovely curve, every exacting proportion is the product of a hand driven by a high desire to create a better standard . . . May these halls become a rallying

place for high ideals and aspirations; may they crystallize a greater love of beauty; may they be a happy democratic meeting place for all groups, all races, all creeds, all men, who call the mid-west their home.

Nichols liked what he called pictures 'with heart appeal and story-telling qualities'. 'We are not,' he said, 'building a collection for the highbrows and while we do not want to lower our standards of quality it is up to us to select pictures which will have broad appeal.'

Duveen, the personal guest of Nichols (whose wife was shocked that the dealer brought his own satin sheets), was also the star of the opening. As the *Kansas City Independent* commented, 'perhaps the greatest interest in a single guest centered around the person of Lord Duveen of Milbank, house guest of J.C. Nichols. Lord Duveen is a distinguished figure in the world of art, [and] assisted in building the Nelson Collection by finding some of the most distinguished pieces in it.' The presence of an English lord lent a special tenor to proceedings:

> While sitting at the end of the long luncheon table at Mission Hills Club, at one of the many festivities during the week, he chatted with his new Midwestern friends as casually as if he were drinking a cup of his own specially blended tea. An adoring Kansas City woman who had better be nameless remarked in an aside that he really should be called Lord Divine.

Duveen toured private houses and commented on collections (such as they were) and gave talks to women's clubs. He was at his most magnanimous and charming.

The publicity and public discussions surrounding the opening of the Nelson–Atkins Museum was dominated by the themes of local boosterism and, as Nichols' remarks showed, by a populist notion of art. Woodbury Parsons, in a talk to the Kansas City Chamber of Commerce, reassured his audience that 'in a few years the William Rockhill Nelson Gallery will be the topic of conversation at tables in London, Paris, Athens and Rome'. The visit of two art historians, one Italian and the other German, to view the collection, led one newspaper to reflect on how things had changed: 'Two years ago there would have been no reason for it; today they could scarcely avoid coming here because the city now possesses art treasures that both needed to see in connection with their work.' Maybe, the *Kansas City Times* pondered, this would put paid to some myths about the Midwest:

> Through the connivance of certain American authors, Europe has come to look upon the Middle West of the United States as the home of barbarism and ignorance. Now European critics are finding it necessary to visit the Mid West to complete their study of Titian and Piranesi and other European masters. It is interesting to see what effect this fact will have upon the fiction of our barbarism.

The *Kansas City Star* put it more positively, 'Like a pupil that has outstripped its teacher, so has Kansas City passed New York in the ability to create something marvellously beautiful'.

Even more important than the sense that Kansas City had placed itself on the cultural map was the deep commitment to the idea that art was not the special province of snobs and experts. Woodbury

Parsons, though himself a confirmed elitist, felt it wise to tell his audience of businessmen that, 'Art, primarily created for the rich man, has become the possession of the people, the paintings painted for kings and potentates, sculptures made for the homes of historic wealth are now accessible to all who have learned to enjoy them.' In an article headed, 'The Layman's Art', the *Kansas City Star* applauded the decline of cultural snobbery: 'it is evident that art in Kansas City has begun to lose its Oxford accent with the opening of the new gallery'. Visitors

> who have supposed that it was something that could be appreciated only by experts, have discovered to their surprise, that the Nelson Gallery contains much of beauty of which they can readily see without special training. The old myth that art is a mystery to be understood by a few initiates is rapidly being exploded, whenever there is a modern gallery organized along the lines of the Nelson Gallery.

Another item, 'Exposure to Beauty', published the same day, continued to urge the accessibility of great art: 'The layman in art is inclined to imagine that the things he ought to like are determined in some mysterious way by the art experts, and will probably be beyond his comprehension. But that is not the case. The test of a great painting or a great piece of sculpture in general is simply its power to attract enduring interest.'

The conclusion drawn by the press and local commentators was that, though the new museum was of benefit to out-of-town scholars and experts, and was an invaluable advertisement for Kansas City and its culture, 'it is intended primarily for the pleasure of the inhabitant of the city and surrounding territory. Surely we who live nearby have no excuse for failing to take advantage of facilities that are attracting visitors from abroad.'

The discussion in Kansas City about the importance of their new art museum mixed pride with anxiety: pride that citizens now had their own museum (and a fine one to boot) and that they had caught up (and perhaps even surpassed) other cities in pursuit of a civilizing mission; anxiety because the people of the town, even members of its elite, were not sure of their competence to judge their achievement and the art that sustained it. Hence the repeated claims that appreciation of a great work of art was not the province of a special elite or clique of connoisseurs but was possible for ordinary citizens provided they looked at art with care and attention. This insecurity was compounded by the view, expressed even by art enthusiasts, that the art world was a racket, full of forgers and fraudsters, constantly on the look out for an opportunity to bamboozle the credulous and ill-informed. Figures like Woodbury Parsons and Nichols tried to reassure the public that they would be constantly vigilant in their interests.

Andrée and Harry Hahn had played on these same feelings of pride and anxiety in Kansas City back in 1920 and had made considerable headway when they had tried to sell their version of *La Belle Ferronnière*. Nichols and his friends were attracted to the purchase as a bold, spectacular gesture, but they also quickly came to realize that such an audacious move was fraught with risk. It seemed more like the crap shoots that existed in the gambling dens down town than the steady calculations of high-end real-estate development that financed the new museum. The civic leaders preferred business risk to gambling. And so it was that Duveen was able to exact a sort of revenge for his setback in the New York court, to steer wealthy Kansas citizens away from the Hahns and their picture and back into the gallery showrooms and dealerships that controlled the business of Old Master art. It is puzzling that, after their success in 1929, the Hahns stopped trying to sell their painting. *La Belle* languished in a New York bank vault until after the Second World War. No doubt the Hahns had other matters on their mind, but it seems probable that Duveen's success in Kansas meant that what they saw as their best chance of a picture sale – one that appealed more to civic pride than art expertise – had been pre-empted. It was not until after the Second World War, and with the publication of Harry Hahn's controversial polemic, *The Rape of La Belle,* that the Hahns renewed their long-standing battle for the acceptance and sale of their painting. Duveen (who died in the spring of 1939) had bested them on their home turf, but he had not been able to change the populist, anti-elitist values that were as much a part of Midwesterners' view of art as of politics, and these were the views that the Hahns again exploited when the case of *La Belle* re-emerged in the 1940s.

CHAPTER 8

The Rape of La Belle

Throughout the 1930s and during the Second World War, the Hahn *La Belle Ferronnière* languished in a New York bank vault. After the verdict and settlement, the Hahns returned to Dinard in France. The two Hahn children, Jacqueline and Harry Junior, were entering their teen years and the family had the comfortable nest-egg of $60,000 (£12,350) courtesy of Sir Joseph Duveen. They had incurred, of course, a large number of legal expenses, but these had largely been offset by agreements promising their lawyers a percentage of the price when *La Belle* was finally sold. Relations between Andrée and Harry, however, were deteriorating, compounded by disputes over the distribution of Duveen's money. (Andrée wanted her 'aunt' Massot to share in the spoils.) Some time in the 1930s Harry returned alone to the United States and, after trying and failing with a wine import business in New York, moved to Wichita, Kansas. The couple divorced and both married again, Harry to an American, Marjorie, and Andrée to an hotelier from Dinard, Roger Dupas.

The war itself dispersed the family. Jacqueline was sent first to relatives in Nice and eventually escaped via Portugal to the United States and was reunited with her father in Kansas in 1942. Harry

Junior joined the Free French in England, fought in North Africa and was badly wounded, losing contact with the rest of the family until the end of the war. Andrée remained in Dinard. However, in 1947 she, Roger and Harry Junior travelled to Kansas to join her daughter, who rented an apartment for them. They did not stay long. Andrée hated the Midwestern climate and there were few opportunities in Wichita for Roger who wanted to work in the hotel business. In 1948, the rest of the Hahns left Harry and his second wife for a new life in California.

Just before the family was briefly reunited, Harry began to search for a publisher for a book he had been working on about *La Belle* and the art market, and which he described as the research he had undertaken for the retrial with Duveen that never took place. He turned for help to a Kansas City businessman, Frank Glenn, who ran a rare book and manuscript business. Frank was born in Bearmouth, Montana, and had, like Harry, served in the air corps in the First World War. When he came to Kansas in the 1920s, he roomed with the family of Conrad Hug, the dealer who had helped the Hahns in their negotiations to sell *La Belle* in Kansas City in 1920. According to his widow, Ardis Glenn, Frank regarded the Hug family as if they were his own kin and he came to view his involvement in *La Belle* as a vindication of his mentor. Largely self-educated – he never finished secondary school – Frank sold books for the Grolier Society, before setting up his own book business in 1933.

Glenn approached a number of publishers late in 1945, including Little, Brown in Boston and Crowell in New York, but, much to his irritation, everyone turned him down. Already, even after a few weeks, Frank began to see the publication of Harry's book as a vital crusade. 'This book,' he wrote to Harry after another rejection letter, 'is going to be printed if I have to set every word of the type myself.' In January 1946, Glenn the bookseller decided to go into the business of publishing and, in so doing, launched another phase of the remarkable career of the Hahn *La Belle Ferronnière*.

The publication of what was eventually entitled *The Rape of La Belle* (it had earlier been called 'Duveen Summons the Clan') was the collaborative effort of three men – Glenn, who put up the money and bore the risk, Harry Hahn, who wrote a first version of the text, and Thomas Hart Benton, who rewrote much of the general discussion of the art world in the book, and who provided both publicity and a strident introduction. Of the three men, Benton was much the best known. The rebel son of a Democratic congressman and lawyer, he had studied art in Chicago, Paris and New York, and taught at the Art Students League in Manhattan (one of his pupils was Jackson Pollock), before denouncing modernism, Europe and the New York art scene, and decamping to Kansas City in 1935. Only five feet two inches tall, dark-haired, moustachioed, intense and often dressed in working-man's clothes, Benton was a leading figure in American Regionalism (other exponents included Grant Wood) who became nationally famous for his scandalous murals of the history of Indiana, exhibited at the *Century of Progress Exhibition* in Chicago in 1933. (Particular objection was made to his depiction of the activities of the Ku Klux Klan.) By 1934 he had achieved national fame, appearing on the cover of *Time* magazine, feted as America's most influential and controversial artist. Political and aesthetic conservatives disliked Benton's progressive and reformist vision of Indiana's history and his 'distorted' depiction of the human form; modernists dismissed his 'realism' as provincial and regressive. It was all grist to Benton's mill. He described history not as a scholarly study but as 'a drama', one, we must add, in which Benton himself was a leading character. 'I saw it,' he wrote in his autobiography, *An Artist in America* (1937), 'not as a succession of events, but as a continuous flow of action having its climax in my own immediate experience.' During much of the 1930s Benton travelled with his sketchpads and paint brushes back and forth across the United States, seeking out the history and soul of the nation. He became a prolific illustrator of the American way, whether in vast murals or as an illustrator of such books as Mark Twain's *Tom Sawyer,* John Steinbeck's *Grapes of Wrath* or Leo Huberman's Marxist American history, *We, the People.*

It would be a mistake, however, to see Benton's politics as Leftist (or, indeed, as some have asserted, almost Fascist). At heart he was, like the father he fought with but embraced at the end of his life, an American populist. He had a strong appreciation of the richness and contradictions of American society, a powerful sympathy for the underdog and a penchant for low life. He also had a singular talent for self-promotion. (He was a great believer in the press as an engine of progress.) Tom Benton found it hard to stay out of a fight. When he returned to Kansas City he maintained his notoriety. Asked by the Missouri legislature to paint a series of murals depicting state history in the Capitol Building in Jefferson City, he outraged many regional boosters by depicting Bosses like Tom Pendergast, the Kansas City stockyards, and its bars and speakeasies. Given the themes and content of his earlier murals, Benton's 'realist' history, with its working folk, both black and white, and his unjaundiced depiction of the ways of American politics, was hardly unexpected, but the legislature seems to have been gulled into commissioning his work on the naive assumption that Missouri's most famous artist would be sure to idealize his native state.

It was not long before he was sacked from his job as a teacher at the Kansas City Art Institute. He had painted two realist nudes, *Persephone* and *Susanna and the Elders*, versions of the female form, complete with pubic hair, which shocked local sensibilities. These finally reached breaking point when Benton declared in an interview to the *New York World-Telegram* on 4 April 1941 that he would rather 'sell [his pictures] to saloons, bawdy houses, Kiwanis and Rotary Clubs, Chambers of Commerce – even women's clubs', than to a museum: 'the typical museum is a graveyard run by a pretty boy with delicate curving wrists and a swing in his gait'. Benton believed that art should be a part of society, not fastidiously cut off from the everyday. He hated the pretensions of the art world and he was also, it should be added, a life-long homophobe. Benton was fired and his *Persephone* ended up on the walls of the Horseshoe Night Club in New York, run by the songwriter and theatrical showman, Billy Rose. However, Benton stuck it out in Kansas City, except for the summers when he retired to his mother's farm in Martha's Vineyard, buying a house on Belleview Avenue in Roanoke Park where he converted the carriage house into a painting studio. Here he held court, entertaining a motley crew of visitors and friends that included artists, writers, nightclub owners and anyone he found interesting. There was nothing Benton liked more than an evening's carousing with his cronies.

How Benton knew Harry Hahn is something of a mystery, but

the two men were well acquainted before Benton first met Frank Glenn on a boozy evening in January 1946 when the three men gathered in Frank's living room to swap stories (Ardis Glenn recalls that Tom and Harry brought out Frank's 'Rabelaisian side') and to plot the publication of Harry's book. For all three this project was much more than a simple publishing venture. What they planned was a general assault on what they repeatedly referred to as this 'lush' or 'lucrative' Old Masters 'racket'. Harry's *The Rape of La Belle* was never intended simply to demonstrate that the Hahn painting was a genuine Leonardo; its object was, as many of its reviewers recognized, the public exposure of a general conspiracy to delude Americans into accepting, buying and displaying large numbers of fakes of Old Masters. The chief perpetrator of this plot was the late Joseph Duveen, but he was by no means its sole conspirator. He was the leader of a European movement, sustained by spurious notions of expertise, to trick the American public into buying worthless art. This scenario drew on the plot outlined by the Hahns' lawyers in the 1929 trial, but recast it as a symptom of a general cultural malaise that afflicted the American polity. Its origins were to be found in 'American universities, museums and foundations', institutions that placed an excessive reliance on foreign experts.

Hahn, Glenn and Benton drew, quite explicitly, on a strain of Midwestern populism whose first manifestations in the nineteenth century had attacked big business, excessive wealth, European and Jewish banking, and technical knowledge rather than American common sense. They moved the idea of plutocratic conspiracy from the realm of financial capitalism into the art world, condemning it as corrupt, plush, luxurious and venal, and portrayed themselves as humble, put-upon ordinary citizens, bravely struggling to fight the juggernaut that Duveen had designed and propelled into the United States. And because the Old Masters racket was a plot, whose success depended on the concealment of the truth, the three men saw their task as one of exposure, in the best traditions of American muck-raking journalism, and of persuasion – convincing their fellow countrymen to make public their rejection of the illusions foisted on them by Duveen and his 'gang'. No action, of course, could better demonstrate this than the acceptance of the Hahn portrait as a genuine Leonardo and, even better, its purchase and display in an American gallery of art. At the same time the three men tried to draw on the intense civic and regional pride that was to be found in almost every city in the United States, but which was laced with a sense of cultural inferiority in many Midwestern and Western cities.

All three men involved in the publication of *The Rape of la Belle* had complex feelings about Old Master art and the European cultural heritage it represented. Benton had been educated in Paris. As he commented in his introduction to the book, 'it never occurred to me I could be an artist except by going to Europe and borrowing my forms'. Indeed, despite his subsequent denials, both the subject matter and execution of his later works drew on the art of the great Italian fresco painters of the Renaissance and on such artists as Nicolas Poussin, Correggio and Caravaggio. Yet what Benton most wanted was to shake off what he saw as 'the colonial attitudes' expressed in 'American aesthetic psychology', the knee-jerk obeisance to European taste, whether for Old Masters or modernism. He wanted a vigorous, indigenous American art and a public, including rich collectors, who would patronize it. He blamed the failure to move beyond an American 'imitation' of European art partly on the nation's 'Old Master mania' and on the oligarchs and dealers who supported it by looking 'down with disdain on the poor and struggling workaday world of American aesthetic thought and expression'. He also condemned American intellectuals' cultural cringe to all things European. As he made clear on more than one occasion, he was not much interested in the authenticity of *La Belle* – a question, after all, that was chiefly of concern to those in thrall to the Old Master mania. 'A newly discovered Leonardo is, to my way of thinking, just another old picture – and to hell with it!' he wrote. What mattered for Benton, who was well aware how hard it was to achieve, was a second American revolution in which the artist freed himself (and it was almost always he) from the colonial oppression of Europe.

Harry Hahn, though his aims were very different from those of Thomas Hart Benton, had a similarly embattled and complex relationship to Europe. A callow small-town, Midwestern mechanic with no college education beyond his technical training, he was barely twenty years of age when he joined the American forces in France, and was only twenty-three when he married Andrée. Until 1933, when he returned to the United States, Harry lived chiefly in France and made himself into a passable expert on the works of Leonardo and on such technical issues as the chemistry of pigments. He became fascinated not only with the family picture, but with the business of the art world. During the 1929 trial – it must have been difficult for a man who so much craved the limelight – he had had to take a back seat to Andrée whose good looks and French airs had made her an object of fascination for the American press. He had compensated for this by making himself into an 'expert', one of the breed he claimed to loath, albeit one, as he endlessly repeated, who concerned himself with 'facts' rather than metaphysical speculation. In returning to his Kansas roots, he discovered in himself a refurbished nativism – though he spent much of his time trying to teach his new American wife, Marjorie, French ways – that he polished in the speeches and talks he gave to Rotary Clubs and on Kansan radio stations. Hahn was an extremely intelligent and charismatic figure, a notable in Wichita, but also someone who, as several reviewers of *The Rape of La Belle* observed, seemed to have a chip on his shoulder. As he was well aware, his book was not just an authentication of the picture but a personal vindication – a demonstration that this ordinary Midwesterner was every bit as good as any snobbish connoisseur or college aesthete. It would also make the Hahn Leonardo just as much Harry Hahn's picture as that of his wife.

Frank Glenn, like Harry Hahn, had little formal education. Forced to begin work as a teenager, the sole breadwinner in a fatherless family, he was an autodidact whose enthusiasm for books was first nurtured by his repeated reading of the twenty-volume British children's encyclopedia *The Book of Knowledge*. Ironically, he began his bookselling career by peddling the same reference work for the Grolier Society in the Midwest. In 1931 he became the manager of a Grolier rare book shop in Kansas City, and a few years later opened his own business. Frank, whose mother was German, had a typically European notion of '*bildung*', a powerful commitment to personal and public cultivation. He provided lists of good books for children in his 'The Children's Treasury Room' and lectured in schools and museums in the South and Midwest, accompanied by examples of these 'treasures'. In the 1950s he created the 'Magic

Carpet on Wheels', a specially fitted mobile home that contained a 'History of the Book' and toured schools and rural communities in the United States and Canada. Frank's business sold the classics – rare editions of Edmund Spenser's *Faerie Queen*, John Milton's *Paradise Lost*, Shakespeare quartos and the like – but he was also a pioneer in the collection and sale of Western Americana and his favourite author (a taste he shared with Tom Benton) remained Mark Twain. An inveterate traveller – he made more than forty-six trips abroad, chiefly in Europe but also in Asia – he nevertheless cultivated a no-nonsense Midwestern manner that despised affectation and pretentiousness. And like his two partners, he had grand aspirations – wanting to patronize learning and encourage education, to spread knowledge, so that it was available to all. He was, as his widow puts it, 'a raconteur and a promoter', a man full of schemes and visions. When he became involved in the cause of *La Belle*, Glenn was somewhat in the shadow of his two partners, whom he clearly regarded with some awe, but, more than either of them, he persisted in his attempts to sell both the book and the picture.

In the early months of 1946 Harry Hahn and Frank Glenn, having recruited Tom Benton to the cause, worked tirelessly on the preparation and promotion of the book. They targeted several groups of potential readers. First and foremost, they wanted to win the major collectors, both private and institutional, to their view that they had been cheated into buying fakes and copies of the European masters. This meant that they took their message to the fat cats and plutocrats they openly despised. The two men drew up impressive lists of major art collectors and dealers, combing telephone books and paying a company to provide them with lists of notables throughout the United States. Harry proudly sent Frank what he typically called 'a high-priority, triple-plated list of Old Master buyers and others closely allied with the plush art traffic'. Such a priority may not have been the wisest marketing strategy, but it accorded with the tradition of muck-raking journalism, on which both men drew, of directly confronting the enemy. Then they wrote to the main institutions and associations that represented contemporary American artists which they assumed would be hostile to the European Old Master trade. In order to reach American painters of every stripe, they concluded a deal with the Association of American Artists, an organization of which Benton was a founder member, to take a large number of copies at a cut price. They also sent galley proofs to a number of political columnists known for their journalistic exposure of scandals, in an attempt to get them to help expose 'the art racket'. These included Westbrook Pegler (described by Glenn as 'every inch an American, and not afraid to speak your piece'), who worked for Scripps Howard newspapers and whose columns appeared in 170 newspapers with more than 10 million subscribers, and Drew Pearson whose investigations in 'The Washington Merry-go-Round' printed in the *Washington Post* had brought him fame as a fearless reporter. The decision to seek their support makes clear that Glenn and Hahn saw the 'art racket' as a political matter. Indeed, Glenn wrote to an Illinois Congressman, Cecil William 'Runt' Bishop, asking him to initiate a 'congressional investigation of this whole art racket', which he claimed had 'taken America for better than a billion dollars'. Bishop was sympathetic, but took no action.

Glenn began to recruit salesmen for the book from New York, New England and Britain, where he was negotiating with George

Allen and Unwin to publish an English edition of the book. A German publisher took out an option for *The Rape of La Belle*'s translation rights, while galleys were sent to *Reader's Digest* and the *Saturday Evening Post* in the hope they would publish extracts. However, most of Glenn's efforts went into producing a flyer soliciting pre-publication orders. He had 10,000 copies printed up soliciting subscribers at a heavily discounted price. Its claims were not modest. The brainstorming of Frank, Harry and Tom, aided by a steady diet of liquor, created a document high on hyperbole. They promised 'Sensational revelations'. *The Rape of La Belle*, they asserted, 'drops an ATOMIC BOMB on the World of Art'. 'You,' they declaimed, 'as a member of the art world, should know these revealing facts. See how love of money has replaced love of art and sought to debauch the entire art world.' Asking 'what has he done to the art loving American people?', they denounced Joseph Duveen as 'a man who was a self-confessed fraud and felon – a man who built a great fortune and reputation in art circles but who intentionally tried to defraud the United States Government'. The overstatement continued unabated:

> So revealing and astounding are the facts in this book that the entire art world will feel its profound effect. So authentic are the facts they are beyond dispute. So important are the revelations that further frauds may be stopped ... Hundreds of thousands of dollars and thousands of hours of work in the archives have gone into producing the facts you'll read in this amazing book.

Benton contributed to this hyperbole, but, after a preliminary burst of enthusiasm, he seems to have left the promotion of *The Rape of La Belle* to Hahn and Glenn. The latter's expenditures was as lavish as his friends' prose. He laid out several thousand dollars on publicity, taking out full-page advertisements in a number of art journals and magazines, including *American Artist, Publishers Weekly, Art Digest* and *Art News,* and box ads in numerous newspapers, among them the *New York Herald Tribune, Chicago Tribune, Philadelphia Inquirer, Cleveland Plain Dealer* and the *San Francisco Examiner.*

The pre-publication sales of *The Rape of La Belle* were not huge – as Glenn commented to a friend, he knew the book was not in the same league as *Gone with the Wind* – but they were promising. (Buyers included the judge of the 1929 trial, Justice Black, who eagerly solicited a copy.) Then disaster struck. The Scooley Printing and Stationery Company, the business Glenn had hired to print the book, and to whom he had already paid $700 (£174), refused to continue printing, because they thought the book libellous. Glenn and Hahn were furious and both believed, though without any evidence, that the printers had been 'got at' by sinister forces associated with the art world. From the outset Hahn had been anxious that somehow the publication would be subverted. In January 1946, when Glenn had excitedly told him that the famous French writer who was in New York, André Maurois, was interested in the manuscript of *La Belle,* Hahn had warned him against revealing too much. André Maurois, he told his partner, 'is Jewish and a notorious apologist for all that is Jewish. I have nothing against him on that particular score except for the fact that my manuscript deals a heavy hand to an art dealers clique which is in the main Jewish.' He suspected that somehow word of his work had got through 'to the Duveen organization or to Wildenstein', and that they were trying 'to find out what it is all about' through Maurois. Now their worst fears seemed to be realized.

Glenn sought legal advice about the book from this attorney, Harrison Johnson who, in an astonishingly one-sided opinion, told him that in his view no libel action against the book could be successful. 'I have come to admire very much,' he wrote, 'Mr. Hahn's uniform pattern of assembling his facts, giving his sources before drawing his conclusions, and to admire likewise his restraint and genteelness in launching his conclusions that I found always justi-fied. This book is an expose of a very lucrative racket and publicity is just what they don't want, either by this book or by a suit concerning it.' In a later letter elaborating his views, Johnson repeatedly took Hahn's side. Commenting on the accusation that the art historian Robert Langton Douglas was guilty of 'gross incom-petence or questionable professional integrity', he shrugged off the remark by saying that there was ample evidence that this was true.

Johnson's spirited endorsement of *The Rape of La Belle* must have been reassuring, but Hahn nevertheless modified some of the text, as some of the passages discussed by the lawyer do not appear in the published book. And Hahn, always adept at getting others to take responsibility for him, seems to have persuaded Glenn to take out an indemnifying bond accepting responsibility if they were sued for libel. This might also have assuaged the printers, but they were not willing to take the risk. Fearful that there were sinister forces afoot, Frank and his wife Ardis took a secret plane journey up to Iowa (she recalls the excitement of this cloak-and-dagger trip), telling no one of their destination. At Council Bluffs they succeeded in signing up Ainsworth Printing Company as the new producer of the book.

In the long term the Scooley company's withdrawal initiated a protracted lawsuit between Glenn and them that was eventually resolved in 1956. Glenn lost. The judge ruled that some passages about Duveen were indeed libellous and found for the printers, who were awarded $1,252.84 (£447.44), 'representing the cost of Scooley's preparations for printing the book'. In the short term, the loss of the printer threw out all of Frank Glenn's carefully laid publication plans. Production of the book was delayed by several months, and soon he was inundated with letters demanding copies or the return of payments. Glenn wrote hundreds of letters and continued to promote the book as much as he could. He struggled to cut deals with art associations across the country, urging them to take bulk orders at cut prices, but found that his profit margins were constantly eroded.

Nevertheless, when the book finally appeared, Glenn remained sanguine about its prospects. He wrote to one Boston correspondent that 'it was quite conceivable this book will put an end to the Old Master racket in the United States' and, though his original business plan was for an edition of 5,000 copies, he began talking to the printers about a further edition of 5,000.

The Rape of La Belle covered much of the territory crossed by the Hahns' attorneys during the trial. It emphasized, yet again (and to considerable effect), the disagreements, contradictions and changes of mind among Duveen's expert witnesses, and it drew, even more starkly than during the trial, a contrast between scientific evidence and what Hahn called 'the degraded philosophic twaddle' of art connoisseurs. The core of the book is a detailed examination of the technical, scientific and historical evidence in favour of the Hahns' painting. Hahn laid out three grounds for authentication: 'authentic documents and historical evidence', facts revealed by 'accurate scientific analysis and by measurements of the materials used in the execution of the subject painting' and 'valid technical criticism of a painting . . . given by one who is himself a first-rate painter technician'. Using A.P. Laurie's work on pigments and his own research in the archives (but adducing no evidence from 'painter technicians'), Hahn argues not just that the Hahn *La Belle* is genuine, but that the Louvre picture is a seventeenth-century copy. In other words, his position inverts that most commonly held by Duveen's experts. There is a good deal of *ad hominem* attack in the book, which talks of Duveen's 'lust for power and . . . selfish ambition to dominate the art world', dismisses Bernard Berenson as 'the Dean of the Dilettante' and condemns the testimony of young Alan Burroughs, Duveen's x-ray expert, as 'brazen perjury'. More telling, however, is its general critique of the art world, most fully elaborated in the final two chapters of the book, entitled 'Certificate of "Genuineness"' and 'Happiness consists in being well deceived'.

The art racket, Hahn maintains, is sustained not just by dishonesty, but most importantly by social snobbery. Taking up a dictum, 'the price of a picture always depends on the hook from which it hangs'. Hahn adds:

> if the hook happens to be on the plush walls of the world's greatest art dealer, the dependent picture is worth five or six figures; if the hook is sticking in the plaster of a gallery 'just around the corner' off Fifth Avenue, the same painting is expensive at four figures; and if the hook is in the gallery of a small art dealer in Kansas City, the painting is worth what you can get for it.

The high-end art market plays on the social pretensions of its clients:

> The art game, as it reaches into fancy figures, is based not on documented information nor on historical veracity, but on the nicely calculated effects of a pair of striped pants and a set of affected continental mannerisms, on the insecure cultural pretension of parvenues suddenly vaulted into high social position ... documented facts have been made to appear crude and lacking in gentility. Art and especially high priced art, has been carefully kept from any disgusting contact with reality.

Only this snobbery, and the deference to 'art critics' and dealers, could explain why men otherwise shrewd, skilful and brilliant in business could be gulled into buying bad pictures and fakes. These collectors continued to resist the proper scientific examination of their pictures, because they are afraid that their errors of judgement would be exposed. 'What the picture collectors of America need,' concludes Hahn, 'is a little moral sense and civic courage ... In the full light of day this traffic in spurious paintings would soon die out.'

Hahn estimated that 85 per cent of Old Masters in museums and private collections 'are backed by no factual documentary historical evidence worthy of consideration'. He implied that practically all such pictures were fakes, copies, restorations or pedestrian paintings puffed up as great masterpieces. He could draw, of course, on many instances in which false attributions had been made and errors exposed; as we have seen, fakery, misattribution and skullduggery were part of the boom market of the first half of the twentieth century. For most within the art world, such crimes, errors and misdemeanours were an inevitable but marginal part of the art boom, one that improved connoisseurship of the traditional sort had helped to combat, reducing the number of attributed works to many artists, identifying new painters and bringing coherence and order to much of Europe's cultural heritage. However, to Hahn – and his view was shared by many others who peered in on the art world – perfidy for profit was the name of the art game. *The Rape of La Belle* was a call to arms of all those outside the art world to recognize its moral emptiness, and of those who had been tainted by its practices – American collectors and museums – to recognize the error of their ways.

The critical reception of *The Rape of La Belle* was largely positive and enthusiastic. It was chiefly reviewed in magazines and journals for artists, such as the *American Artist Magazine* and *Art Digest*, and by newspapers from around the country, though chiefly by those in the Midwest. Its greatest coup was to get a full-page review in the *Times Literary Supplement*. The *Chicago Tribune* described it as 'a unique book' in which 'the men who have been responsible for putting the seal of authority on our Old Masters make a pretty poor showing'. A *Los Angeles Times* reviewer remarked, 'what the trial showed, and it was the most famous since Whistler sued Ruskin, is that a set of art experts whose say so will make a painting stand or fall as a masterpiece, will change their supposedly infallible opinions, when the man who put butter on their bread, Duveen, cracked the whip.' Most of the trade journals echoed, in one form or another, the sentiments of Albert T. Reed of the American Artists Professional League, who said that the book 'should be required reading for every museum attaché in the country'.

Glenn complained to his correspondents that newspapers in almost every metropolitan area reviewed *The Rape*, but that the New York press totally neglected the book, but this, as he knew, was not true. On 1 December 1946 the *New York Herald Tribune* published a piece in its weekly book review. Its author had some sympathy for Harry Hahn's scepticism about art experts: 'His impatience with art connoisseurship,' he wrote, 'is not without justification.' Otherwise, the reviewer condemned Hahn's 'passionate bias', quizzically commenting that the most remarkable feature of the book was Hahn's feat in sustaining his 'intemperate emotion', for over fifteen years. 'Readers of this book,' he concluded, 'will not have the benefit of calm, judicious guidance ... [the author] obviously expected the book to create a considerable furor. Its failure to do so can be blamed chiefly on his lack of self discipline and to a minor degree on some of the grubbiest illustrations that ever got into a $5 book about painting.'

For Glenn the publication of *The Rape of La Belle* had always been part of a larger strategy. Three days after he had signed a book contract with Tom Benton and Harry Hahn, he wrote to Andrée Hahn asking if he could act as her sole agent in the sale of *La Belle Ferronnière*. As a sign of his good will he told her how much he had spent advertising Harry's book, and he asked her about the liens on the picture that he knew were owing to Andrée's New York lawyers. The negotiations took a while, as Andrée had now appointed Jacqueline, who was living with her father in Wichita, as her legal representative, but by July Glenn and Andrée had a deal in which he had a two-year option on the painting which would have brought him 25 per cent of the gross if it were sold. With the book and picture in hand, Glenn now tried to buy up all the surviving copies of the six-colour print of *La Belle* produced in the 1920s by the American Lithography Company. He was turning into something of a monopolist.

Glenn's chief hope was that he would be able to persuade the Nelson–Atkins Art Museum in Kansas City to buy the painting. He had launched *The Rape of La Belle* with a party held at the Kansas City Rotary Club (there were more than 400 members) after a rousing thirty-minute talk from Harry Hahn on 18 July 1946. The presentation had an electrifying effect and, as Glenn continued to boast, was still talked about months after its delivery. Unrestrained by anxieties about libel, facing an audience he felt sure was on his side, Hahn gave full force to his populist rhetoric. He began, said one report in the *Wichita Beacon*, to talk about the 'plush art salesrooms of the monocle and spats boys' filled with devious and unscrupulous dealers. Closeted with these men, 'Our hard-fisted business tycoons are as helpless as a canary bird in the presence of a boa constrictor.' At the centre of this plot was 'a highly organized clique known as art experts'. The mastermind Joseph Duveen was 'responsible for the beautification of this inner-sanctum of crystal-gazers'. Nor was his power confined to art showrooms: 'The tentacles of this highly-rigged fancy-packaging organization extend all the way from the plush art salesrooms in London, Paris and New York deep into the inner sanctum of the direction of public museum and the art research departments of great universities.' Harry Hahn, never modest on such occasions, portrayed himself as the best-informed opponent of the art racket, a single voice crying out against fraud. 'For 25 years,' he told his audience, 'I have worked single-handed against the great forces of the essentially commercial nature of the Old Master business.' Its tentacles, he claimed, reached everywhere into modern society, subverting American values: 'I have experienced the abuses of a subsidized press that continually indoctrinated the American public with European ideas of art and artistic culture quite foreign to our own.' No one praised 'living American artists' (a line no doubt inserted to please Tom Benton); no one but he was prepared to expose what he baroquely described as 'foreign art dealers reaching deep into the fat purses of swag-bellied American museum markets'. Hahn's audience was entranced by his passionate and purple prose. The Rotarian's party was a great success, creating fertile ground for the idea that the *La Belle Ferronnière* might return to the city where it had first been publicly shown.

Frank Glenn knew J.C. Nichols – his first bookshop at 312 Ward Parkway was part of the Country Club Plaza rented by the developer – and he knew that Nichols had the clout to push the museum trustees into considering the acquisition of *La Belle*. He made sure that Nichols had a pre-publication copy of the book and sent him favourable reviews. In September 1946 he discussed *The Rape of La Belle* with Nichols, who liked the book and praised it. Within days Glenn had persuaded him that it would be a good idea to get 'the painting back out here for exhibit'.

Armed with the knowledge of Nichols' support, Glenn wrote a formal letter to the trustees of the Nelson–Atkins Art Museum. He began by claiming that Hahn's book had finally given *La Belle* proper legitimacy: 'Through the publication of this book the painting of La Belle Ferronnière is reborn and attains its rightful place not only as a Leonardo da Vinci but also as the most thoroughly documented and scientifically tested Leonardo da Vinci in the world with the possible exception of the Mona Lisa.' He sent a collection of reviews to show that the press accepted this view and pointed to the use of the book in courses at universities and art schools. He reminded the trustees of the previous showing of *La Belle* at the Art Institute in 1920, when it drew '5,000 persons in a single afternoon'. He pointed out that *La Belle* was 'the only Leonardo da Vinci in America, and is probably the only one America will ever have', and told of his plans to 'take this painting on a tour of the world for its vindication'. Finally, appealing to the trustees civic pride, he concluded that it 'was only proper that this book should be published in Kansas City and since *La Belle* Ferronnière has had a rebirth, it would be fitting if some of the press was vindicated and her first showing would be at the William Rockhill Nelson Gallery of Art.'

Glenn was anxious about the trustees' response because he believed that the museum's first director, Paul Gardner, and its chief buyer in Europe, Harold Woodbury Parsons, were both 'Duveen' men, and therefore ill-disposed to *La Belle*. At all events, Nichols and Glenn got their way, though the board stipulated that 'It will be made clear that no claim of endorsement of the painting by the Nelson Gallery', when the picture went on show. Nichols agreed to make arrangements for the exhibition.

La Belle herself was still languishing in a bank vault in New York, where she had remained ever since the court case had ended in 1929. Harry Hahn persuaded Glenn to put up the $1,500 (£372) of insurance money required to secure the release of the painting, and on 4 November 1946 the picture arrived at Kansas City's magnificent Union Station in the hand luggage of the New York attorney, James Farrell, a member of the law firm that had represented Andrée in the 1920s and which had a 25 per cent interest in the painting. After being placed in 'a rubbed antique gold frame of Florentine type with a red velvet liner', it was taken to the museum and displayed to the public between 8 December and 5 January in the main entrance hall. Glenn fantasized about getting 50–60,000 people into the gallery to see the picture, and was sure that if its exhibition was a success, then the pressure on the trustees to buy it would be overwhelming.

The show did not quite match up to Glenn's expectations, but it was a popular hit. The *Kansas City Star* ran a big spread in its Sunday edition before the opening, telling the story of *La Belle* very much from Harry Hahn's point of view. As in so much of the Midwestern press coverage, the paper treated the painting more as a living person than a thing:

> That sensational lady in red, La Belle Ferronnière, of Milan and Paris, who has wept dry tears these seventeen years in a dark storage vault in New York at last is coming back to Kansas City to show her face again ... Whether Leonardo da Vinci painted her, or whether he didn't, the lady in red got her real start not on the banks of the Seine but right here where the Kaw joins the Missouri. For that reason there should be a certain dash of local pride in the piquant La Belle.

Despite heavy rain on the first day of *La Belle*'s exhibition, 1,800 visitors were reported to have viewed her. Glenn later claimed that 25,500 people had seen the picture.

Hahn and Glen enjoyed similar success a few weeks later when *La Belle* was taken to be shown in Wichita, where Harry Hahn now lived. The doors of the local art association had to be closed 'to prevent more from entering', as 4,500 people squeezed in to view the picture. The exhibit, sponsored by the *Wichita Beacon*, whose deputy editor was a friend of Hahn's, was held over for three days and local children were dismissed early from school so they could see the painting.

Frank Glenn was exultant, especially as he was getting very positive signals from J.C. Nichols, who was urging him to lobby other trustees and Paul Gardner, the director of the Nelson–Atkins Museum. Nichols did not want his name mentioned in any discussions, as his colleagues 'probably feel I have always been very sympathetic to this picture', but he urged on Frank nonetheless. However, discussions ground to a halt by March 1947. Gardner's attitude, in particular, was totally non-committal about the Hahn painting. Trustees like Nichols were impressed by popular interest in the picture, and by the stories that surrounded it as an object that had a Kansan history, but the likes of Gardner, who had to answer to the museum world as well as his trustees, thought about *La Belle* in a completely different way. Like many insiders in the art world, he thought of the Hahn *La Belle* as a tainted picture.

Hahn and Glenn now tried a new tactic to promote *La Belle*. In the previous summer Hahn, having completed *The Rape of La Belle*, began work on a synopsis of a film about the painting. The idea of producing a movie had been mooted in the book contract the two men had signed in the spring of 1946, where Glenn had been given a sizeable 50 per cent of motion picture rights. They had signed up agents, Oceana Publications, who were liaising with Warner Brothers about a film deal. However, the two men began to fall out about Hahn's synopsis, which Glenn – and for that matter every other reader we know about – did not like.

The document Harry Hahn sent to Hollywood is an extraordinary mishmash of portentous self-justification and Hollywood cliché. It begins with an account of the struggle with Duveen, gives a detailed history of the Hahn picture (according to Harry Hahn) and finishes with the story of Lucrezia Crivelli, the supposed subject of the Hahn *La Belle Ferronnière*, and of her daughter, 'Djem'. In *The Rape of La Belle* Hahn had argued that the jewelled headband on the painting had been added by the French court painter Francesco Primaticcio at the orders of Francis I. The original Leonardo, he argued, was of Crivelli without the headband, painted when she was the mistress of Ludovico il Moro in Milan. Later her daughter, who bore a startling resemblance to her mother, became the mistress of Francis I, and he had the painting altered so as to remind him of his new mistress. Taking these 'facts', and basing his account on a mid-nineteenth-century French study, Hahn concocted what he called 'a love-drama of the debauched court of Ludovico il Moro'. In Hahn's treatment the monarchs are lusty, the mistresses are beautiful, the courts are glamorous, the emotions are exaggerated, and the plot implausible. Perhaps it is surprising that it never made it to the silver screen. However, its plot, subordinate to demonstrating how the jewelled headband was added to the painting, is too complex for a Hollywood story. Nor was Hahn's treatment subtle. Describing the meeting of Crivelli and Ludovico, he writes, 'In the moment of meeting Lucrezia, Ludovico knows his search has ended. Here is a woman who surely shares his concepts.'

Hahn was typically boastful and blustering about what he described as 'an action scenario'. Reminding Glenn that whatever he produced would be rewritten according to 'the Hollywood slant on history', he explained that he had 'simply put down the historical background of Milan and the court of Ludovico il Moro that permits the writing of anything that Hollywood wants to concoct'. 'In fact,' he added, 'my synopsis puts down the basis for a story that would make the life and loves of Benvenuto Cellini look like an ice-cream social.' It would be 'a grandiose production in Technicolor', a story where 'the imagination of a director could run riot'.

Never lacking in ambition, Harry Hahn planned to sell both the painting and the treatment to a studio in a single package. He wanted to use *La Belle* not just to make money but to launch his own Hollywood career.

Frank Glenn's quarrel with Hahn over the film treatment was the first of a growing number of disagreements. Hahn could be astonishingly charming but he tended to hector and bully others when he did not get his way. He was beginning to browbeat Glenn, to try to push him around. Airily dismissing his publisher's criticisms of the script, Hahn told him to 'take my tip and have the synopsis typed as is, and send it that way. I bet you a plugged nickel that Hollywood will quickly see what to do with it.'

The relationship between the two men began to fray. Harry Hahn, who always seemed short of money, kept asking Glenn to help him out with loans and 'advances'. From the very start of their relationship, he had insisted on payments. He wanted to be paid to come from Wichita to Kansas City to meetings about the publication of the book, even though Glenn was bearing the brunt of the costs of publication and had promised him royalties. He pestered Glenn for small loans, claiming that the time he was working on *La Belle* was undercutting his earnings as a salesmen.

Things came to a head in late March 1947 when the chance to take the painting to Hollywood came up. Hahn refused to get on the train to Los Angeles when only paid $350 (£87) towards his expenses, saying he would not go for less than $500 (£124). The letter he wrote to his publisher was alternately wheedling and peremptory. He conceded that Glenn had made him repeated advances and spoke of his fear that he might be 'jeopardizing his moral reserves', but he played on Glenn's fear that his friend's debts might distract him from the task of selling the picture in Los Angeles and emphasized how much was riding on the success of the California trip. 'I know,' he wrote disingenuously, 'that at the moment you are in a thousand times better position to take care of the matter for me than I am,' but then ended by saying, 'Please send this $150 by return air mail special delivery as I have matters that must be attended to before Saturday morning.'

Glenn was exasperated with Hahn's request, but sent the money 'in spite of my better judgement'. He complained that Hahn kept on asking for money, but did not carry out simple tasks, like sending him the photographs of *La Belle* he needed. 'Your account with me,' he wrote testily, 'is getting considerably out of line and to work quite a hardship on me. I just can't keep on handing out money. In fact I promised myself that this is the last regardless. If the painting sells, well and good. And if it doesn't then each step must pay for itself.' Glenn had recently opened another new shop and, as he admitted to Hahn, was 'drained mightily low myself'. He was beginning to realize that his author had skilfully arranged matters so that he, the publisher, bore all the risk and undertook most of the work marketing *The Rape of La Belle* and the picture.

The sales of the book that was supposed to bring the art world to its knees were disappointing. In the end Glenn only managed to sell about half of the original edition of 5,000. It was becoming apparent that, unless the painting was sold, Glenn was going to incur a pretty heavy loss. Harry Hahn knew this and was able to extort more funds from his publisher, for whom the California trip had become like the last throw of the dice. The men buried their differences, lured by the prospect of a glamorous sale in Tinseltown.

Before he left for the West Coast, Glenn made one last attempt to get the trustees of the Nelson–Atkins to take the picture. He wrote to one of Nichols' fellow trustees, another real-estate developer, Herbert V. Jones, telling him that the picture was about to be sold in California. He painted a glowing picture of *La Belle*'s future: 'A millionaire of Los Angeles is backing *La Belle* with everything he has, and I am positive, ere a year goes by, you'll find she is accepted throughout the world as one of the finest Da Vincis. Such is the power of the press, the radio and movies that she will be accepted without question.' He was writing this letter, he slyly said to Jones, 'so that you and your Board would have the full details of it, and so there can never be any criticism of me, for not having made every effort possible to keep the painting in Kansas City'. Don't blame me, says Glenn, but you'll be to blame when it turns out you've let America's only Leonardo slip through your fingers.

It would be easy to interpret this as a cynical sales pitch, but letters that Glenn wrote the same day to Harry Hahn and to Conrad Hug Jr, the son of the Kansas City Art dealer who had tried to sell *La Belle* back in 1920, show that he was fully convinced that a sale was imminent. The picture, he was sure, would 'never leave Los Angeles'. Glenn had every confidence in the Hartwell

Galleries, who were paying him to exhibit the picture, and their owner's ability to secure a sale. Yet what is striking in his letter to Herbert Jones is the strength of his belief, which was clearly a delusion, that somehow it was possible to secure the attribution of a picture by popular acclamation. Hardheaded businessmen like Jones and J.C. Nichols happily expressed populist sympathies – as long as they did not intrude on their businesses – but would never have made decisions based on popular sentiment rather than commercial expertise. Which is why, in the end, and despite a deep wish that *La Belle* was a genuine Leonardo, Jones and Nichols were not going to buy the Hahn picture. They may have had their reservations about the European experts and New York art dealers – Nichols liked to tell anecdotes at Duveen's expense – but they understood that their legitimacy, as trustees of their institution, depended on the cooperation and endorsement of the major players in the art world.

Yet how would *La Belle* fare in Hollywood? Glenn, his wife Artis, and Harry Hahn left Wichita station with the picture on the afternoon of Saturday, 5 April 1947. As they clambered aboard 'The Scout', photographers from the *Wichita Beacon* were on hand to catch their departure and send pictures on to Los Angeles down the Associated Press Wire Photo service. Early on Monday morning they arrived at Union Station in downtown Los Angeles, to be met with an armoured car and a police escort that drove the painting to the Hartwell Galleries on the West Side on the city. The Glenns and Hahn checked into the Knickerbocker Hotel on Ivar Boulevard. Hardly the most convenient location for the Hartwell Galleries, which was a couple of miles away, it was, however, right in the heart of Hollywood, exactly where Harry Hahn wanted to be. The hotel, still frequented by stars – the famous director, D.W. Griffith, who lived in the hotel, was to collapse and die under its famous lobby chandelier in the following year – it seemed impossibly glamorous to the party from Kansas. The next evening the picture went on display with a gala opening whose proceeds were dedicated to the Nursery School for Visually Handicapped Children. Guests were asked to pay $5 to enjoy 'the Premier Showing in the West' of what was described as 'the only historically documented Leonardo Da Vinci painting in the United States. Valued at $1,000,000 [£248,000]'.

Hartwell's had mustered an impressive line-up of patrons and sponsors for the evening. It included Hollywood moguls Walt Disney and Louis B. Meyer, and rich businessmen and philanthropists like Arthur Atwater Kent, the millionaire radio manufacturer who had ostentatiously bought $2,500 (£620) of tickets, Harvey Mudd, the head of the Cyprus Mining Corporation, Robert Ellsworth Gross, the head of the Lockheed Company, and Herbert Kalmus, the inventor of Technicolor. Among the collectors present were Walter Arensberg (once a key figure on the New York modernist art scene), Bror Dahlberg and Edward G. Robinson, who was not just a famous actor but, before his divorce in 1956, the owner of one of the finest private art collections in the United States. The rest of the Hollywood crowd included the producer Frederick Brisson and his more famous wife, the actress Rosalind Russell, the art director William Ferrari, Travis Banton the costume designer and teacher of Edith Head (who also attended the opening), the retired actor and busy philanthropist Harold Lloyd, the actresses Irene Dunne, Merle Oberon and Benay Venuta, and the former actress turned gossip columnist, Hedda Hopper. Also present at the opening were Vincent Price, who was to prove one of Hollywood's most discerning art collectors, Natalie Draper and Hurd Hatfield.

The glamour of the opening left Ardis, the young wife of Frank Glenn, giddy with excitement, though a little shocked at the extravagant fashions. Travis Banton's wife, she told her mother back in Kansas, wore 'the most hideous black evening hobble skirts and plumed hat that I ever hoped to see'. Her husband, who loved the chivalrous gesture (he had dictated to her a proposal of marriage when she had worked as his secretary), told her that, though surrounded by stars, she was incomparably the most beautiful woman in the room. Glenn and Hahn revelled in the occasion and loved being photographed in front of the painting with Hedda Hopper and the wife of Edward G. Robinson. All looked well for a quick sale. Hopper's great rival, Luella Parsons, was one of several journalists who covered the event, commenting (according to Ardis Glenn), 'This is the first time movie producers have been offered an art masterpiece with the right to film the story behind it.'

However, by the end of the week, the shine of Hollywood was wearing a bit thin. As the Kansas crowd came to learn, a good party is much easier to stage than a million dollar sale. One of the guests, Walter Arensberg, was an enthusiast for *La Belle*, but he collected modernist not Old Master art, and his opinions carried little weight against the opposition of a formidable foe, the co-director of the Los Angeles County Museum, Wilhelm Valentiner.

Valentiner had been one of the first experts to examine the Hahn *La Belle* in Hyacinthe Ringrose's office in New York and he had been deposed in 1921. He had been categorical in his rejection of the painting, condemning its weakness of execution, its clear status as a copy and asserting that it had clearly never been on wood. Young at the time of his deposition, Valentiner had gone on to become one of the foremost art historians and museum officials in the United States. Raised under the tutelage of Wilhelm von Bode at the Kaiser Friedrich Museum in Berlin, he had worked at the Metropolitan in New York, single-handedly developed one of the great American collections at the Detroit Institute of Art and founded and edited two of the most important art journals in the United States – *Art in America* and *Art Quarterly*. The author of several *catalogues raisonnée* and a strong supporter of modern art – he staged the first American exhibition of German Expressionism in New York in 1923 – he was immensely erudite, an intellectual with a broad range of interests not just in art but literature and music. His preeminence in the American museum world was confirmed in 1939 when he was appointed director general of the 'Masterpieces of World Art' exhibition at the Chicago World's Fair. Valentiner had arrived in Los Angeles in 1946, when he was asked to come out of retirement to help develop the collections at the Los Angeles County Museum of Art. What he saw did not impress him: the collections were poorly organized and displayed; the community of local collectors – the Hollywood crowd – had money but, in his view, little taste. His advice was sacrosanct, and he was working on an exhibition on Leonardo that was to open at LACMA in 1949.

In his characteristically swashbuckling way, Hahn had taken several swipes at Valentiner in *The Rape of La Belle*. He repeatedly impugned his skills as a connoisseur, accusing him of misattribution in his catalogue of the Widener collection and of error in his choice of a 'highly dubious' Franz Hals for the Chicago World's Fair exhibit. More generally, Hahn singled out Valentiner as 'one of the most active authenticators ... who has on various occasions rendered yeoman service to art collections that have been largely formed under the selling auspices of the late Sir Joseph Duveen'. Then he scoffed at the scholarship that had made Valentiner famous: 'Dr. Valentiner has compiled numerous de luxe art catalogues sprinkled with highly speculative guessing about the authenticity of dubious paintings, and of some outright fakes.' And when Hahn complained about the state of Rembrandt scholarship, Valentiner was once again a prime suspect: 'Had certain American museums and collectors ... given less heed to the babblings of Bode, Bredius and Valentiner, there would be about one-fifth the number of pictures in the United States that are now sporting shiny brass plates on their frames inscribed with the illustrious name of Rembrandt.' We can be sure that Valentiner was not amused.

Harry Hahn knew that Valentiner's presence would be one of the main obstacles to selling *La Belle* in Los Angeles. In his begging letter to Glenn requesting extra funds, he had argued that he needed the money because 'I ... want to be as free from worry as possible ... in as much as I fully believe we are going to be in for a fight with Valentiner.' Not that he was going to admit to a weakness. He went on to claim that 'it does not worry me as much, as I am loaded for bear-hunting on that aspect of the trip', but he clearly was anxious and with good reason. As Ardis Glenn explained in a letter to her mother, 'Dr Valentiner at the museum up to now had tried every way to block us'. We don't know how decisive Valentiner's opposition proved to be, but within days the euphoria of the opening night at the Hartwell Galleries gave way to a growing anxiety that interest in the painting was waning. Frank and Ardis Glenn returned to Kansas City and their book business. Harry Hahn hung around Los Angeles, where he 'talked at swanky clubs, and appeared before Junior League groups, and was in constant demand for lectures'. But he had not reckoned with Hollywood's extraordinary short attention span and was soon grumpily complaining to Glenn that the Hartwell Galleries were doing too little to promote the picture. Short of funds, as usual, he checked out of the Knickerbocker – sending the bill to Glenn – and headed back to Wichita, where he gave a graphic account of his Hollywood triumphs to the *Wichita Beacon*. It soon became clear that the Los Angeles venture, though it began with a bang, had ended in a whimper.

The failure in Hollywood (and its expense) rekindled the conflict between Frank Glenn and Harry Hahn. In May 1947 Glenn wrote to Hahn about his failure to turn up to a meeting in Kansas City: 'my plans for last week were entirely disrupted ... but not even a word from you as to why you didn't come', he complained bitterly. Hahn shrugged off the incident, telling his publisher they should put aside their differences and 'keep up the push'. Then he announced that he was returning to Los Angeles to work as manager of the Hartwell Galleries at least until the autumn and possibly longer. Harry Hahn had charmed his way into the job. During the summer Glenn negotiated a deal with a buyer in St Louis, in which the money paid for the picture was to be deposited in escrow for a year, while the purchaser got opinions on the picture, but the deal fell through when Hahn ignored his requests for the documents necessary to complete the transaction. Glenn was especially angry as he had come to think that such an arrangement was the best way to sell the painting: 'Let the world know the painting is sold and let anyone take pot shots at it. I don't think anyone would be so foolish.'

Frank Glenn was getting increasingly desperate and he now approached the National Dry Goods Association, attempting to recoup some of his losses by displaying the painting for a fee when new supermarkets and department stores opened. The fee was $150 (£37) a day for four days and $100 (£25) thereafter. The painting seems to have been shown in San Francisco, Dallas and Houston, but the loans did nothing for the sale of the painting and Glenn and the Hahns quarrelled over the distribution of the profits. By October 1947 relations between Glenn and Hahn had completely broken down. Glenn had come to realize the full extent of his losses. He sent a stiff, formal letter to Hahn in Los Angeles offering him the remaining stock of *The Rape of La Belle* – 2,350 copies – at the knock-down price of $1.60 (40p) each but only provided he took the entire stock. He told him his accountant was drawing up a final statement of the royalty account, dryly commenting, 'I am under the impression that a considerable amount will be due to me'.

Two weeks later he received a long letter from Jacqueline Hahn in Wichita. Glenn assumed (almost certainly correctly) that it had been dictated by her father. In it she vetoed any escrow agreement for the sale of *La Belle*. Nothing more, she said, could be known about the painting to make a potential purchaser change their mind: 'there is no information that could be derogatory to my mother's painting, and its case is clearly set forth by documents and it is in the basis of these documents and court testimony that it is unattackable [*sic*].' She told Glenn that the price of the picture was $450,000 (£111,700), and not a penny less, and that it was his responsibility to promote the picture at his own expense, tartly adding, 'if I am obliged to make promotions for myself, I do not need a sales agreement'. Finally, she refused to provide Glenn with an account of the profits made when the picture had been taken up to San Francisco by Harry Hahn to be exhibited.

Frank Glenn was deeply hurt by this letter and the recent passage of events. 'I was in this thing to fight to the end and that the painting should be sold and accepted as a Leonardo', he protested to Jacqueline; reminding her that it 'would have remained in storage had I not published the book'. The Hahns' attitude, he complained, was 'discouraging'; 'from now on,' he added, 'my interest will of necessity be one of pure business'. As for her father, he told Jacqueline, 'I will do nothing further . . . if it involves working with Mr. Harry Hahn'. Hahn had reneged on his verbal agreement to allow the sale through escrow. He wasn't formally obliged, Glenn admitted, to inform him about the receipts from San Francisco, but 'since Mr. Hahn is indebted to me for money advanced to him to make the trip to Los Angeles, it is his moral obligation to repay that advance with the proceeds of the exhibit'. Glenn had had enough of Harry Hahn. Their mutual effort to sell *La Belle* on the back of *The Rape of La Belle*'s publication had ended in failure.

Matters did not end there. Jacqueline and Andrée used the opportunity created by Glenn's refusal to work with Harry Hahn as the occasion to gain possession of the painting. In an agreement made in January 1948 and set up by Frueauff, Burns, Ruch and Farrell, the firm with an interest in the painting, Harry relinquished *La Belle* in return for being 'relieved of any and all responsibilities' towards the New York lawyers. They, in turn, understood that Jacqueline would pass the picture over to Glenn 'for safekeeping during the duration of his contract'. If *La Belle* did not sell, it was to be returned to New York. In fact, Andrée and her daughter took the picture off to Los Angeles, where they had just moved, and set about selling the picture on their own account. They approached Frueauffs, asking about the cost of redeeming their interest in the picture, and some months later began negotiations with their two Parisian attorneys, Michel Brault and Anthony Manley, trying to fix a fee in return for relinquishing their interest in *La Belle*. They even managed to get the picture examined and cleaned at the Los Angeles County Museum, despite the continuing presence of Valentiner.

In 1950, Andrée was in touch with Paul Drey, the proprietor of a gallery in New York and a well-known Old Master dealer who had sold pictures to many major museums, including the Museum of Modern Art in New York, the Art Institute in Chicago and the Detroit Institute of Art. Drey was both sympathetic and businesslike. He explained to Andrée that he believed that 'the painting is old and of the period and of very fine quality'. He set aside her fears that the trial had tainted the picture. On the contrary, he told here, it was advantageous because 'it blackened the Louvre painting'. The real problem, he said, was Harry Hahn's book: 'It is correct in many points, and inaccurate in many others. The main fault is that it is so very aggressive and so rudely attacks all and sundry.' The very qualities that Harry had admired in his own work were those that damned it in the eyes of dealers, critics and connoisseurs. Drey also warned Andrée that he might not be able to get the sort of price she wanted. As he counselled, 'don't be downhearted, but also not yet too optimistic'. Like many subsequent supporters of the Hahn *La Belle*, Drey believed that its cause would be best served if it were displayed alongside the Louvre version of the picture. 'I am trying,' he told Andrée, 'to show the Louvre version and your painting side by side. If I can overcome the difficulties and obstacles involved and should succeed in this, half of our battle will be won.'

Meanwhile Frank Glenn and Harry Hahn, both unhappy about the way in which *La Belle* had slipped from view, were gradually reconciled. In April 1952 Hahn wrote a long, blustering letter to Glenn, prompted by some correspondence he had had with the well-known New York playwright, S.N. Behrman, who had just published a slim volume with Random House based on a witty, gossipy series of New Yorker profiles of Joseph Duveen. He had written praising *The Rape of La Belle* and told Harry that the book had been recommended to him by 'a distinguished don at Oxford'. Hahn used this news as the occasion for a remarkable denunciation of his former friend:

It is with some sadness and regret that I look back to the time when you allowed yourself to be swayed by those who were intent on destroying the sale and distribution of The Rape of la Belle. Petty jealousy, animosity and envy finally triumphed over your better judgement and brought to an unhappy climax an effort of yours that will, in spite of your actions, turn out to be the most important social and intellectual contribution of your lifetime. The book you tried to cast into oblivion has turned out to be the most remarkable art book of the twentieth century. The ironic part of it all is the fact that the very publishing of my book brought you world-wide prestige as a courageous publisher. As the years pass away may you see and understand how gross was your unfairness to me.

Hahn closed by saying, 'Some day, Frank, when you come to your good senses, write to me.'

One might have expected this arrogant, deluded and deeply unjust letter to have severed relations between Hahn and Glenn once and for all. However, Frank Glenn did not rise to the provocation. Instead, he responded to Hahn's diatribe with remarkable restraint: 'I too am sad about the turn our relationship took, but I can't find anything in the past I could have done that I didn't do to promote your book.' He told his former friend that he had just been negotiating with Doubleday to issue a reprint and ended by ruefully commenting that, 'I wish I had half of the loss on La Belle in my pocket right now, to say nothing of the time that was spent on it that could have been more productive.' Glenn managed to turn what looked like a moment of inevitable rupture into a patched-up reconciliation.

Within a few months the two men were talking with one another and trying to get the painting back from Los Angeles. Andrée was deeply resistant, saying that her plans for the picture no longer included its exhibition. In fact, she had now given an option to an art dealer in Nice in France, where she hoped to return with her daughter. She also seems to have told the dealer, D. Kellerman, that her ex-husband was no longer living, which would have come as a surprise to Harry Hahn and to Glenn, who also still believed that he had an option to sell the picture.

Ironically, both Glenn, acting with Harry Hahn, and Robert

Kellerman (D. Kellerman's nephew), acting on behalf of Andrée and Jacqueline, were now in contact with the same expert in Europe, the Dutchman Maurits M. van Dantzig. Van Dantzig, whose part in the history of *La Belle* is fully discussed in the next chapter, was not a part of the Dutch art-historical establishment – indeed, he hated it – but he had become well-known in the United States in the postwar era. He first came to prominence in January 1947, just after *La Belle* had been exhibited at the Nelson–Atkins Museum. The international press had been full of news about the sensational trial, already discussed in Chapter 6, of the Dutch painter Han van Meegeren and his Vermeer forgeries. The American scriptwriter and journalist Irving Wallace had gone to the Netherlands to write about the case and the trial. On 11 January 1947 he had published a long article in the *Saturday Evening Post* entitled 'The Man who swindled Goering'. The article caused a sensation – as articles about forgers are prone to do – and was widely extracted, syndicated and discussed in the American press. Wallace had included a paragraph about the Hahn *La Belle* at the beginning of his essay, but the article was chiefly concerned with the disarray among art experts who had once attributed van Meegeren's work to Vermeer and were now having to concede that the paintings were forgeries. Wallace talked to eight Dutch experts in all, but mentions only one, van Dantzig, by name; a large part of the article was devoted to his views both about van Meegeren's work and how to make attributions.

Van Dantzig liked publicity and was far less circumspect than other experts and museum officials, which is why he made such good copy. Wallace described him as 'a caustic and peppery little art detective', adding:

Incidentally, Van Dantzig's favorite indoor sport consists in haranguing his fellow experts with his claim that 60% of the paintings owned by museums and collectors are, like Van Meegeren's Vermeers, fakes. Van Dantzig arrived at this somewhat arbitrary figure by a private alchemy which none of his friends understands. His colleagues have long ceased to argue with Van Dantzig about the percentage which they regard as preposterous, but they do agree wholeheartedly with him that there are a large number of fakes floating about in high places.

Wallace may have portrayed van Dantzig as a somewhat eccentric and difficult character, but it did not stop him quoting him at length:

> The so-called art experts are often unable to discriminate between copy and original. A masterpiece is accepted as genuine because others before insisted it was genuine and so the legend builds. But really you cannot simply glance at an oil and say it is authentic ... You must look through a painting to the personality behind it. In an Old Master's original, the color, composition, all the elements go together. That is because the originator does it all at once, creatively in one fresh stroke. The copyist, the forger, does each thing separately because he isn't inventing or creating but rather thinking, analysing, imitating. But many experts do not see this, and that is why collectors own masterpieces no more authentic than Van Meegeren's Vermeers.

Van Dantzig went on to explain the differences between Vermeer's and van Meegeren's brushstrokes, spots and dots, and portrayal of hands and human hair. In Wallace's article, he emerges as the embodiment of the well-informed expert.

Both Frank Glenn and Harry Hahn knew about the van Meegeren trial and Wallace's article. Hahn had originally included a chapter dedicated to the Vermeer scandal in *The Rape of La Belle*, but he and Glenn had decided to exclude it as too great a distraction from the main argument. However, Hahn continued to work on the van Meegeren case, and when Glenn died in 1960 he had in his possession the manuscript of Hahn's essay on the Vermeer forgeries. Glenn had written to Wallace about his article in the *Saturday Evening Post*, complaining about the inadequate coverage of the case of *La Belle*; Wallace, like a shrewd hack, saw the letter for what it was: an attempt to puff Hahn's book.

Van Dantzig's American reputation was further enhanced by the exhibition he organized about forgeries, called *True or False in Art,* which toured American cities in 1953–4. The American public was fascinated and, when Van Dantzig appeared on the CBS syndicated program *Omnibus* on 24 January 1954 to discuss the exhibit, he was inundated with requests to make attributions for viewers. In the following year, van Dantzig began work on a new project on Leonardo and, in the summer of 1955, while working at the Louvre, met Marcel Wallenstein, a dapper aesthete who eked out a living in Paris as the European arts correspondent of a number of American newspapers, including the *Kansas City Star*. Soon, news got back to Kansas about van Dantzig's project and his belief that the Louvre version of *La Belle Ferronnière* had not been painted by Leonardo.

Glenn was tremendously excited about this news. In all the recent campaigning on behalf of the Hahn *La Belle*, he had not been able to secure the support of a bona fide art expert to support the painting. He was quick to see that van Dantzig's arrival on the scene would be an enormous help in selling the picture. What he did not know was that van Dantzig, for all the publicity he had received, was not viewed by most museum experts and connoisseurs as reliable. Quite the opposite: he was seen as a maverick. Nor did Glenn know that Andrée's agent in Europe, Kellerman, was already in touch with van Dantzig about the painting. Buoyed by his ignorance, Glenn had visions of finally selling the picture.

In the spring of 1956 Frank Glenn had several irons in the fire. Dr Assis Chateaubriand, the owner of a large chain of newspapers and radio stations in Brazil, and founder of the Museum of Art at São Paolo, which was chiefly dedicated to major European paintings, had been making inquiries about *La Belle*. Glenn had sent him Hahn's book and other materials he thought helped authenticate the picture. He offered the picture and all supporting documentation to the so-called 'King of Brazil' for $400,000 (£143,000). Chateaubriand and his Italian curator, Pietro Maria Bardi, eventually pulled out of the deal, but Glenn regarded this approach as symptomatic of renewed interest in *La Belle*. The news he was getting from Marcel Wallenstein (much of it, it must be said, founded on baseless rumour) was all positive and, in March 1956, he was approached by John Carter, a British expert from Sotheby's, who wanted to come to Kansas City to see the painting.

John Carter was not an expert in European painting, but one of the most distinguished figures in the antiquarian book trade. For many years he had worked as the managing director of Charles Scribner's Sons, but in 1955 he joined Sotheby's as an associate director whose task was to persuade Americans to sell their books, paintings, china, silver and furniture through the London auction house. Tall, monocled and an Old Etonian of great intellectual distinction, he was the author of a number of important works on book collecting and was famous for his exposure in the 1930s of an elaborate series of literary forgeries by the collector, Thomas J. Wise. Together with his collaborator, Graham Pollard, he had combined textual criticism and the scientific examination of paper to expose Wise's fakes. Glenn mentioned their work in his publisher's preface to *The Rape of La Belle* as an instance of how corruption and forgery could be rooted out of the antique book trade.

Carter, as he was to reveal during his visit to Kansas City, was the author of the review of *The Rape of La Belle* published in the *Times Literary Supplement* in April 1947. No doubt the editor, knowing Carter's interest in forgery and authenticity and his reputation as a great sleuth, and seeing his name mentioned in the preface, though him an apt reviewer, though no art expert. In his review Carter expressed his dissatisfaction with the book's weaknesses – 'Its catchpenny title, repetitious and over-emphatic style, confusing presentation of the evidence and air of uneasy defiance' – but warned readers that this should not detract from its theme 'and the problems it tries to solve'. Carter was impressed by Hahn's demonstration that Duveen's experts had contradicted their earlier opinions about the Louvre *La Belle* (their views, he remarked, were 'comically contradictory') and he sympathized with Hahn's portrayal of the connoisseurs as 'a self-bolstering and Duveen-bolstering cohort'. Carter was convinced that Harry Hahn had demonstrated pretty conclusively that the Louvre picture was a seventeenth-century copy of an earlier work and that the Hahn picture had been sold to a private collector in 1796, but he was troubled by Hahn's failure to trace the more recent provenance of his picture. Hahn's evidence was not conclusive, but it should not be ignored. Ironically, he concluded, the only way that the American *La Belle* could be proved to be a Leonardo was through the subjective judgement of the expert eye that Hahn scorned. Despite his misgivings, Carter was intrigued and sympathetic – hence his detour to Kansas City. He was prepared, if suitably impressed by the painting, to talk to his colleagues at Sotheby's and help put it up for auction. Glenn scurried around trying to clear up the question of the surviving liens, so that he could make a proper estimate of his potential profit. He told James Farrell, the Hahns' lawyer in New York, that there was now a 'better than 9/10 chance of selling the painting'.

However, there was one problem: Frank Glenn and Harry Hahn did not have *La Belle*; the painting was in Los Angeles and Andrée and Jacqueline Hahn were proving uncooperative. With the renewed interest in the painting and the imminent arrival of John Carter from London, Harry Hahn had first telephoned and then written to Jacqueline about a sale. Andrée had prevaricated, telling Harry that she wanted to clear $250,000 (£90,000) for the picture, and then revealing that she now had her own agent and therefore could not do anything for the present. This was the first inkling that Andrée and Jacqueline Hahn had plans to sell the picture independently, and it infuriated Harry who sent an irate six-page letter to his daughter. In it he reminded her (and Andrée) that her mother was not the sole owner of the painting, and that the lawyers in New York who held a 25 per cent interest had given Glenn sole rights to sell the picture for them. He also pointed out that the Hug family still had a claim on the picture, maintaining they were owed $30,000 (£10,700) in expenses and held a 25 per cent interest

in it. Given Glenn's position with the lawyers and his close friendship with the Hug family, he urged the two women to cooperate
with him and help effect a sale. Harry tried hard to allay what he
saw as his ex-wife and daughter's suspicions of him: 'If you folks
will just get it into your noggins that I am trying to help you keep
out of a mess of legal complications instead of taking the attitude
that Frank Glenn or myself or someone else is trying to ill advise
you for their own personal gain you would be a whole lot better
off.' And he reminded them of Glenn's efforts on their behalf: 'I
have a bundle of letters a foot high from Glenn,' he wrote hyper-
bolically, 'where he was trying to do something to sell the painting
while your mother was hiding from the Boche . . . and how much
he contributed to keeping the Hug estate from putting a seizure
on the painting is more than you can imagine.' 'Frank Glenn was
never my enemy,' declared Harry. 'We simply misunderstood each
other. After all he has done to help me and the painting and publish
my book I am heartily ashamed that I once listened to the stories
which were brought to my ears about him.'

Harry Hahn's letter, with its pages of legalese – 'this case is so
darned complicated it would take forty Philadelphia lawyers to
figure it out' – was largely intended to intimidate Andrée and
Jacqueline into cooperating with Frank Glenn. A few days later
the publisher himself weighed in with a long rambling letter to
Andrée in which he outlined his efforts to sell the picture – 'during
these years I left no stone unturned' – expressed his conviction that
'the period of prejudice' against *La Belle* was now over and urged
her to allow the picture back to Kansas City. He also pointed out
that if she had appointed another agent to sell the painting, this
was not legal and that she would have to pay his 25 per cent

commission on the sale. In the following week he flew to Los Angeles and seems to have persuaded Andrée to release the picture for a short while so that it could be viewed by Carter in Kansas City.

Carter's visit to the Midwest was a success. He stayed as a house guest of the Glenns for almost a week and, according to a number of letters Frank Glenn wrote after Carter returned to London (not all of which are reliable), the man from Sotheby's was enthusiastic about the picture, believed he could recruit Kenneth Clark into supporting it and thought that a reserve of £100,000 ($280,000) was reasonable, but that bidding might reach half a million. Harry Hahn was producing a digest of *The Rape of La Belle,* a document that at Carter's advice was stripped of 'personal opinions' and arranged as a series of thirty-three questions and answers about the Hahn *La Belle* and the picture in the Louvre. 'FACTS, FACTS, FACTS are simply involved', Hahn wrote to Glenn, though he could not resist including in his letter a tirade against 'bush-league erudites', 'stinkers' and 'academic bastards'. After Carter's visit, Frank Glenn was exultant. Sending him a copy of Sortais's opinion on the Hahn picture, he speculated that any experts formerly opposed to *La Belle* would now support it: 'people like Mr. B[erenson]'. 'This would erase,' he said, 'an ugly scar on an otherwise fair character.'

However, Glenn still had to contend with Andrée Hahn. As he told Harry, she was now telling him that she was in no hurry to sell, that she wasn't interested in a Sotheby's auction and, although it would be nice if the painting were bought by the Nelson–Atkins and remained in Kansas, she fully expected to bequeath the picture to her children. Andrée Hahn seems to have decided to prevaricate while laying plans to return to Europe and her reluctance to act is hard to explain except as a way of cutting Glenn and her ex-husband out of any profit that might have been made on a sale. Glenn soldiered on. He knew that the Nelson–Atkins could not buy the painting outright, as he'd been told by one of the trustees that they had just committed themselves to buying a very expensive picture. He toyed with the idea of negotiating a sale with an instalment plan and even suggested to Harry Hahn that they could put together a consortium of twenty buyers, each contributing $20,000 (£7,140). At the same time he was wooing the Oklahoma oil baron and collector, Thomas Gilcrease, sending him letters full of optimistic reports about European interest in the picture, urging him to buy it as a patriotic gesture that would 'keep it from going to any European combine which is interested in its acquisition for exploitation'.

In the summer of 1956 Glenn went to Amsterdam to visit van Dantzig and spent two 'most delightful' days with him. His conversations with the Dutchman convinced him more than ever that *La Belle* could now be sold. He rushed over to London to see if Carter had made any more progress in arranging a sale through Sotheby's. His new plan was to have the picture exhibited for charity in different European cities before returning it to London for auction 'to which all the nobility of Europe and the wealthy collectors would be invited'. However, Sotheby's would do no more without the opinion of Sir Kenneth Clark and he was away for the summer.

In the autumn Glenn's plans fell apart. In September John Carter wrote to him, telling him that Clark's rejection of the Hahn picture, and assertion that the Louvre picture was indeed by Leonardo, meant that 'the consensus here is that ... we ... do not feel justified in encouraging you to take a gamble on the picture with the idea of putting it up for sale in London'. At the same time Andrée Hahn refused Glenn a new option and refused to sell him the picture for $150,000 (£53,600). This last suggestion, made after he had discovered that Andrée Hahn was already in contact with van Dantzig through her agent in Nice, was a desperate last throw. Glenn tried to approach Andrée a couple of times before he died in 1960, but she showed no interest. She was focused on Europe and on the expert she believed would solve her problems without recourse to either Frank Glenn or, more importantly, Harry Hahn.

Frank Glenn and Harry Hahn's campaign to sell the Hahn *La Belle Ferronnière* and to create a crisis of confidence in the art world had failed. Glenn's strenuous efforts to sell the painting foundered in the face of Hahn's wayward conduct. The author of *The Rape of La Belle* was chiefly interested in basking in the publicity, excitement and glamour produced by the picture and was probably mindful that these would vanish once *La Belle* was sold. But even if Harry Hahn and, indeed, the other members of the family, had been more cooperative, a legitimate sale – one that recognized the Hahn *La Belle* as a Leonardo – was virtually impossible. A triumphal progress through Missouri and Kansas did far more for Harry Hahn's ego than for the sale of the picture itself; showing *La Belle* at supermarket, department store and shopping mall openings gave the painting a new public, but downgraded it as a collectable among the sort of buyer Glenn was seeking. The ploy of selling both painting and script to Hollywood was a tribute to the ingenuity and shamelessness of Harry Hahn, a brilliant stroke if it had succeeded, for the painting and its story would have reached an audience of millions and would have been the perfect platform from which to preach the populist critique of the art world. But the project was bungled, not least because of Hahn's over-confident insistence that he should control the entire project, acting as salesman, scriptwriter, author and promoter. If it had progressed further, he would doubtless have insisted that he play a part such as that of the French king, Francis I.

As long as the two enthusiastic promoters of the *La Belle* remained outside the art world, they were able to draw on a well of scepticism about its workings, and, especially in the Midwest, on a populist tradition that was deeply suspicious of elitism and expertise. The sympathy they were able to garner and which reassured them in the rightness of their cause created an illusory security. The closer they came to the portals of power, the weaker their position became. Figures as varied as Jesse C. Nichols, the Kansas City booster, and John Carter, the English Old Etonian with a monocle, were willing (though for very different reasons) to revive interest in the painting from within the art world, but they were never going to allow either popular enthusiasm or Harry Hahn's roughhouse hectoring (no matter with scientific evidence) to override the opinions of museum curators, auction house specialists and art experts with whom they had to work and establish trust. Naturally, this reinforced Glenn and Hahn's view that the art world was full of vested interests, which indeed it was; no business, scholarly industry or institution could be otherwise. Whether it was the sort of conspiracy outlined in *The Rape of La Belle* was altogether another matter. And, as many critics pointed out, Harry Hahn's experiences hardly made him a dispassionate critic.

Besides, one of the features of the campaign to legitimise *La*

Belle in the 1940s and 1950s was its almost total reluctance to involve figures that had any real influence in the art world. Nichols and Carter both were on its margins. Hartwell, the proprietor of the gallery in Los Angeles, was a wealthy oilman from the Midwest, not an art expert. His gallery was a rich man's plaything and was soon to close. Paradoxically, experts from within the art world were not consulted because, in the eyes of Glenn and Hahn, their very competence was grounds for their exclusion. Their expertise disqualified them from making a proper judgement because they were part and parcel of the Duveen conspiracy. Nevertheless, it is striking that Hahn made no real attempt to recruit chemists and technical experts like A.P. Laurie to support the conclusions he reached. In *The Rape of La Belle*, he quoted evidence from the trial, but he made no serious attempt to set up a new forensic investigation of the picture. Instead, he embarked on a campaign of self-promotion at Frank Glenn's expense.

Andrée and Jacqueline Hahn observed much of this spectacle from afar and, on occasion, thought that it might produce what they most seemed to want, namely a sale. The emergence of Maurits van Dantzig, who seemed, at least to them, to have some influence in the art world, as a supporter of the Hahn picture, together with an increasing nostalgia for France, led them to seize the initiative from Harry Hahn, to take physical possession of the picture that he had agreed to cede them as their legal property and to take it to Europe, where they hoped to begin life anew. Andrée's concern with the painting had not changed: she cared little for the publicity it provoked but continued to hope that it would provide her and her children with the level of prosperity she aspired to, but, in doing so, she began another chapter in the saga of the picture, one that once again raised issues within the art world about the nature of connoisseurship and art expertise. This was not a deliberate move on her part, though the experience of the previous decade made clear that there was no hope of selling the Hahn *La Belle* as a Leonardo without support from within the art world. Her connection to van Dantzig was almost serendipitous and her anxieties about money meant that it was difficult to persuade her of the need to take time to assemble a case for the authenticity of her painting. Nevertheless, over the next decade and more, the case of *La Belle* was taken in hand by two men, van Dantzig and Helmut Ruhemann who, though they were controversial figures in their own different ways, had more expertise and greater influence in the art world than any earlier supporters of Andrée and Jacqueline Hahn's painting.

CHAPTER 9

True or False in Art

The trial of Otto Wacker in Berlin in 1932 for trying to sell a large number of van Gogh fakes and of Han van Meegeren in 1947 for faking Vermeers, paintings whose authenticity continued to vex art historians, created, I have argued, something of a crisis of connoisseurship, one that powerfully affected public perceptions about the weakness of prevailing modes of attribution and which also troubled some within the art world itself. However, these cases also had a more direct effect on the fate of the Hahn *La Belle Ferronnière* because they involved two figures, the German conservator Helmut Ruhemann and his protégé, the Dutch connoisseur Maurits van Dantzig, exciting in them a life-long interest in fakes and copies, in the nature of attribution and in the pursuit of a more certain means of identifying pictures. Drawn into the affair of the American Leonardo, they both came to see the Hahn painting as a means to further their views about art connoisseurship.

Van Dantzig and Ruhemann were what Thomas Hoving, the former director of New York's Metropolitan Museum, has called 'fakebusters', men involved not just in detecting forgeries, but in exposing forgers' tricks to a larger public through van Dantzig's major international exhibition, *True or False in Art*. Between the late 1950s and their deaths (van Dantzig in 1960 and Ruhemann in 1973), the two men worked tirelessly on *La Belle*, which was deposited first in Amsterdam, and then in a vault in Coutts Bank, round the corner from London's National Gallery. The men's interest in the picture was quite different from that of the Hahns and of the dealers and businessmen to whom they had offered sale options. Van Dantzig and Ruhemann, as they constantly reiterated, had no commercial interest in the picture. Their concern was exclusively professional – about vindicating their own methods of connoisseurship and persuading other art experts to change their mind.

Ruhemann and van Dantzig had much in common, though the former was twelve years older than his pupil. Both were born into prosperous Jewish families whose members loved the arts. Ruhemann's father was the head of an American insurance company based in Berlin; van Dantzig's family ran a bank in Rotterdam. Both young men had ambitions to become artists. 'As far back as I can remember', Helmut Ruhemann wrote in a brief autobiographical sketch in his *The Cleaning of Pictures*, 'everybody at home and at school seemed to take it for granted that I was to become a painter.' He studied art in Karlsruhe, Munich and Paris, and spent the First World War in Spain, with fellow artist Martin Bloch, in part supported by a bursary from the Berlin art dealer, Paul Cassirer. In Madrid, he began to copy Old Masters in the Prado and study their techniques, making his 'first attempts' at restoring pictures. Back in Germany after the war, Ruhemann wanted to make his living as a portraitist, but a combination of postwar hyper-inflation and his own ineptitude (everyone I have talked to has commented on how hopeless he was with money) forced him into the restoration business. A dealer friend asked him to work on a picture and then produced a Rubens. He completed the work, but the enormity of the task led to his collapse from nervous exhaustion. However, when he recovered there was, as he himself said, 'no turning back'. At first he worked as a restorer for major dealers and collectors. By all accounts he was brilliant at retouching and in-painting, and soon he had a large clientele. In 1929 he began work at the prestigious Kaiser Friedrich Museum; six months later he was made head of conservation.

Van Dantzig's career began more slowly. For many years he worked with his brothers running the family bank, but at twenty-six and to 'the great astonishment of his family', he quit business, cut a deal with the family which gave him 6 per cent of the bank's profits and embarked on his studies as a painter, first in The Hague and then, because of his interest in the techniques of the medieval and Renaissance masters, in Berlin. When he returned to Amsterdam in 1933, van Dantzig became a member of the 'De Brug' society of painters and exhibited his work at the Stedelijk Museum. Though he always thought of Ruhemann as his teacher and mentor, he never really practised as a restorer or conservator, devoting himself first to painting, and then to connoisseurship and criticism.

In 1931 Ruhemann and van Dantzig travelled together to the Netherlands to carry out research into the work of Vincent van Gogh. Ruhemann was working as an expert witness in the trial of Otto Wacker for passing off more than thirty fake van Goghs. The Wacker trial sparked in Ruhemann a life-long interest in the question of fakes and forgeries, but for van Dantzig it marked something more. The young Dutchman was shocked and appalled by the proceedings of the Wacker case. He felt it was blatantly obvious that the daubs that Wacker had foisted on the experts and that had proudly hung in the most fashionable Berlin galleries were fakes. As he wrote later in the draft of a manuscript describing his theory of pictology:

> these paintings appeared so badly done and so much like the other Wacker pictures, that I really was astounded to see people in their favour, and I then understood how easy it is to get under the suggestive spell of the pictures, of a name, or the place it is shown, a spell that hampers our feelings and our brains, and that troubles our judgement for years.

Van Dantzig became convinced that connoisseurship, the question of attribution, had to become more certain, objective and scientific. The evaluation of art, if it were not to remain riddled with fraud, had to become more rigorous. This was the cause to which the serious young Dutchman was to devote much of the rest of his life. Even as he lay dying some thirty-seven years later, he was still hard at work, dictating in a whisper an article on the authenticity of works by Georges Braque and Pablo Picasso.

The political events of the 1930s and 1940s kept Ruhemann and van Dantzig apart. Ruhemann loved his job at the Kaiser Friedrich Museum and looked back on it as the most fulfilling and exciting time in his career. Certainly, he was an incredibly active head of restoration. He worked closely with the museum's director, Max Friedländer, on such projects as the detection of forgeries; he collaborated with firms like Siemens and IG Farben to develop new methods of restoration; he invented new tools of the restorer's craft; he experimented on new synthetic varnishes; and he tried to formalize restorers' training and education. However, Ruhemann was Jewish and by 1933 it was clear that he would be dismissed from the museum and deprived of his rights as a German civil servant. Fortunately, he had befriended a young Englishman, Philip Hendy, whom he had met in 1931 when Hendy had brought a disputed painting from the Museum of Fine Arts in Boston, where he was a curator, to be cleaned and examined by Friedländer. The painting, now known to be Rogier van der Weyden's *Saint Luke Drawing the Virgin*, was beautifully restored by Ruhemann, and, when Hendy took the newly attributed picture back to Boston, the two men remained in contact. Two years later Hendy, now back in Britain, helped orchestrate Ruhemann's flight from Germany. Together with W.G. Constable, the head of the Courtauld Institute, and Kenneth Clark, the director of the National Gallery, he helped set up Ruhemann's new life in London, where he began a long career as a lecturer teaching at the newly founded Courtauld and working as consultant restorer at the National Gallery where he was de facto head of restoration until 1972, the year before his death. Hendy and Ruhemann remained life-long friends and worked closely together when Hendy succeeded Clark as head of the National Gallery in 1946.

While Ruhemann began a new life in London, van Dantzig had returned to Amsterdam, where he continued to paint while beginning a new career as an art critic and connoisseur, writing regularly in art magazines and newspapers. In 1936 he published his first book, *Pictorial Art, Hackwork, Fakes*, and in the following year he achieved fame (if not notoriety) for his criticism of a Frans Hals exhibition in Haarlem in which he identified a large number of the pictures as doubtful or palpable fakes. (Attacking a major exhibition's attributions was one way in which connoisseurs made their reputation. Bernard Berenson's scathing critique of the Italian Old Masters show in London in 1894 first brought him to the attention of the art world.) The war and German occupation of the Netherlands put a stop to van Dantzig's public career: he was banned both from publishing and exhibiting his work. He turned to the private study of psychology and graphology while secretly working for the Dutch resistance, using his skills to fake documents and identity papers. (At one point, in homage to the Netherlands' greatest painter, he created an entire new identity for his family, in which the van Dantzigs of Amsterdam became the van Rijns of Blaricum.)

When van Dantzig returned to his work as an art critic after the war, he quickly became embroiled in the van Meegeren affair. As we have seen, van Dantzig featured prominently in the publicity surrounding the scandal, being singled out by Irving Wallace in his much syndicated story, 'The Man who swindled Goering', published in the *Saturday Evening Post*. The exposure of the inadequacies of the experts in the case was all grist to Mau van Dantzig's mill. As early as 1939 he had pointed out in a talk at the University of Amsterdam that van Meegeren's masterpiece was a fake and he reiterated that view in articles he published at the end of the war. His book on the van Meegeren case (*Johannes Vermeer, De 'Emmausgangers' en de Critici*), published in 1947, was a devastating indictment of the art-historical establishment. Only one chapter deals with the painting itself. The rest of the book is devoted to a painstaking analysis of the errors and confusions perpetrated by critics and experts in the Netherlands, France, Britain and Germany. For van Dantzig the widespread critical acceptance of van Meegeren's famous 'Vermeer' of *Die Emmausgangers* (*The*

Disciples at Emmaus) by art 'experts' was symptomatic of what was wrong with the entire practice of art attribution. He wrote:

> The admiration that was common amongst the critics is a symptom of the imperfection of understanding on which the experts base their judgement of a piece of art; moreover, it's a symptom of the impurity of our judgement of art in general. However, the admiration for the 'Emmausgoers' is merely a symptom ... Recently a lot of notorious trials about forgeries went public. The Frans Hals' forgeries prove that the entire terrain of painted art is littered with irregularities, to say nothing about modern art.

Van Dantzig mocked the credulity of the experts, calling them 'shallow enthusiasts', and excoriated them for their lack of evidence, facts and rigour. The contrast with Paul Coremans' treatment of the case in his *Van Meegeren's Faked Vermeers and de Hooghs*, which appeared in the same year, could not be more pronounced. It would have been easy for Coremans, whose scientific analysis of the pictures proved them fakes, to gloat over the errors of the connoisseurs who had authenticated van Meegeren's pictures. Instead, he went out of his way to absolve them. Discussing the discovery of *The Disciples at Emmaus* and subsequent forgeries, he concluded, 'once the *Disciples* was admitted to be an authentic Vermeer it was quite logical that the other paintings, although of lesser and decreasing quality, should also be incorporated amongst Vermeer's works, especially as they possessed, in varying degree, similar characteristics. In these circumstances, surely no blame can be attached to the Dutch specialists.'

Van Dantzig was never so diplomatic. Of course, he had long been at odds with what he saw as the cosy and corrupt world of art historians and art experts. His essay on Frans Hals had been the first salvo in what was to be a life-long barrage of criticism against the sloppy and unsystematic speculations and attributions by members of the art establishment. His book on the *Disciples of Emmaus*, his articles in 1954 claiming that a large number of the newly acquired Rubens drawings at the Museum Boijmans Van Beuningen – the most important postwar find of new Rubens materials in the Netherlands – were doubtful or outright fakes, his book on van Gogh and his unpublished work on Leonardo were all intended as direct public challenges to art-historical orthodoxy. To his admirers he was a crusader, 'a living conscience' pursuing what the *Vrye Volk* newspaper called his 'unblemished urge for the truth regardless of rank and person'; to his detractors, many of whom were art historians and museum curators, he was paranoid, seeing 'ghosts on a clear day', 'tilting at windmills', 'an iconoclast' and 'a charlatan' who irresponsibly took pleasure in parading questions of attribution that should be confined to the charmed circle of experts in newspapers and magazines before a general public. Even his apologists in *Vrye Volk* admitted that he 'gave the impression that he truly liked to tarnish reputations' and that his belief that 'not only the malpractice of art dealers and the people who falsify paintings is below any standard, but that the blind aesthetic views of art historians and critics also revealed a moral inadequacy', made him 'a very difficult person'. Of course, the art historians fought back. When van Dantzig applied to the Prince Bernhart Foundation in 1949 for a grant to publish a much expanded version of his study of Frans Hals, a huge tome of 562 pages with more than 334 illustrations, it was condemned by Henri van de Waal, an expert in Dutch iconology and the head of the Print Cabinet in Leiden, for trying 'to prove the common opinion of art historians is incorrect, in a highly aggressive manner'. The proposal was rejected because van Dantzig was 'not respectful to official art historical knowledge'.

However, outside the world of the art dealer and museum van Dantzig had his admirers. He wrote regularly for *Vrye Volk*, a reputable Amsterdam newspaper which often endorsed his judgements and admired the way in which he challenged received opinions. He was asked for attributions in Germany, the Netherlands and Switzerland, working for art dealers and even, at one point, for the Thyssen family. He also ran a successful business, using graphology and psychological testing to vet potential employees in businesses in Europe and the United States. However, what particularly irked his critics were the large claims he made for what he called 'pictology' as a method of scientific attribution and aesthetic discrimination. As one of his obituaries pointed out, 'he was an art connoisseur with his own and passionately defended method of looking at and judging pictures', which grew into a new science he called pictology. 'This fact itself was enough to make most art dealers and critics call him a charlatan.'

Van Dantzig's pictology started from the not uncommon premise that a great work of art was the distinctive creation of its maker. In its totality a picture bore the characteristics of the artist who painted it. These features were not matters of style but rather distinctive personal attributes which were an expression of an artist's feelings and personality, rather as handwriting was seen as a sign of individuality in graphology. Van Dantzig's method depended upon the systematic accumulation of these features of an artist. The examination of a large number of works taken as more or less indisputably by a particular master was used to build up a profile of his characteristics. In the case of Leonardo, for example, van Dantzig identified more than seventy pictorial elements. These ranged from the particular ways of rendering line, space and light to materials and painting techniques.

The identification of pictorial elements was both a means towards accurate attribution and a way of making aesthetic discriminations. Van Dantzig assumed that the works of great masters were an expression of their entire personality and that they were marked by a totality, spontaneity and boldness that were absent in copies and fakes. As described in his book on pictology, the latter were inevitably the expression of two sets of principles 'those of the painter himself – he cannot eliminate himself – and those (supposedly) of the master he is copying or imitating. These pictures show a mixture of characteristics of the painter and those of the painter he was copying, mostly in a mutilated form'. The simulacrum lacked coherence and also betrayed a kind of meticulousness that was the inevitable consequence of the imitation.

These views, it is fair to say, are pretty mainstream, not unlike many comments of the period on the difference between a masterpiece and a copy, and embody many of the assumptions about the way in which fakes were executed, but a number of features of van Dantzig's method excited the hostility of art historians and other connoisseurs. First and foremost, they disliked what they saw as the extremely mechanical way in which he used his list of pictorial elements. He argued that the presence or absence of these features should be aggregated. If more than 75 per cent were present the work could securely be attributed to the master; 50–75 per cent made the picture problematic; less than that made it clear that the work under consideration was not genuine. Such an approach seemed to give all characteristics equal weight. And, as several commentators pointed out, it did not seem to allow for change and development in an artist, so that his work differed at different times in his career. More tellingly, in its plodding aggregation it appeared the very opposite of a critical judgement that depended on a powerful general impression of the picture as a whole – the first *aperçu* beloved of traditional connoisseurs. It seemed to make the appreciation of beauty a matter of working through a check-list of features. Moreover, van Dantzig's democratic claim that his method could be used by anyone – any layman visiting an exhibit or viewing a picture – went against a notion of expertise as some-thing that was painstakingly accumulated over many years and depended on the trained eye.

The debate about van Dantzig and his method is redolent of the discussion surrounding Giovanni Morelli's 'scientific' connoisseur-ship. Both men claimed to transform connoisseurship into a science, were extremely disparaging about traditional art 'experts', seemed to hold out the possibility of a more publicly accessible method of attribution and were criticized for adopting a mechanical approach. Contemporaries described Morelli as a natural precursor of van Dantzig, though the Dutchman does not seem to have acknowl-edged any connection. What is striking, however, is that both Morelli and van Dantzig claimed to be scientizing art attribution at times when it seemed as if scientific method would help unlock the secrets of social life. Whereas Morelli's method connected to the conjec-tural sciences and forensics of the late nineteenth century, van

Dantzig drew quite explicitly on work in social psychology and graphology, including his own and others' research at the University of Amsterdam. At the time there were great expectations that new methods used for psychological profiling (like those of van Dantzig in his business evaluating company employees) would permit the accurate analysis of states of mind and human feeling, making it possible to build up a distinct picture of an individual's psyche. The application of such approaches to works of art promised to lend 'scientific' precision to the task of locating the exact 'profile' of the artist.

Van Dantzig always recognized that the appreciation and enjoyment of art involved an emotional response to a work as a totality. However, he was determined to find a more objective, scientific way of understanding this response that would help avoid the sort of collusion and collective delusion he believed he had observed among art connoisseurs and which he saw as so perfectly embodied in the van Meegeren affair. He did not help his cause, though, by setting up nearly every debate in which he engaged as a Manichean struggle between himself and a benighted art-historical profession. The American painter and museum director, Thomas Buechner, who studied with van Dantzig in the 1940s and remained one of his most loyal followers, wrote as follows about the draft of an article van Dantzig sent him in 1954:

> It starts out about art in general and soon becomes an attack on forgers, art historians, scientists and abstractionists. The negative aspects are emphasized at great length, and often with keen sequential logic, the positive aspects are brief and sandwiched between the text. You go into great detail about the art situation

today, rightfully blaming the misleading authorities and snobbish collectors. I think this is a mistake. By so doing you put
yourself in the class you criticize. You are trying to pick a fight
to show how weak your adversaries are. You are forcing the
intelligent bystander to choose between you and everyone else
in the art world.

This was typical. Van Dantzig found it difficult to understand why
he managed to alienate so many art historians. In 1954 he tried
to get one of his long-time opponents, Arthur van Schendel, to
explain why he kept ignoring him. Van Dantzig had often criticized van Schendel's judgement but, as he explained to him, he did
not dislike him, only his opinions. Van Schendel was at a loss for
a reply. Three years later van Dantzig was to alienate one of the
few major figures in the art world who supported him, Willem
Sandberg, the director of the Stedelijk Museum, by attacking the
abstract art his friend so admired because he believed it to have
no aesthetic value. Sandberg patiently tolerated van Dantzig's criticisms until he finally could take no more. In November 1957 he
exploded: 'I have the impression that, apart from a radio and a
car, you are not at home in our modern days, just like the paintings you are studying,' He castigated van Dantzig's negative attitude and attacks on abstract art; he even told him that he regretted
giving him a special pass to the Stedelijk Museum. For once, van
Dantzig was shocked and mortified. Writing in a script that did
not need a graphologist to see his agitation, he told Sandberg:

We have known each other for twenty-five years. We went through
the war together in which we could count on each other. Nothing

ever happened until now. I lived in the steady conviction that our relationship was rock steady and could never be tarnished. Probably you think this is naive, but that's the reason your attitude gives me so much grief. I know I have lost a friendship that is very dear to me.

The loss of Sandberg's support was a bitter blow. For more than four years he and van Dantzig had been talking about setting up a foundation for the study of pictology and together they had mounted the exhibition, first shown in the Stedelijk Museum, entitled *True or False*. This exhibition subsequently toured much of Europe and the United States in the years between 1952 and 1954, and made van Dantzig's reputation outside the Netherlands.

The tensions between Sandberg and Van Dantzig were already apparent over the content and presentation of *True or False*. To van Dantzig and his American protégé, Thomas Buechner, who had become the director of the Corning Glass Museum in upstate New York, the exhibition was intended as a showcase for pictology. For Sandberg it was a general analysis of the different ways in which fakes could be exposed. In his introduction to the catalogue that accompanied the exhibit, he emphasized how important collaboration across fields had become in the detection of fakes. 'Several sciences,' he wrote, 'have devoted themselves to this problem of recognizing new ways to recognize the genuine. Physical and chemical methods have been refined, pictology has joined iconography and art history, and the ever-growing number of "oeuvre catalogues" facilitates the study of the pedigree' of pictures. However, in the American edition of the catalogue, Buechner introduced the exhibit as 'a new approach, by a prominent authority, to this important subject'. Though the catalogue essay by van Dantzig concluded with a propitiatory gesture towards scientific means for detecting frauds and conceded that 'We are indebted to the art historians for almost everything we know about art and, in fact, for the preservation and formation of the world's great collections', the bulk of the text comprised a detailed exposition of the main principles and methods of pictology. This was not what Sandberg had wanted. He had told Buechner that if he and van Dantzig planned to make the exhibition a 'platform' for pictology, then they would have to do it on their own. He made it very clear that he preferred the show to be more general, 'like the original in Amsterdam'. However, Buechner worked tirelessly to promote the exhibition as an exposition of pictology, and managed to interest not just the Corning Museum, but the Toledo Museum of Art, the Boston Museum of Fine Arts, the San Francisco Museum of Art and the Brooklyn Museum. When the Brooklyn Museum dropped out, he was able to have the show exhibited at Wildenstein's New York Galleries, sponsored by the Menninger Foundation.

The response to *True or False* was predictable. Both *Art News* and the art critic of the *New York Herald Tribune* dismissed van Dantzig and his theories. The *Tribune* wrote that 'Mr. Van Dantzig's theories, expanded in charts and diagrams, are so arbitrary, so mechanical, so patently absurd, that when they manage to be intelligible at all, they are highly shocking as the work of a serious scholar.' But the public reaction was altogether different. On 24 January 1954, van Dantzig appeared on the CBS syndicated program *Omnibus* to discuss the exhibit and explain his theories. The show was an enormous success and van Dantzig was inundated with requests from viewers from all over the United States that he expertize their works of art. It was probably at this time that the Hahns first became aware of him as an art 'expert'.

The following year van Dantzig began work on a new project on Leonardo. In the summer of 1955 he spent some time examining the Louvre Leonardos in Paris and, after reading Harry Hahn's book, *The Rape of La Belle*, told Tom Buechner that he was almost certain that the Paris *La Belle* was not a genuine Leonardo. Before the end of the year the *Kansas City Star* reported on van Dantzig's views about the Louvre picture. By that time he had already been approached by Robert Kellerman, a psychologist in Utrecht whose uncle, D. Kellerman, an *expert des tableaux* in Nice, a man of Hungarian origin who spoke English, French and German, had been given an option to sell the picture by Andrée. As we have seen, at the same time van Dantzig was contacted by Frank Glenn who wanted him to help sell the picture.

Van Dantzig did not at first realize that he was caught up in a family squabble. Andrée was trying to sell the picture on her own; Harry was trying to get her to deal through Frank Glenn. Van Dantzig was not interested in family matters, but was eager to expertize the picture, though this was not easy. As Robert Kellerman explained to him in a letter, 'As I understand it Mrs. Hahn only wants to see money and as soon as possible, and she is hardly interested in any expert investigation, especially when this costs money.' His uncle, he observed, had just lost a potential buyer in part because he lacked adequate documentation in Nice to authenticate the picture. 'I believe he suppressed the fact that expertised judgement has to be done. Even if he was convinced of this fact Mrs. Hahn is in dire need of money and my uncle is in dire need of time.' Glenn was no more accommodating. He rather patronizingly told van Dantzig that his views on the Louvre *La Belle* were probably drawn from Harry's book, added that Harry had lots more new information, but then tried to recruit van Dantzig as a vendor:

> Because this painting should come to an eventual home in some great museum or in the collection of some worldwide collector, I am sure that you would be better fitted then most to arrange for the sale of the painting, if an interested buyer presents himself. I am in touch with Mr. Hahn and his daughter and could furnish you with such information and aid as you desire towards an eventual disposition of the picture. In any event I should be glad to hear from you as I value your opinion very highly.

Van Dantzig made clear that he was not going to be involved in any dealings with the painting unless he was allowed to examine it: 'Not having seen the picture itself I am not responsible for any opinion concerning that painting ... If someone wants a judgement I have to see the painting. The photographs sent to me appear to lack the information I want for sufficient argumentation.'

Over the next year, van Dantzig and Glenn courted one another. Glenn offered to publish van Dantzig's book on van Gogh in America, and in the summer of 1956 he visited Holland and met Mau van Dantzig and his family. However, the Dutchman was only one of several irons in the fire. It was during that same summer that, as discussed, John Carter, the representative of Sotheby's, flew out to Kansas City to view the picture and seemed enthusiastic about a London sale. But then Glenn received the bad news. As he told van Dantzig:

Sir Kenneth Clark whom, as you know, we had hoped to assist us in getting to show La Belle Ferronnière in London ... is now perfectly convinced that the Louvre picture is a genuine Leonardo. Since, in addition to this inconvenient conviction, on the basis of photographs, [he believes] that the Hahn picture is not even from the Leonardo studio, I am afraid that we have come to a dead end for the time being.

Sotheby's dropped the Hahn picture like a hot potato. For Glenn it was further proof 'that the art racket is as strong as ever.'

The news of Clark's views piqued van Dantzig's interest, but he persisted in pressing Glenn for the painting. 'Of course the art racket goes on and on,' he wrote to Glenn, but:

I have not yet seen the picture itself. You will remember you promised to send it to me, for without that I cannot examine and judge the picture itself. I can only compare photos and I gave you the outcome of my preliminary investigation. It showed how the Hahn painting is better than the Louvre. The Louvre is not genuine, of that I am certain about for I examined it in the Louvre. But I can't possibly say whether the Hahn is an original or a good copy as long as I have not the possibility of close inspection. If it is badly damaged or too much restored it is even possible that I will never come to any certainty at all. I would love to have the picture for one or two months with me for a most detailed description.

He then went on to outline his plans for an ambitious pictolog-ical analysis of Leonardo's work in which, if he thought it genuine, the Hahn portrait would play a major role. As he made clear to Glenn, van Dantzig wanted to recruit Leonardo on his side in his struggle with the art historians. His plans grew more and more ambitious. He asked Glenn:

> I wonder whether it would be possible to start a big, interna-
> tional action, asking the foremost experts how they form their
> opinion on pictures, such in view of the many pictures hanging
> in public and private collections on wrong names that were
> accepted on mere feelings or art historical guess work. Whether
> it is their feelings that they have to go on, or what they intend
> to do to clarify artistic attribution; also Berenson and Kenneth
> Clark could be asked, and the possible positive answer could be
> applied to the Hahn picture.

Typically, he thought the results of such an investigation could be published not just in professional journals but also made available to a larger public in magazines such as *Life*. Perhaps, he mused, the *Kansas City Star* would be interested in funding such a project?

Glenn then met several times with the *Kansas City Star* corre-spondent whose articles had prompted his negotiation with van Dantzig, but nothing was promised other than a continued deter-mination to break 'this art racket'. Glenn was particularly incensed by Kenneth Clark's remarks to a representative of Sotheby's:

> What disturbs me more than anything else is the intellectual dishon-
> esty that prevails in the racket. AND WHY? Why do they not try
> to be honest? Why will they of all people pass off on the public
> pictures if they knew what they doing were fakes, near-fakes, copies

and forgeries? The obvious answer is they do not know but assume a knowledge where there is no knowledge.

Given Clark and Berenson's opinions, would it be possible, he asked van Dantzig, to sell the painting in a reasonable period of time? How much weight would van Dantzig's and Coremans' opinion carry in the art world? Glenn ended his letter with a characteristically sententious declaration: 'I have been dedicated to this fight since 1933 and probably always will be. It has not profited me one penny. On the contrary it has cost me considerable. But God willing I will stay in it, until there is some honesty in the art world.'

In September 1956 van Dantzig responded to Glenn's queries. His reply betrays the sort of assertive self-aggrandizement to which he was all too prone:

In my opinion, the influence of Berenson and Kenneth Clark can be turned down to almost nothing if I could interest other people. They could be found in several European museums and research institutions e.g. Coremans in Belgium, others from Zurich, Stuttgart and Rome. I would start with my closest friends and with their help get others, even the Louvre and the London National Gallery.

However, as he explained to Glenn, it was essential that these people were not commercially involved in the Hahn *La Belle*:

These people always have one big and important condition: NO PUBLICATION BEFORE AND DURING THE RESEARCH;

afterwards only with their consent. They are purely scientifically interested and they refuse to work when the object is offered for sale during or just before the time of their research. They stand or fall with their reputation and they can't afford anything being published but by themselves or with their approbation.

The task of engaging them would be difficult, but he could accomplish it: 'I am certain that my friends would work with and for me, but I am certain in this particular case, with so much already published, they would not accept the commission from anyone else.' He told Glenn that he would need the painting for a year (including six months for scientific analysis) and that he would not accept the picture unless it was fully insured.

More than two months later, van Dantzig had heard nothing from Glenn and wrote a querulous letter to him accusing him of not fulfilling any of his promises. He had not published the van Gogh book and he had not sent the picture. Perhaps Mrs Dupas (the remarried Andrée Hahn) had lost faith in her picture? As van Dantzig shrewdly commented:

I think Mrs. Dupas can't take a decision to take the risk of a refusal on my part or on the part of the other specialists. There must be some doubts in the back of her mind otherwise she would risk it when she'd seen the list I gave to you. I mean her attitude shows that she herself is less than certain of the picture than she consciously knows.

In fact, though van Dantzig did not know this, Glenn was conducting this negotiation with him without Andrée's knowledge and without being in possession of the picture, which had been returned to Los Angeles from Kansas. When Glenn finally did contact Andrée, he was shocked to be told that she was already in contact with van Dantzig. 'I do not recall you're ever having mentioned to me you're having any direct contact with her,' he wrote, somewhat accusingly, adding for good measure, 'She is most difficult to deal with'. In fact van Dantzig had not had any direct dealings with Andrée, only with her agent, Kellerman and his nephew in Utrecht, and he continued to treat Glenn as if he were privy to her intentions. After a trip to London in January 1957 to examine the Leonardos in the National Gallery, van Dantzig wrote to Glenn asking if he knew what Andrée wished to do. He also sent a copy of the pages on *La Belle* in the most recent edition of Kenneth Clark's book on Leonardo, commenting on the changing views of art historians in general and of Clark in particular.

Van Dantzig was pointing out to Glenn how Clark had shifted his ground on *La Belle Ferronnière*. In the 1939 and 1952 editions of his *Leonardo da Vinci: An Account of his Development as an Artist* he attributed the Louvre version of the picture to Boltraffio. Speaking of Leonardo's protégé, he writes, 'It is reasonable to suppose that Leonardo, occupied in multifarious commissions for the Sforzas [dukes of Milan], allowed this promising youth to complete work from his designs, and that under his guidance the pupil achieved a delicacy absent from his later, independent work.' He goes on to say, 'Some such hypothesis seems to me necessary if we are to explain the authorship of the portrait in the Louvre, known as La Belle Ferronière.' He then cites his teacher Berenson's view that 'one would regret to have to accept this as Leonardo's own work', and criticizes its 'commonplace pose' and 'insensitive drawing', while conceding that the ribbons on *La Belle*'s shoulder seem 'close to Leonardo' and that the face is beautifully modelled. Clark concludes, 'No one who prefers truth to finality should be dogmatic about La Belle Ferronière, but for the time being I am inclined to think that the picture is by Boltraffio, working in Leonardo's studio and under his guidance.' But in the 1958 edition of the book, Clark makes a number of changes that are not, like his revisions of his views on *The Virgin of the Rocks,* pointed out to the reader. Much of the text remains the same – the discussion of Boltraffio, the citation of Berenson, the analysis of the picture – but Clark distances himself from the hypothesis he once embraced, saying only that it 'has been used' rather than 'seems to me necessary' to explain the authorship of the picture, which he now praises more fully – 'the face, too, has great beauty of modelling, easily appreciated when the numerous copies of the Louvre picture are compared with the original, and photographic enlargements of her features show the extraordinary knowledge of structure with which they are drawn'. He concludes 'I am now inclined to think the picture is by Leonardo, and shows how in these years he was willing to subdue his genius to the needs of the court'. What made Clark change his mind? We do not know, but perhaps his acquaintance with the photographs of the Hahn *La Belle* in 1956 and his knowledge that the picture was on the market led to his re-evaluation. If so, it would not be the first time that the Hahn picture had led an expert to change his mind about the painter of the Louvre *La Belle.*

While van Dantzig and Glenn swapped derogatory remarks about Clark, Andrée took matters into her own hands. She decided to bring the picture to Europe herself. As Robert Kellerman wrote to van Dantzig, 'Apparently Mrs. Dupas finally realized that the knowledge of connoisseurs is crucial for the sale of her painting. Her personal arrival in the Netherlands is most probably motivated by financial desires and to close this business once and for all – at least that is what we think.' Van Dantzig was delighted, telling Kellerman that he was 'very anxious how this riddle will develop'. He even thought of visiting the elder Kellerman in Nice before the picture arrived.

In May 1957 Andrée and Jacqueline travelled from Los Angeles to New York to sail to Europe, accompanied by *La Belle* in her special packing case. They boarded the *New Amsterdam* and set sail for Rotterdam. They were two of the more than a million passengers who crossed the Atlantic that year, at the end of the postwar boom in transatlantic oceanic traffic before its eclipse by the jet planes that were to transform travel between the United States and Europe. The great ocean liners were by-words of the sort of luxury that Andrée enjoyed. The *New Amsterdam* was a smart vessel with its dark hull, white trim and orange and black funnels, but it was half the size of the great oceanic liners like the *Normandie*, the *Queen Mary* and the *Queen Elizabeth*, and it lacked their flamboyant opulence. Andrée and Jacqueline needed to be frugal. Andrée probably chose the flagship of the Holland-America Line because it was one of the first ships to include two rather three classes for passengers and to offer amenities in tourist class that were not far behind those for the Holland-America's richest clients. She was no longer in a position to travel first class, but she wanted her creature comforts. For Jacqueline the surroundings were a stark contrast to her last transatlantic voyage sixteen years earlier, when she had sailed from Lisbon to New York in a refugee ship, sharing a small, ill-lit cabin well below the water line with her beloved dog and other fugitives from the Nazis.

On 18 May the *New Amsterdam* docked in Rotterdam and Andrée and Jacqueline took the train to Amsterdam, arriving the same day at van Dantzig's house on Richard Wagnerstraat. Three days later he deposited the Hahn *La Belle* in an Amsterdam Bank. Andrée and Jacqueline remained in Amsterdam until 25 May, when they travelled on to France. The visit seems to have been a success. Van Dantzig promised to write a book about the picture and agreed not to have dealings with Glenn or any representative of Harry Hahn (Andrée was extremely nervous about his possible interference), while Andrée came to feel that at last she had found the man who would see that her picture was finally sold. A few months later she sent van Dantzig a florid letter expressing her thanks. (She wrote, as she usually did when expressing strong emotions, in French; for her, English was the language of business.) At last, she said:

> my dream is realized. I knew that one day I would find a person who for love and knowledge of art, complemented by an absolute honesty, would come to range themselves on the side of truth and not that of money and lying like the majority of men who are taken up in this affair ... men void of all honesty, honour and *amour propre*. I am happy now. I never lost hope that the truth would triumph. I have exerted a great deal of patience ... I have so much confidence in my picture and its provenance.

Van Dantzig was soon working away on the picture and on Leonardo more generally. He was in London in June 1957 examining the

National Gallery version of *The Virgin of the Rocks*, and in September he showed the Hahn *La Belle* to David Röell, the outgoing director of the Rijksmuseum, whom he described to Andrée as 'most impressed' by the picture. However, he also warned her that getting support for the picture would take time. 'Museum people usually are slow,' he told her, adding, 'and I fear I will have to fight, especially in Paris.'

By the following spring Andrée was fretting about the slow progress van Dantzig was making. It was more than a year since her trip to the Netherlands, she pointed out, what was happening about her picture and about his promised book? Van Dantzig sought to reassure her, but the only good news he had was that the book on Leonardo was finished, although it had yet to be translated from Dutch into English. He was also having terrible problems obtaining good reproductions of the Leonardos in the Louvre. He felt the authorities there, especially Germain Bazin, the chief curator at the Louvre, whom he described as an 'old enemy', were being obstructive.

At this point van Dantzig turned for help to his old teacher and friend, Helmut Ruhemann. He knew he was an expert on fakes and that he was as independently minded as it was possible to be. If he could be convinced of the authenticity of the Hahn Leonardo, he would win over a powerful ally who would also help him win support in other museums and countries. The two men had remained friends since their days together in Berlin. They had lost contact during the war, when van Dantzig was in hiding and Ruhemann was busy restoring pictures from the National Gallery's collections when they were in safe storage. After the war they were soon back in contact. Helmut Ruhemann's son, Frank, has fond memories of the van Dantzig family visiting London and of the closeness of the two men. Ruhemann visited van Dantzig in Amsterdam at least twice in the years immediately after the war. On one occasion they spent an afternoon together in the Rijksmuseum debating the authenticity of its latest acquisitions. On another visit, Ruhemann reported to his boss Hendy, 'Mr. Van Dantzig expounded to me his most interesting method of applying graphology to style criticism.' In 1952 Doortje, van Dantzig's daughter, moved to London and lived with the Ruhemanns in St John's Wood while she trained under Helmut's instruction to be a restorer. When van Dantzig organized his *True or False* exhibition of fakes that toured Europe and the United States in 1953–4, Ruhemann, who had a collection of forgeries he used for teaching purposes, lent a number of objects for the show, including an Italian School *Adoration of the Magi*, and two versions of the *Virgin and Child* by imitators of the fourteenth-century Sienese fresco and panel painter, Lippo Vanni.

Van Dantzig had asked Helmut Ruhemann to come to Amsterdam specially to see the Hahn picture and to hear his critical evaluation of it. When Ruhemann accepted his invitation in 1958, van Dantzig sent a jubilant yet agitated letter to his mentor. 'Hurray!' he wrote, before urging his friend to come as soon as possible, as he feared the Hahns might want their picture back. After more than a year of research, van Dantzig was ready to make his case to the man who he respected, perhaps more than any other, in the art world. Using his 'pictology', van Dantzig had already identified more than seventy characteristics of Leonardo's work. He had then constructed a checklist of these or their absence in both the Louvre and Hahn paintings. The Hahn picture had come out well ahead, though the Louvre picture also included many features typical of the master. At first, Ruhemann was deeply sceptical, both about the picture and the plan to write a book on Leonardo, but van Dantzig was determined to convince his former teacher – in some ways an even greater challenge for him that persuading the Dutch art-historical establishment. Ruhemann, for his part, was deeply committed to the principle that the good art historian should always remain open-minded. He listened with patience and looked with care. After twelve hours of deliberation, he announced himself convinced. He wasn't certain that the painting was a Leonardo, but he was sure that it was an older picture than the version in the Louvre which he concluded was a copy of the Hahn *La Belle*.

Back in London a few days later, Ruhemann wrote to Mau van Dantzig thanking him 'for the wonderful hospitality and for what you have taught me!' He warned him, however, against placing too much trust in his own methods as opposed to more traditional forms of art connoisseurship – 'don't be like a doctor,' he wrote, 'who fails to apply medicines that help, because he wants to prove that one he invented cures on its own'. (In fact, Ruhemann was never very convinced by van Dantzig's pictology; he endorsed his copy of van Dantzig's pictological analysis of *La Belle* as 'virtually useless'.) However, his former pupil had made a tremendous impression on him and Ruhemann hastened to see Kenneth Clark, the former director of the National Gallery, and the man who had helped him stay in Britain, about the exciting news. The two men had recently been working together on a television programme that Clark was planning called *Do Fakes Matter?* in which they were to discuss the strengths and limitations of scientific evidence in detecting forgery. They met at the Arts Club in London on 20 June 1958. As Ruhemann told van Dantzig in a letter he wrote a few days after the meeting, Clark told him that he had always taken the Louvre picture as a Leonardo, 'though he regarded it as inferior as it was the only real portrait he consented to paint'. He added that he had never seen the Hahn picture or a proper photograph. (Here, of course, Clark was being economical with the truth. He had, as we have seen, not always taken the Louvre *La Belle* to be a Leonardo, indeed, for nearly twenty years he had been on record as attributing it to Boltraffio, and he had seen photographs of the Hahn *La Belle*, when he had given his opinion to Sotheby's in 1956.) Ruhemann responded to Clark by telling him, 'I have seen one and that it is clear that the Louvre version is the copy, it showed definite copyist's mistakes.' Clark, he added, seemed 'shaken'. Ruhemann interpreted Clark's reaction as one of surprise at the news, but it is also possible that Clark was upset by the revival of the old controversy over the Louvre and Hahn pictures which he had helped bury in 1955.

Ruhemann's meeting with Clark in June 1958 was the first of many attempts to gain the former director's support. He turned to him not just as a mentor and friend but also as the most publicly visible Leonardo expert in Britain. Kenneth Clark had catalogued the Leonardo drawings in Windsor Castle and his Leonardo monograph was the most accessible but scholarly work in the English language on the Italian master. As a protégé of Bernard Berenson, Clark was an acknowledged connoisseur of Italian art and as the young, rich and energetic director of the National Gallery between 1933 and 1945, he was a highly visible public figure of great influence. He was also the sole foreigner on the committee that oversaw the French Museums, and he was therefore in a position to help Ruhemann in the delicate negotiations with the Louvre that would have been an inevitable part of the vindication of the Hahns' *La Belle Ferronnière*.

Van Dantzig was delighted with the news about Clark, whom he described as 'gentlemanlike' in his response to the analysis of the Hahn *La Belle*, but he took less kindly to Ruhemann's advice. His methods, he said, were 'objective' and 'scientific'; he was working with a statistics professor who vetted his work, and as long as he approved of his methods he would continue to pursue them. He also told his friend that Arthur van Schendel, the director of the Rijksmuseum, had returned to see the picture and had politely declined to take it, mentioning the many 'difficulties' that surrounded its attribution. Van Dantzig planned to show the picture to the Mauritshuis at The Hague, but thought they would not be interested. He suggested to Ruhemann that the picture go to London to be seen by Hendy, though he was not sure what the owners wanted. By the autumn, van Dantzig had not only talked to van Schendel, but also to David Röell again, who was far more enthusiastic than his successor at the Rijksmuseum and urged van Dantzig to take the painting to Paris. Van Dantzig mulled over this idea, but felt that he needed to find some way to 'leave national feelings out of the game'. He and Röell discussed the possibility of approaching Coremans, head of the Institut Royale du Patrimoine Artistique in Brussels, and a German scholar, Kurt Wehlte. Röell told van Dantzig that 'he did not dare say whether it was a Leonardo or not', but he believed that, if not by the master, then it was probably the work of one of his pupils, possibly Boltraffio. He could not hold out the hope that the picture could be purchased in the

Netherlands, and he estimated that it was worth half a million Dutch guilders (£50,000) if by Boltraffio, but between 5 and 10 million (£500,000 and £1 million) if by Leonardo.

By the autumn of 1958, everyone involved with the American *La Belle* seems to have been optimistic about an imminent sale. D. Kellerman, whose option to sell the picture had just been extended for a year, wrote to van Dantzig of his 'great work' and how everyone was 'waiting to see it crowned with success'. Like Andrée before him, he praised van Dantzig to the skies: 'the nobility of your soul, your zealous enthusiasm, your great work gives us all hope that everything will come out well'. The Dutchman himself must have told Tom Buechner in New York that he was confident of success, for his protégé wrote to him, 'What a genius you are! What an even greater one you'll become with Van Schendel, Roell and Ruhemann mere caryatids supporting your pedestal'. Andrée wrote approving van Dantzig's suggestion that the picture remain in the Netherlands: 'you are the only gentleman who trusted me and my painting, so that gives me the feeling of wishing that your country should become the proud owners of a Leonardo da Vinci'. More prosaically, she explained the financial arrangements in which she was to have $180,000 (£64,300) for the picture – mostly deposited in a Swiss bank account – and that Kellerman was to have 15 per cent of that fee.

In January 1959 van Dantzig wrote to tell Helmut Ruhemann that Coremans, whose report had been so important in the van Meegeren case, planned to come to Amsterdam before the end of the month and that if he liked the Hahns' picture Röell would approach the Louvre. However, he had become more guarded, less optimistic of quick success. He was resigned, he said, to moving forward slowly and would be patient. His forbearance is partly explained by the troubles he was now having getting his book on Leonardo published. He had been negotiating with Meulenhoff in the Netherlands and Doubleday in the United States, but the project was consistently criticized as too expensive because of the number of illustrations and the cost of translation. Röell, like many museum directors, was shy of publicity; perhaps, van Dantzig told Ruhemann, it was for the best if the book appeared after the Hahn painting was sold.

Then van Dantzig's plans were thrown into disarray. He was taken seriously ill. He had, he wrote to Ruhemann, a disease of the blood 'rather serious' though the doctors 'don't give it a name'. He was soon confined to hospital. Yet even in his sickbed he continued to pursue the cause of *La Belle*. He told Andrée that, while in hospital, he had been visited by three experts from major European museums and had managed to convince them of *La Belle*'s authenticity. 'We now have three great Museums on our side!' he wrote gleefully. Yet his health problems persisted. He was advised by his physician to spend time in a warmer climate, and he and his wife Ella flew to Sicily, where they stayed for some months at the Hotel Times in Taormina. There, despite remaining weak and sickly, he planned to set up a small international committee, consisting of figures from five major museums in different countries, to compare the Hahn and Louvre versions of *La Belle*, hoping to outmanoeuvre the Louvre which he rightly identified as the most hostile to the American *La Belle* because of 'nationalist sentiment'.

On 18 January 1960, before he could fulfil his ambitious plans, Mau van Dantzig died. A few days earlier, his wife, Ella, had received a letter from Harry Hahn in Kansas addressed to her husband. Harry had written one of his typically bold and peremptory letters to van Dantzig, telling him he was planning to contest his wife's claim of sole ownership of *La Belle*, and that he wanted to know where the painting was, whether it had yet been sold and who had paid for it to come to Europe. He added, for good measure, that he had heard from Frank Glenn, his publisher, about van Dantzig's work and about his theory of pictology. 'You have, Sir, I am sure,' he wrote rather pompously, 'injected an important facet of scientific appraisal as one of the reliable standards of identification. You have, I am happy to say flashed a brilliant beam into the dark corridors of "subjective guessing".' Ella van Dantzig was too heartbroken to answer Harry's queries. She wrote a brief note saying that life was too short for her to be involved in such quarrels.

However, Ella van Dantzig did not abandon her husband's cause. She wrote to Andrée Dupas and told her that she and her daughter planned to take the picture to London and leave it in the custody of the National Gallery, where it would be examined by the director, Philip Hendy, the curator in Italian art, Martin Davies, and her husband's old friend, Helmut Ruhemann. On 13 May 1960 the two women flew to London with the picture (and without any formal documentation of its importation into Britain). Ella Dantzig explained what happened to a friend: 'We went directly to the National Gallery where Ruhemann was present. In the afternoon we went with Ruhemann to Sir Philip Hendy who looked at the painting and said immediately, "not a Leonardo!"' Ella tried to explain her late husband's theories to Hendy but he waved them aside. Then he proposed that they go in the gallery and compare the Hahn *La Belle* with the painting of *The Madonna of the Rocks*. Ella and her daughter were shocked:

> To our great dismay, Dora [Doortje] and I, we had to confess that La Belle next to a real Leonardo is incomparable. It has been a very disappointing experience . . . but I have to be honest and to tell you that Mau himself never did this test. Sir Philip Hendy lifted the painting next to the Madonna and I have to say that La Belle is much sweeter, less powerful. In the real Leonardo there is much more relief, much more contrast between light and dark. I think this is all very awkward, but I'm quite sure that if Mau had done this test, he would have arrived at the same conclusion.

Despite his opinions, Ella van Dantzig was impressed by Hendy: 'Sir Philip was very co-operative and very nice, and willing to help us – much different from Röell, because he held up the painting several times, next to several pupils of Leonardo like Luini and de Predis which La Belle resembled very much actually, and Boltraffio.' Hendy liked the picture, even though he did not think it a Leonardo: 'He thought it was very pretty, and was much prettier than the picture in the Louvre. But it was not a Leonardo.' The two women left the National Gallery 'very depressed'. Röell, who was on a visit to London, was supposed to meet them about the picture, but never contacted them. Ruhemann tried to console them. At a dinner at his house in St John's Wood, 'he offered very politely to write a letter to Sir Philip to ask him for a written expertise and opinion'. Ella van Dantzig was so down, she even began to doubt Helmut Ruhemann's commitment. He 'is very cooperative, very friendly, very civil,' she wrote, 'but I am afraid he is also afraid to get too much into this matter. Still he appreciates Mau's work and understands what he has done in the past.'

On 1 June, Ruhemann deposited the picture at Coutts Bank on the Strand, a stone's throw from the National Gallery, in a repository that he often used to store private client's pictures that he was restoring. He promised Ella that he would help keep Mau van Dantzig's cause alive.

Ruhemann was as good as his word. Over the summer and autumn he worked tirelessly to get the picture to the Louvre and to arrange the comparison that he felt would show that the Hahn *La Belle* preceded the Louvre picture. He turned once again to Kenneth Clark, whom he had been helping prepare one of his television broadcasts on the nature of art. But Clark was reluctant to get involved. In May of 1960, he responded to Ruhemann's persistent cajoling by admitting that, 'It would interest me to see the Hahn Belle Ferronière,' but he added that, 'this picture has been the subject of so much troublesome controversy that I am rather nervous of expressing any opinion on it.' He went on to suggest that he should see the picture in secret: 'If it is in the National Gallery could I not slip in one day and look at it? I would not care to see it in the company of Mrs. Hahn's representative.' He seems to have followed up on his suggestion. Years later (in a letter to Kate Steinmetz, who had a friend whose possible Leonardo Clark refused to look at in 1966), he ruefully recalled how, 'When the Hahn Bel Faronier [*sic*] was in London, I could not resist going to see her, and I literally put on a disguise and swore to secrecy the restorer who showed her to me.' But even this could not prevent Clark becoming involved in the debate about the picture: 'it did no good,'

he remembered, 'and I found myself involved in unpleasant controversy'. In August 1960 Clark wrote to Ruhemann telling him that
he had taken a photo of the Hahn *La Belle* to the Louvre. 'Most
interesting,' he wrote. 'I think I could persuade a jury – even a
jury of laymen; but it would take an hour or so, and they would
have to pay attention.' The letter was a masterpiece of mandarin
ambiguity, but Ruhemann seized on it as an endorsement of the
Hahn *La Belle* and it gave him the confidence to press for a
'confrontation' between the Hahn and Louvre versions of the picture.

Ruhemann also turned for help to Ludwig Goldscheider, a
Viennese art historian who had fled Austria in 1938 and who was
co-founder and director of Phaidon Press. Ruhemann knew that
Goldscheider had written about the Louvre version of *La Belle*,
and had argued that it was neither by Leonardo nor, as others had
argued, by Boltraffio, but by Francesco Melzi. He also enlisted the
support of LeRoux Smith LeRoux, who sometimes worked for the
family firm of Wildenstein. This alliance was a strange meeting of
opposites. LeRoux was a notorious character on the art scene in
London, a leading figure in the so-called 'Tate Affair', the uproar
about administrative bungling and alleged illegalities that engulfed
the Tate Gallery and its director, Sir John Rothenstein, between
1952 and 1954. Remarkably charming at first acquaintance,
endowed with an inexhaustible appetite for skullduggery and
intrigue, a master at fiddling an expense account, LeRoux had
charmed a naive Rothenstein, who had met him on a visit to South
Africa, into helping him leave his native Pretoria to work as one
of the keepers at the Tate. Despite being the protégé of the director,
LeRoux worked tirelessly to get his boss dismissed, succeeded in
turning some of the trustees against him and repeatedly leaked

information to the press and the director's enemies about supposed incompetence and malfeasance at the Tate. (Page after page of Rothenstein's memoirs, *Brave Day, Hideous Night*, catalogue LeRoux's perfidies, but also reveal their author to be an astonishingly inept politician and slipshod administrator.) It took Rothenstein two years to get rid of his subordinate, who even to his supporters was 'a devious South African rogue'. Thereafter LeRoux worked as an art-adviser for Lord Beaverbrook, whom, according to Rothenstein, he defrauded of thousands of pounds, before getting a job at Wildenstein's in the spring of 1960. Three years later he was found dead after having been dismissed from his latest post. It was rumoured that he had killed himself rather than face evidence of his malfeasance.

LeRoux had employed Ruhemann as a picture restorer for his private South African clients, and after he left the Tate he tried to take advantage of their acquaintance once he began dealing in Old Masters. His work on *La Belle* began as a private arrangement between friends, but then became one of his first assignments for Wildenstein's. He spent much of June 1960 working on *La Belle* and discussed taking out an option on the picture with Ruhemann. He read Harry Hahn's *The Rape of La Belle*, went to the Louvre to examine their version of the picture and read through the museum's files on the painting. He was persuaded that the Hahn version preceded that in the Louvre but, as he reminded the thick-skinned Ruhemann, they could 'go a long way to abolishing the status of the Louvre picture', which would cause a sensation and make them lots of enemies, but this would only be worthwhile if they could vindicate the Hahn version. Ruhemann, on the other hand, had became 'more and more convinced' of the authenticity of the painting, especially after he had concluded that it had been executed by an artist who was left-handed, just like Leonardo. In his notes he described the sale of the Hahn painting as a 'kind of duty to Mau'. His enthusiasm affected LeRoux, who helped arrange the shipment of the Hahn *La Belle* to Paris in October 1960. When it arrived he jotted down a note to Ruhemann: 'Advised that our beautiful Lady has landed safely', and told him the painting would be kept securely in the safe of the Wildenstein office in Paris. The head of the firm was returning from New York to examine the picture.

The financial arrangements surrounding the painting were becoming increasingly Byzantine. In October, Schwarz wrote to Ruhemann telling him that he was assigning to him an exclusive option to sell *La Belle* for the months of October and November. (This arrangement, in which Ruhemann was effectively acting as Schwarz's seller, was as close as he came to breaking his vow not to be involved financially in pictures.) The plan was to sell the picture to Wildenstein, who had a number of possible buyers, and to deposit the money – Schwarz was asking $3 million (£1.07 million) – in an American bank account. However, Schwarz was worried about LeRoux. His first involvement in the picture had been as an independent agent, in which he would have got a 10 per cent cut of the final price, and therefore had a real incentive to push the purchaser to pay more. This arrangement was still in place, but LeRoux was now a director of Wildenstein, whose interest as a middle-man was to pay low and sell on high. Schwarz was smart enough to know that LeRoux was a slippery customer and well-aware that Ruhemann was not adept at financial negotiations. He feared that Wildenstein would sell on at a huge profit and that

Andrée, with whom he had agreed only to sell to intermediaries who paid the full price, would demand that he make up the difference.

On 14 October 1960 the Hahn *La Belle* made her second pilgrimage to the Louvre. She was fortunate to be accompanied by Helmut Ruhemann, who had among the junior staff of the Paris museum a number of friends and admirers whom he had visited at least once a year over the previous decade. What exactly happened on this occasion is obscure. It would seem that Bazin, the Louvre's chief curator, would not have anything to do with the Hahn picture, possibly on instructions from his superior, Henri Seyrig, head of the French Museums. Some of the curators and restorers at the Louvre saw the Hahn picture, but no proper comparison took place, and no high-ranking official was involved. Just before the proposed 'confrontation', as it was always called, LeRoux wrote to Ella van Dantzig in high spirits claiming that the meeting of the two *Belle*s would considerably enhance the value of the Hahn painting, and that he had a number of important prospective buyers in view. He warned her not to agree to any sale until the research on the two pictures was complete. However, the response of the French authorities shifted his mood. After the failure of the October mission, LeRoux and Wildenstein were no longer interested.

The situation seemed to be going from bad to worse. Despite their close friendship, Ruhemann had been unable to persuade Hendy to support his cause, nor was he able to draw in Goldscheider. After the failure in Paris he had written to Kenneth Clark asking for his help. On this occasion, Clark was far more direct than he had been in August. 'I ought to warn you,' he wrote, 'that I fear you misunderstood my last letter to you.' He confessed that he had expressed himself 'in this indefinite way because I did not want to be drawn into any controversy regarding the Hahn picture'. Now Clark wanted to make himself clear: 'I must, therefore, state definitely that I was completely convinced that the Louvre picture is the original of the Fifteenth Century, and the Hahn picture a post-Raphaelesque copy.' (It is noteworthy that Clark did not say that he thought the Louvre picture by Leonardo, but only 'the original of the Fifteenth Century'.) He went on to add that:

> I believe that by taking a group of authentic drawings and pictures by Leonardo, and demonstrating his type of modelling and then taking a number of post-Raphaelesque heads and showing their type of modelling, it would be possible to prove that the Louvre picture fell into the first category and the Hahn picture into the second, even though the Hahn picture is an extremely close and skilful copy, in which the copyist has rectified one or two small irregularities in the original.

This was a severe blow. Ruhemann scrapped a letter he had drafted to Clark and deferentially apologized for the misunderstanding, though he added that he had 'no monetary or other interest in these matters of attribution or recognition, except that I am passionately interested in the truth. I have never or ever will take a commission.' Bridges were mended and Clark, in turn, offered Ruhemann a half-apology: 'I see that my previous reference to the picture was far too guarded.' The mutual respect of the two men, so clear in all their correspondence, remained intact, but Clark had once again dealt the Hahn *La Belle* a severe blow. To cap it all, on 28 October 1960 Ruhemann was hit by a car coming out of an alleyway off

Kensington High Street and was hospitalized for more than two weeks with a broken hip. As Ella wrote to him three days before he was allowed home, 'It is incredible that you still care for my troubles.'

Schwarz, the van Dantzig's family adviser, was thinking of abandoning Europe in pursuit of a sale. He had heard rumours of the possible sale of Leonardo's earliest portrait, *Ginevra de' Benci*, to the Metropolitan in New York; couldn't they, he asked Ruhemann, contact van Dantzig's old pupil and protégé in New York, Thomas Buechner, who was now the director of the Brooklyn Museum, and find an American museum buyer? But Ruhemann was determined not to give up on the Louvre. Unlike others, who had a financial stake in the sale of *La Belle*, his interest was professional. In the following years, he would sometimes aid Andrée and her agents in attempts to take the painting to market, but this was not his chief concern. Throughout his life he never deviated from his determination to get the Louvre and its officials to recognize what he saw as a professional truth – that the Hahn *La Belle* was, if not a Leonardo, then an original, and that the Louvre picture was a copy. His first aim was to get the Louvre to buy the picture and to display it together with their own version of *La Belle*. He wanted them to admit that they had made a mistake and that they were willing to rectify it.

Persistent as ever, by January 1961 Ruhemann had persuaded Seyrig to permit a formal 'confrontation' between the pictures. He then turned once again to Kenneth Clark. A surviving series of drafts of a letter that Helmut repeatedly reworked in order to win over Clark show how important he regarded his support. He desperately wanted Clark to attend the meeting at the Louvre.

Ruhemann began by emphasizing his disinterestedness in the case. He had, he stressed, no financial interest in the sale of the picture. 'I have been offered large sums but flatly refuse them. I only charge for restoration. For *La Belle* I only receive a modest fee and expenses. My gratification is in finding the truth.' He then tried to deal with the obvious objection that the Louvre would hardly be amenable to a re-evaluation of their picture. He pointed out that they had agreed to place the pictures together, even though he had explained that doing so might lead to a reassessment of their *La Belle*. One of his colleagues at the Louvre, after examining the Hahn *La Belle* had told him, 'If you propose to put this picture in the place of ours. I would not oppose it'. The time was ripe for change. Then Ruhemann appealed to Clark's vanity. 'You have already shown', he wrote, 'that you are capable of the same kind of greatness that distinguished Berenson, by letting yourself be convinced and change your mind in public . . . with your extraordinary tact you will know how to deal with this delicate situation.' He then transcribed some notes from a lecture he had written on forgery and misattribution:

B[ernard] B[erenson] greatness in correcting his errors himself. Errors exist – Friedländer – their errors will go into history coupled with their name. I will be glad to hear your argument but you won't convince me. That is the attitude of the little man. He will remain infallible only in his own eyes not in the eyes of posterity . . . It is a pity that some of the most instructive of my experiences must remain untold. They must hurt people's feelings or even business . . . but by being hushed over the error does not disappear, it lives on and spreads under the surface like dry rot, which when revealed and cut out can be made innocuous. It can be stopped only be revealing it and cutting it out.

We do not know if Ruhemann ever included any of this in his final letter – he probably did not – but it very much conveys his general attitude with its emphasis on critical open-mindedness. Ruhemann even suggested that the case of the two *La Belle*s, along with the reassessment of other works, would enable Clark to rewrite the Leonardo canon. He sent Clark the materials he had assembled for his report on *La Belle*, entreating Clark to study the differences between the two pictures: 'you may at least be able to admit that it is the original from which the L[ouvre] version has been copied'.

Clark's response was polite and evasive. Telling Ruhemann of a recent illness, he mentioned that he was going to the south of France to recuperate for a week or two and doubted whether he would be able to see the pictures on his return: 'I'm very sorry not to have had the opportunity to see them as I know you would not have written to me about them if they had not been of real interest and importance.' When pressed again by Ruhemann to attend the 'confrontation' in Paris, Clark simply failed to reply. Ruhemann was by now convinced that Clark's position stemmed from his fear of an embarrassing row between the National Gallery and the Louvre. Alluding to the ongoing controversy between the two museums over the status of their respective versions of Leonardo's *The Virgin of the Rocks*, he wrote to Schwarz, 'Poor Sir Kenneth must be in a frightful quandary. He senses of course that this is only the thin end of the wedge, that the Vierge aux Rocheaux comes next.' Clark kept Ruhemann's materials for three months.

At the end of April 1961, Ruhemann was disappointed to receive a note from Clark's secretary, Gillian Ross, together with his materials on *La Belle*. She told him that Sir Kenneth, who was now in Italy, had instructed her to return them to him: 'He has asked me to return the enclosed folder, since he does not wish to inconvenience you any longer.' Nothing was said about the picture. Ever the diplomat, Clark was not going to get involved in a messy quarrel between Ruhemann and the Louvre.

Lacking Clark's support, Ruhemann turned again to Philip Hendy, but the director of the National Gallery, despite his close friendship with Ruhemann, remained unconvinced by the Hahn painting. He conceded that the Louvre picture was probably not a Leonardo, but said he 'liked it better'. Ruhemann persisted, but Hendy would not shift his ground. As he told Ella van Dantzig, 'Sir Philip vaguely admits that our *Belle* is no worse than the Louvre one, but he doesn't want to commit himself like all the other faint-hearted people.'

Meanwhile, it had been agreed with the Louvre that *La Belle* was to travel back, once more, to Paris in June. This was a less clandestine affair than the trip of the previous year and Ruhemann became anxious that Bazin, who had been forced by his superior to agree to the 'confrontation', might try to seize the Hahn *La Belle* 'to annoy us' on the grounds that it had originally been illegally exported. That way the Louvre could get the picture free of charge. However, in Amsterdam Schwarz took legal advice and reassured him that any action by the French authorities would be extremely unlikely. Besides, Schwarz had now brought in a new figure to help ease the picture's way, the well-known gentleman-dealer, connoisseur and art historian, Vitale Bloch.

Bloch was a good choice to help *La Belle Ferronnière* for a number of reasons, of which perhaps the most important was his close friendship with Bazin, whom Ruhemann regarded as the greatest obstacle to the acceptance of the Hahn picture. Bloch, a Russian by birth, a cosmopolitan by inclination (he was fluent in six languages), had been an art dealer in Berlin in the 1920s, then moved to Amsterdam and Paris. He had been instrumental in many extremely important art sales – including that of a Giorgione to the National Gallery – had a fine personal collection (eventually donated to the Museum Boijmans Van Beuningen in Rotterdam) and was widely regarded as one of the best, most fastidious connoisseurs in the art world. Writing about him after his death in 1974, the *Burlington Magazine* said:

> Anyone who had the privilege of going around a museum or exhibition in his company soon realized that he would respond with equal sensitivity to the Italian Quattrocento or the Nabis; and he had that rare gift in conversation of opening one's eyes to the magic of colour and form, wherever throughout the last six centuries it happened to spout or blossom.

A follower of Ruhemann's old boss, Max Friedländer, for whom he had worked (in rather dubious circumstances) during the Second World War, a deft talker and elegant writer who abhorred the pomposities of academic art criticism, this brilliant aesthete – if he liked the Hahn painting – would undoubtedly have greatly enhanced its value, even if he had not succeeded in showing it to be by Leonardo. Schwarz could barely conceal his delight in recruiting him and began calculating that they would all make millions. Ella van Dantzig wrote to Ruhemann asking if she could attend the 'confrontation' at the Louvre. She would remain as unobtrusive as possible, she told him, but she wanted to be present at the moment that would see the crowning moment of her late husband's work.

All seemed to be going well. Schwarz visited Ruhemann in London to complete preparations and the restorer took his students to Coutts to see *La Belle* shortly before her departure for Paris. No doubt he took the opportunity to rehearse the remarks he planned when there and which he had now drafted as a report on the Hahn picture. However, they were having difficulties pinning down Vitale Bloch. The original plan had been to show him the painting before going to the Louvre. Schwarz got the Louvre to agree that Bloch could be present at the confrontation – they said they saw him as an art historian and not a dealer (the latter they added would definitely be excluded) – but Bloch understandably wanted to preserve his independence. At first, he said he wished to be able to be present and to give his opinion on the picture 'yes' or 'no'. Then he shifted his ground once more, saying that he did not want to be involved in the confrontation, though he might help sell the Hahn *La Belle*. As Schwarz explained to Ella van Dantzig:

> Bloch will look at the painting if I, as a non-expert invite him to do it, but he, for whatever reason, is not prepared to look at the painting in the presence only of experts. He is not willing to give his opinion then, so he will have the liberty to be silent if he wishes, which he supposes to be possible if I am there but to him seems not possible if he is surrounded by fellow experts who are aiming for a confrontation.

Finally, Bloch got cold feet. He told Ruhemann that he did not want anything to do with the picture and certainly would not help sell it 'because he would not have another quiet night for the rest of his life if he did'.

This disappointment was an augury of what was to come. Again, the confrontation proved a damp squib. The Louvre staff did not turn up; nothing was resolved; the situation did not change. As Ruhemann explained in a letter to Andrée, 'Our last meeting in Paris was again most disappointing. I had been led to believe that some authority from the Louvre would be present at the confrontation of the two pictures, but only a public relations lady appeared'. He added:

> I found only one person of standing to agree with us, but he won't have the courage to admit it officially. He is in a high position at the Louvre but does not want to be named. He said to me that your picture that I showed him was much superior to the Louvre's. Unfortunately other people who matter are not convinced or do not admit it.

Ruhemann blamed Bazin, who he believed to be determined to thwart any proper consideration of the authenticity of his picture. The junior curators, for whatever reason, maintained their silence. Schwarz's hopes of millions vanished. The blow must have been considerable to Ruhemann because, despite his promise not to give up the fight, for almost a year there is almost no sign of the case of *La Belle* among his surviving papers. He had taken on the Louvre twice and on both occasions his efforts to have a proper evaluation of the two pictures had been rebuffed.

As Ruhemann retreated, Schwarz, who had become increasingly frustrated at the failure to sell the painting, decided to take matters into his own hands. A hardnosed businessman, for some time he had been concerned at the growing expense of trying to sell *La Belle*, complaining to Ella van Dantzig that he had already spent several thousand guilders. He clearly felt that their efforts had been undertaken with insufficient care and planning so, after the failure in Paris, he drew up a series of proposals. Faced with such little support in Europe and what he called 'the unconquerable obstacle' of the Louvre's hostility, Schwarz returned to his idea of getting van Dantzig's protégé, Tom Buechner, to become the focus of an American campaign to sell the Hahns' *La Belle*. Buechner would approach museum directors and would also orchestrate a press campaign to revive interest in the painting. He wrote to Andrée about his plans, but warned her that she might have to lower her expectations. The existence of the Louvre version of *La Belle*, he reminded her, 'makes it very difficult for people to take the risk and pay such a considerable price for the painting'. She might have to sell at a reduced price.

Tom Buechner was a willing recruit to the cause, but he quickly discovered how difficult a task he had undertaken. As he told Ella van Dantzig, 'the Duveen trial stigma is still very much in effect'. He quickly discovered that 'the present administration at the Metropolitan [Museum of New York] is too timid to venture into such a controversial area', and when he approached Sherman Lee, the director of the Cleveland Museum of Art (and an oriental specialist), he was told that the museum was not interested 'because of the old controversy'. Buechner bewailed what he described as 'the cowardly attitude of museum directors', but as he ruefully admitted, 'I am convinced of the Hahn picture, [but] my opinion is worth nothing in the art market and museum field.'

Schwarz was at a loss to know what do to. He toyed with the idea of publishing Mau van Dantzig's book on Leonardo, but admitted that such a stratagem was of little use if no art experts believed in the painting. As he wrote to his lawyer in New York, 'This question [of *La Belle*] is getting on my nerves. It has cost me a lot of money so far, and no result has been obtained.' He was almost ready to give up. He wanted an American to take out an option on the painting, pay for its insurance and also cover the costs of researching the picture. When Andrée wrote to him saying she was shocked at his difficulties, he could barely contain his exasperation:

> You say once the art dealers, critics and connoisseurs have seen the painting they generally agree on its authenticity. This is not so, alas. As I said before, Mr. Kenneth Clark, at the National Gallery London, the greatest expert on the paintings of Leonardo, wrote a book on those paintings, a big art dealer in Paris, the recently deceased Director of the Rijksmuseum of Amsterdam, the actual Director of this Museum, are not prepared to say that it is genuine. Most of these people say it is by Boltraffio.

He made clear that if he did not sell the picture soon, he would lower the price and look for someone he described as a 'speculator' to take a chance on the painting. Instead, Schwarz persuaded his American lawyer, Martin Roeder, a partner in the firm Roeder, Guggenheimer and Untermeyer, to try to sell the painting but made little headway. He wrote to Schwarz, 'It is well known that the picture is for sale, but that it is impossible to get a price for it.' No one, he pointed out, would be interested in the picture 'unless some indication of price was given'.

By 1963 Schwarz had abandoned his American campaign and attempts to sell the painting were foundering. He was giving way to Kellerman senior, who once again was taking a more active role in seeking a sale. Kellerman seems to have been behind the initiative, in which Ruhemann acted as an intermediary, to put *La Belle* up for auction at Sotheby's in London. On 12 February, Ruhemann had lunch with Carmen Gronau. The head of the Old Masters department at Sotheby's, she was another exile from Hitler's Germany, a formidable woman, short and severe-looking with dark wiry hair and piercing brown eyes behind heavy glasses. She was Sotheby's first female director. Witty, loud, erudite and highly intelligent, she was a central figure in the firm's transformation from a book and decorative arts auction house into a major player and serious rival to Christie's in the Old Master trade. As her obituary in the *Times* in 1999 explained: 'if people were a nuisance or the picture was poor, she was brusque; if she liked the picture, then a doubting or recalcitrant vendor would be won over by equal measures of pressure and charm'. She treated Ruhemann with polite candour. She knew the problems and history of the picture, and she told him that she doubted it would fetch more than £25,000 ($70,000); she reminded him that there was nobody much in favour of the picture.

When Kellerman gave Andrée Dupas this news back in Los Angeles, she was not pleased. She said she wanted to sell for about $200,000 (£71,500), thus leaving about $180,000 (£64,400) for herself after she had paid Kellerman's fee. She was also terrified that the picture would have to be withdrawn if it did not reach its reserve price, and that she would incur costs. She also did not want to pay a seller's premium of 2.5 per cent. When Ruhemann talked again to Gronau in October 1963, she was somewhat more conciliatory. She said she was prepared to produce a special catalogue with colour plates, but she was pretty sure that the picture still would not fetch more than between $60,000 and $90,000 (£21,400–£32,100). This was not good enough for either Kellerman or Andrée Dupas, and negotiations ground to a halt.

Ruhemann's heart does not seem to have been in a Sotheby's sale and when he talked to Gronau he also floated a scheme that he had obviously been mulling over for some time. What, he asked Gronau, did she think of the idea of approaching the maverick French minister of culture André Malraux – going over the head of Bazin – and offering the Hahn picture for public exhibit at the Louvre? Gronau thought it worth a try, but did not think it would succeed. Ruhemann, though, was very taken with the idea. As he told Kellerman, 'The other day a friend of mine in Paris offered me to submit the case to Malraux if I provided the material, photos and letters. He will try to arrange an audience for me.'

In January 1964 Ruhemann began gathering together materials for his report for Malraux. He had four new photographs and two new x-rays taken of *La Belle Ferronnière* and Joyce Plesters, his colleague at the National Gallery Laboratory, prepared a technical and scientific report on the Hahn picture, which he sent to Ella van Dantzig for her approval. He sketched out notes for his meeting in Paris with G. Rosetti, his contact with Malraux, and drafted a letter – never sent – to the minister of culture asking that the two versions of *La Belle* be put together. What happened to this initiative is not clear. Rosetti seems to have wanted fuller documentation before approaching Malraux. What we can assert with confidence is that Ruhemann did not succeed in seeing Malraux or in securing his cooperation.

While Ruhemann continued to pursue the Louvre, a new commercial interest in the picture was taken by the Madden Gallery in Blandford Street, London. Andrée Dupas and Jacqueline Hahn returned to France in the summer of 1964, planning to remain in Europe, and were eager to secure a sale. Probably as a result of this pressure, Francis Madden talked about the Hahn *La Belle* to the *Daily Express* which printed a report that the picture was for sale at the Madden Gallery for £195,000 ($546,000). The story was sensationalized in the *France Soir* much to the anger of Andrée and the annoyance of Kellerman, who felt that Madden was too naive and indiscreet to handle such a delicate matter as the sale of *La Belle*. Both Kellerman and Ruhemann were relieved when Madden's brother-in-law, Sol Rissen, took over the sale of the picture in the following year. As Ruhemann wrote to Kellerman, 'Mr. R makes an excellent impression, a calibre very different from Mr. M, a quite successful businessman'.

Over the next few years Ruhemann was occasionally brought back to *La Belle*. He was asked to adjudicate over the expenses claimed by Schwarz when Ella van Dantzig died in November 1965. He responded by saying that he had nothing to do with business arrangements, though he would let anyone trying to sell the painting use his report, provided it was used anonymously. However, in September 1969 he made one last attempt to interest the Louvre. He knew that his old foe, Bazin, had been marginalized by Malraux and he thought, as he told Andrée, 'the moment was propitious to take another step forward'. He took his report and photos with him, first visiting Hughes de Varine-Bohan, the director of ICOM (International Council of Museums) at UNESCO. De Varine-Bohan gave him a sympathetic hearing and said that he thought that the Louvre should take the picture on loan and that the laboratory of another museum should examine the two pictures thoroughly. Ruhemann then went to see Michel Florisoone, the principle author of a famous catalogue *Hommage à Leonard*, formerly at the Louvre but now another victim of Malraux's policies and sent into exile in the suburbs. Florisoone agreed with de Varine-Bohan, telling Ruhemann that 'it was my duty to draw the attention of the Louvre to your picture before it was sold'. He contacted his former colleague, Mme Beguine in the Louvre and arranged for Ruhemann to see her the same day. As he told Andrée Dupas:

> She received me immediately, though it was late in the afternoon. She warned me that I must not be disappointed if she were unable to speak straight from her heart, she had to follow instructions from above. She was guarded but obviously impressed and wanted to present the case immediately to the new Director, but she said he would not be able to make a decision without drawing in Bazin.

Ruhemann, not surprisingly, was disconcerted by this. I said, he wrote, 'Mr. Bazin is not disinterested in this case, and that he would, rather than give in cause an international scandal.' Ruhemann did not want Michel Laclotte, the new head of paintings, to know about the proposal. He pointed out to Andrée Dupas that Bazin was due to retire in two year's time, and that it would be much better if she could wait until then for him to carry out his plan. He held out the prospect of her painting being examined in the huge new modern laboratory at the Louvre that Malraux had set up. Their findings, together with the opinions of Florisoone and Beguine, he told her, might raise the value of the picture and increase the chances of selling it – to the Louvre. Ruhemann still wanted them rather than a private buyer to take the picture.

Andrée Dupas, who at the same time received a copy of Ruhemann's report, was not happy. She was delighted that his report proved (at least to her satisfaction) that her picture was genuine, but she did not want her painting, she told him, compared to the Louvre *La Belle Ferronnière*; she wanted it compared to a bona fide Leonardo and she wanted, as soon as possible, to find a middle man to sell her picture at a substantial profit.

Ruhemann's counsel of patience went unheeded and Kellerman, presumably with Andrée Dupas's blessing, offered the picture to the Louvre a few months later. In the summer of 1970, the Louvre gave its definitive word: Laclotte wrote to Kellerman on 13 July telling him the museum was not interested in purchasing the Hahn *La Belle*.

Why did Mau van Dantzig and Helmut Ruhemann devote so much energy to the Hahn *La Belle*? In posing this question, I am not implying that either man was not fully and genuinely convinced of the importance of the picture, or that their public professions concealed some sinister ulterior motive. But we do need to ask why they were so persistent in their beliefs and ready to go to such trouble to see them vindicated. Neither, as we have seen, stood to gain financially from the picture. They were not, for instance, like LeRoux Smith LeRoux who was an enthusiastic supporter of the picture when he thought he could make a lot of money from it in the summer of 1960, but quickly backed off when he realized that it was going to be extremely difficult to make a real profit out of *La Belle*. Indeed, van Dantzig and Ruhemann's concerns were often at odds with those whose chief interest was a sale. Both men were far more interested in dealing with major museums – the Rijksmuseum and the Louvre – than with the auction houses or potential private purchasers. Van Dantzig wanted Tom Buechner's support in the United States to show *La Belle* in museums, not to get it to the auction house. The Nice dealer D. Kellerman complained of Ruhemann's commercial indifference. Both van Dantzig and Ruhemann felt constrained by the protocols of the museum and connoisseurship: the former would only mobilize support for *La Belle* provided it was understood that experts would not publish while the picture was for sale; the latter repeatedly made clear that he would not publish anything while the picture was on the market.

It is easier to understand Van Dantzig's commitment to the Hahn painting than that of Ruhemann. The Dutchman had a long history of confrontation with the art establishment and conventional connoisseurs. His attitude towards them was one of pity, tinged with contempt. Of Kenneth Clark he wrote, 'I think that Kenneth Clark is not much worse than any other fine feeling person – there is nothing but his feeling, he therefore is vulnerable, and the more he is, the more stubborn he has to be. Feelings are ridiculous when confronted with pure science.' Van Dantzig shared with the Hahns and their followers the view that the art world was 'a racket', not an opinion ever expressed by Ruhemann. Like the populist critics of connoisseurs he passed moral judgements on their attributions, seeing their errors not as mistakes but moral failings symptomatic of the fundamental flaws in the system of art scholarship. Like the expert in whose footsteps he trod, Morelli, van Dantzig took an approach that was profoundly ahistorical. He felt that art historians were far too concerned with documentation and evidence and insufficiently attentive to what he called 'the literal expressive significance' of the work of art itself, which he saw as unchanging, a sort of laboratory specimen whose proper examination was bound to yield the truth. Leonardo was an ideal subject for pictological analysis, which was concerned to recognize the artist in the work, because 'the more outstanding, the more exceptional, the more extraordinary the painter is' the more obvious was the connection. Of course, using the Hahn painting to demonstrate his theories had, for van Dantzig, the added advantage that it would engender an enormous amount of publicity for his method, mounting a challenge to the very bastion of traditional connoisseurship. And the popularity of Leonardo – no great master was more visible to the general public – sat well with his view that anyone, with the aid of his techniques, could identify a masterpiece and enjoy its beauty.

However, it is hard not to see van Dantzig's project as doomed from the start. This is not only a question of the nature or inherent weakness of van Dantzig's method, but of his need to mobilize support from within the art world to challenge the Louvre and its picture. He wrote optimistically to Frank Glenn and then Andrée Dupas about his ability to get museum directors and curators to assist him, but I have the strong sense that he was deluding himself about the strength of their support. He placed great store on the backing of Paul Coremans, probably the greatest and most publicly visible art scientist in Europe, but Coremans was leery of van Dantzig and his methods. The two major museum curators, van

Schendel and Röell, both felt they had to listen to van Dantzig – not least because they could ill afford not to acquire a Leonardo, if such it was, that had turned up in the Netherlands – but both had born the brunt of van Dantzig's criticism in the past. They had no particular reason to further his cause. Both had been educated in Paris, van Schendel at the Ecole du Louvre and Röell at the Sorbonne; they would not have wanted to disturb the good relations they had in Paris in order to help a man they saw as troublesome, if not hair-brained.

The reasons for Helmut Ruhemann's involvement are more complex. Van Dantzig wanted to replace traditional connoisseurship with a new scientific method. This was never Ruhemann's intent. On the contrary, he went out of his way to explain to his students at the Courtauld and to the general public (especially in his lecture tour of the United States in 1952) that he believed the connoisseur and his eye were paramount in picture attribution. He saw the growing number of lawsuits about paintings as the main reason why the public had come to believe that scientific evidence was more important than traditional connoisseurship. The legal system demanded this sort of evidence – it felt more comfortable with 'scientific facts' – but the crucial judgements were made by art-historical experts. 'Scientific aids,' he concluded, 'only serve for confirmation.' Asking his students, 'Can x-rays or ultra-violet tests decide if a picture is false or not?' he replied:

I believe that all these devices, even if they become more perfect with time, will never be able to compete with the instinct of the true connoisseur, his unaided eye will always be the decisive factor. Just as the great art critic will rarely need to refer to technical tests, one will rarely find the true masterpiece accompanied by scientific certificates.

This, of course, was the position that he and his colleagues had taken back in 1930 at the League of Nations conference on science and art in Rome.

Nor did Ruhemann have any truck with van Dantzig's populism. Skilled attribution was the province of the few. As he told his public audiences, 'The average art lover need not be dismayed if he is not able to distinguish a genuine painting by Rembrandt painted in the seventeenth century from a daub painted in his manner a few years ago.' Expertise depended upon 'a great deal of historical knowledge', and 'there are only a few picture experts who can tell the difference between a clever fake and a genuine masterpiece'. For Ruhemann connoisseurship was the corner-stone of taste and the key to attribution.

His aim was not, like van Dantzig, to render the connoisseur largely redundant, but to reshape connoisseurship itself so as to give a more important place to art conservators and restorers. He was concerned to counter the frequently expressed lack of interest – that sometime teetered into open hostility – of connoisseurs in the material qualities of a painting. As he explained, 'there is no aesthetic quality in a painting which is not at the same time physical matter'. He complained that 'for generations art historians have written about the aesthetic aspects of painting, almost entirely disregarding their physical and technical properties'. Against this he contrasted the modern conservator who did not neglect aesthetic issues. 'I for one have always stressed in teaching and writing the overriding importance of connoisseurship and sensibility in restoration, indeed a sensibility to the least tangible aesthetic qualities.' For Ruhemann good connoisseurship required both a trained eye and a technical knowledge of the physical properties of pictures. So, not surprisingly, he saw properly trained conservators as the equals of art-historian connoisseurs. In his American lectures Ruhemann identified three sorts of experts capable of detecting forgery: the art scholar, historian or style critic; the scientist, including the chemist and physicist; and the paint technologist and restorer who studies the methods and materials of the masters. He portrayed himself as belonging in the third of these categories, but as being conversant with the other two.

There were profound professional and institutional implications to this position. Helmut Ruhemann's career, beginning in the 1920s and ending just before his death in 1973, spanned the years when conservators sought – in part quite successfully – to establish themselves as a professional body which played an active role in the conservation, authentication and presentation of works of art to the museum public. In all his writing, including his magnum opus first published in 1968, *The Cleaning of Paintings: Problems and Potentialities*, Ruhemann spoke eloquently of the growing professionalization and coming of age of the modern conservator, and of his own role in its development. He had been a major figure at the first international congress organized by the League of Nations on the conservation and restoration of art, presenting no fewer than seven different papers as well as taking an active role in the meeting's discussions. He was also the author, together with other colleagues, of the *Manual for the Conservation and Restoration of Pictures* that brought together the conference's results. After the war he played an active role in the Commission on the Care of

Paintings, established by ICOM in 1948 under the leadership of his friend and boss, Philip Hendy, and was a founding member and leading figure in the International Institute for Conservation of Historic and Artistic Works, set up in 1950. Ruhemann's work was marked by a strong commitment to openness and debate about restoration techniques, a willingness to develop scientific methods and a hostility (first nurtured when he peered at murky canvases in the Prado) towards the discoloured varnishes that he believed obscured the original beauties of the Old Masters. In line with his view that aesthetic judgement and the state of the material artwork were inextricably linked, he always maintained that proper cleaning was an important aid to correct attribution.

In October 1969, shortly after the publication of *The Cleaning of Paintings*, Ruhemann gave a lecture to a meeting of conservators in Manchester. In it he examined at length the problems faced by the modern conservator and discussed his task, rights and rank within the organization of the museum. He portrayed the restorer as 'the pivot of a whole team of research workers, trained in such different fields as history, art history, archaeology, physics and chemistry', all of whom 'will be trying to advise not to say control him', though he, and he alone has to perform the tricky task of restoration. According to Ruhemann this task is made even more difficult because, 'although he is called a full collaborator in this team, the hierarchical rank granted by the administration reduces him to the role of a mere executant'. He looked back fondly to his days in Berlin when his rank was the same as a keeper, titled under the director, and where, after five year's service, he was entitled to call himself professor. 'Art historians,' he told his audience, 'look down on you, try to make them look up to you.'

Throughout his career Ruhemann sought to give conservators the prominence and status that he believed they deserved in a reformed system of connoisseurship. This engendered resentments from other figures in the art world. Nowhere was this more apparent than in the conflicts that erupted in Britain immediately after the Second World War when large numbers of pictures that had been cleaned while in wartime storehouses were shown for the first time. Before this, restorers had been largely hidden from public view; now they were conspicuously in the public eye, their handiwork obvious to gallery-goers. Many connoisseurs were horrified with the results. Sir Anthony Blunt told one of Ruhemann's pupils that the president of the Royal Academy thought that the best thing they could do for art was to poison him. It was typical of Ruhemann that his response to these attacks was to organize, with Philip Hendy, a large exhibition devoted to the subject of picture cleaning. This was definitely taking the issue to the opposition and it very nearly cost both Hendy and Ruhemann their jobs, as well as creating friction within the different departments of the museum. After Ruhemann died in 1973, Hendy wrote a letter to his widow praising him as 'a beautiful character', while admitting that, 'We saw eye to eye, but it was he who had the courage in all this silly business over cleaning. What courage I had was mostly due to my complete faith in him.' In fact, Hendy stood solidly behind Ruhemann, defended him repeatedly and helped ensure that the Weaver Inquiry, set up to examine the National Gallery's picture cleaning practices, was staffed by fellow conservators.

The *Cleaned Pictures Exhibition* was a great success and managed to make the conservator (or, at least, Helmut Ruhemann, who was not shy of publicity) a public figure. No fewer than five publishers approached Hendy and Ruhemann, asking them to write books about the picture-cleaning controversy, and a succession of newsreel and film crews asked for permission to show the public how pictures were cleaned. Many members of the public wrote to the National Gallery expressing their enthusiasm for the show. Within the art world the reaction was somewhat different. Some trustees, many artists and not a few connoisseurs – as well as some professional rivals – condemned the National Gallery's cleaning policies; mention the name of Ruhemann and you will still be met with ferocious hostility on the part of art dealers and connoisseurs. His memory survives as someone who ruined 'our' pictures.

Ruhemann himself believed the controversies of the 1940s, and their revival briefly in the 1960s, to be nothing but beneficial. He saw the debates as a way of publicly making a case for his views on conservation and of heightening the profile of conservators. He knew that the display of partially cleaned pictures brought home to their viewers the importance of restorers in determining how the public saw the nation's art. It was this, as much as the brilliance of the hues of some pictures, the loss of the patina of the Old Master, that made his critics so angry. It was an act of presumption, a claim that the conservator had an equal right with the connoisseur to shape how art was seen and understood.

Helmut Ruhemann's engagement with the Hahn *La Belle* appears, then, to have been part of his general campaign – both personal and professional – to demonstrate the importance of the well-informed connoisseur-conservator. It was also bound up with the rivalry between the National Gallery and the Louvre that linked the issue of picture cleaning to Leonardo. Ruhemann always insisted that it was a general failing of the Louvre that it had not cleaned its Leonardos properly and that, if the museum had cleaned its version of *La Belle Ferronnière*, its weaknesses would have been fully revealed. Just as experts in the Louvre took the view that the National Gallery's pictures were over-cleaned, so Ruhemann felt that the French gallery was failing in its duty to reveal all of Leonardo's beauties.

Ruhemann's report on the Hahn *La Belle*, whose final version in 1964 was prepared for André Malraux, though it does not seem to have ever been submitted to him, combined aesthetic judgements about the Hahn and Louvre portraits with technical evidence from the two pictures. It sought to connect the two through a discussion of Leonardo's technique, which had fascinated Ruhemann ever since he had cleaned the London version of *The Virgin of the Rocks* and on which he had published a scholarly essay. Though, in his scrupulous way, Ruhemann refused to attribute the Hahn portrait to Leonardo, his two main technical observations – about the complex way in which the layers of paint were applied and the evidence that at least a part of the portrait had been painted with the left hand – strongly implied an attribution to the master or, at least, to his studio.

At the same time the way that Ruhemann conducted himself in the Hahn controversy also reflected his rather ambiguous relationship to the major museums and his sometimes wilful determination to transcend their institutional imperatives. When, after the Second World War, Hendy set up a scientific and a conservation department at the National Gallery as part of his general aim of rebuilding the museum and its resources, Ruhemann's position was unclear. He was the most senior, internationally famous restorer – indeed, he had trained the head of the conservation department, Arthur Lucas, yet his post was both part-time and honorific. This gave him the opportunity to intervene in all sorts of ways, and fomented inter-departmental rivalries. Ruhemann's special relationship with Hendy – they were the closest of friends and frequently talked privately with one another – compounded the situation.

In many respects, not least in pursuing a policy that asserted the importance of the restorer/conservator and the scientific investigation of works of art, Hendy – whose political skills were considerable – used Ruhemann as something of a stalking horse. He had a strong personal commitment to the development of scientific techniques in the museum and valued the technical skills of conservators. (Kenneth Clark, in recommending Hendy's appointment as director of the National Gallery, is supposed to have warned them that he had 'a bee in his bonnet' about picture restoration.) At the same time Hendy was far more aware of institutional politics than Ruhemann, who operated on principles rather than prudence. When, for example, Ruhemann wrote his great opus on cleaning, it revisited the cleaning controversy of 1946–7 and rehashed the arguments from his point of view. The manuscript also contained a lot of lively personal detail and a robust defence of Ruhemann's controversial views about the National Gallery's Giorgione. In his usual, scrupulous way, Ruhemann submitted the manuscript to Lionel Robbins, the chairman of the board of trustees at the National Gallery, and to Philip Hendy. It brought the mandarin out in both of them. Robbins worried about the personal tone of what was said about what he viewed as National Gallery business, and warned Ruhemann of how his doubtless well-intended comments might be damaging to the gallery. Though well justified, this attempt to moderate Ruhemann was hazardous as it was likely to make him even more determined to tell 'the truth' as he saw it. Hendy was more insinuating. He explained to Ruhemann that his concern was with the coherence and overarching structure of the book, and with the danger that extraneous material might distract the reader from its most important material, which was about techniques of cleaning and restoration. Ruhemann's response was unreservedly enthusiastic. As his drafts show, he cut the personal material, shrank the account of the picture-cleaning controversy and altogether excluded the discussion of Giorgione.

Ruhemann's response to Hendy's comments reveal how, though he was a strong advocate for the Hahn portrait, he probably did not serve the Hahn family as well as they might have liked. Ruhemann was not at all averse to publicity – David Bomford, former head of conservation at the National Gallery, describes his boss's impish pleasure at swabbing a painting in front of journalists, flourishing the discoloured swab stained with brown varnish before his disconcerted audience – but Ruhemann had a strong sense of professional conduct. Indeed, he spent his entire career trying to inculcate it in his pupils and he was incapable of a deliberately confrontational public gesture that might have put pressure on the Louvre and its officials. The closest he came to 'going public' was the plan to confront France's minister of culture, André Malraux, going over the heads of France's museum administration. Given Malraux's personal attachment to the Louvre's Leonardos – he had, after all, acted as an exalted courier of the *Mona Lisa* when it had been exhibited in Washington in 1963 – it is unlikely that he would have received Ruhemann's report sympathetically. However, even this belated gesture of Ruhemann's was conducted through the corridors of power rather than in the pages of the British and French press.

Ruhemann believed that experts should present their findings to a broader public, but he was not a populist. And, in the final analysis, he deferred to his superiors – Clark, Bazin, Hendy – even if he did not agree with them. Here he departed from his pupil, van Dantzig. He agreed with him that museum officials were swayed by institutional pressures but, having worked with such officials all his life, he was inclined to view their pusillanimity as a peccadillo rather than a cardinal sin. Above all, though, Helmut Ruhemann's views were at bottom anti-commercial – he foreswore taking fees for attributions and thereby deprived himself of a handsome income – and much closer to that insistence that the value of a work of art lay less in its market value than in its power to move the beholder. He invested a great deal of time and energy into the cause of the Hahn painting – when one of his pupils painted his portrait he can be seen examining the picture – but came no closer than any of his predecessors to vindicating it.

Indeed, by the mid-1970s it seemed as if the picture had been effectively excluded from the official art world, branded as 'a tainted picture'. Left without supporters in Europe, *La Belle* was to enter a new phase of her career back in the United States, acquiring new backers whose concerns were very different from those of Ruhemann and van Dantzig.

CHAPTER 10

An Investment Opportunity

Throughout the history of the Hahns' *La Belle Ferronnière*, the painting, though never sold, had been the object of a great many complex financial transactions. When *La Belle* returned to the United States on 1 October 1965, the picture was fated to become involved in a series of labyrinthine deals. Though the crusade to vindicate and sell the painting continued, it seemed to become more and more an investment vehicle and a means of raising and borrowing money. As the institutions of the mainstream art world turned their backs on *La Belle*, thereby corroborating the accusations of those who saw the picture's rejection as some sort of conspiracy orchestrated by the successors to Duveen and Berenson, so the picture acquired a new identity and new uses. Most importantly, it was no longer in the hands of experts seeking to use the painting to promote a particular view of connoisseurship, but lawyers and businessmen concerned to use *La Belle* for their financial advantage.

The Hahns' painting had, of course, been used before as a vehicle to raise money. The Hahns, as we have seen, were not wealthy – though they were markedly better off after 1929 when Duveen paid them $60,000 (approx £12,350 at the time) to settle the New York case – and their strategy had always been to use the painting as collateral to pay off their legal expenses and to offload other costs, especially those associated with trying to authenticate and sell the painting, on to others. We do not know the arrangements made by the Hahns with their first lawyer, Hyacinthe Ringrose, though when he was replaced in 1925 by an American lawyer in Paris, Anthony Manley, the new attorney was consigned a 25 per cent interest in the painting. The Kansas City art dealer, Conrad Hug, had apparently advanced $30,000 (£6,200) to Andrée Hahn and also had a 25 per cent interest in the painting. In addition, if Harry Hahn was correct, the Hahns owed their expert witness from the trial, Vadim Chernoff, who had later brought a suit against them, a further $4,000 (£825). After the New York trial Manley's 25 per cent interest in the picture seems to have been transferred to the Manhattan attorneys, Frueauff, Burns, Ruch and Farrell, who had handled the case for Andrée Hahn. After the war, and once her daughter Jacqueline Hahn had taken custody of the painting, Andrée negotiated with Manley and the New York lawyers, seeking to change her percentage agreement into a fixed sum. By 1960 she had a settlement in which her sole outstanding obligations were for a payment of $20,000 (£7,150 in 1960) if and when the painting was sold.

Throughout the time that Andrée was trying to sell *La Belle* in Europe, Harry Hahn had been fretting about the fate of the picture. She had repeatedly warned Maurits van Dantzig not to tell her former husband, or Frank Glenn, or anyone else who represented Harry of the whereabouts or fate of the painting. She also appears to have told D. Kellerman that her husband was dead, creating a great deal of confusion when her agent read about Harry Hahn in the Kansas newspapers.

Harry Hahn, for his part, pursued Andrée with the law (he claimed in his local paper to have involved London's Scotland Yard) and she had to make a new agreement with him that was finalized early in 1961, negotiated by Schwarz's lawyer in New York, Martin Roeder. In it Harry Hahn signed a quit-claim relinquishing all his rights to the picture, in return for which Andrée agreed to inform him of anyone holding the painting who did not have a title to the picture or was a potential buyer. She also consented to pay him a sum of between $20,000 and $40,000 (£7,150 and £14,300) when she sold the painting, depending on how much she received for *La Belle*.

During the postwar era, the Hahns continued their practice of giving options to sell the painting in return for a percentage of the proceeds. Frank Glenn, as we have seen, had such an arrangement and so too did D. Kellerman in Nice. The value of such deals for the Hahns was less in increasing the probability of a sale, than in the way they transferred the expenses of seeking a sale to the option-holder. Glenn, as we have seen, funded not only the publication of *The Rape of La Belle* but also the costs of attempting to sell the Hahn portrait in Kansas, Hollywood and elsewhere. The expenses for *La Belle*'s trip to Europe were born by Kellerman and by Schwarz, the business friend of van Dantzig, who seems to have negotiated a deal with Andrée through his friend's mediation but to have withdrawn when he saw there was no chance of a profit.

By 1974 the future looked bleak for Andrée and her daughter Jacqueline. With Ruhemann's death they had lost their greatest supporter in Europe. And it certainly did not look as if Kellerman was going to manage to sell the picture. For much of the time, Andrée was fending off Harry and his lawyer who were repeatedly pitching schemes for the sale of the painting back in the United States and demanding to know its whereabouts. She wanted to keep him at arm's length, but this only served to increase his anxiety that she had sold the picture and was not letting him know so she could pocket all the proceeds. In 1968 he wrote an angry letter to her claiming she had violated the agreement they had made in 1961 by refusing to reveal the whereabouts of the picture:

> You are well aware of the trickery employed by yourself and our daughter Jacqueline to obtain the painting from my hands in Wichita in 1948 [he meant 1958] so you both could quickly spirit it out of the country and run to Europe with it without telling me a word about your intentions beforehand. I know all about your dealings with Glenn and Van Dantzig and other dealers in Nice and elsewhere that you were keeping on the quiet in order to cheat me out of forty years of work and thousands of dollars advanced by myself and family as well as others towards the liquidation of this painting matter. Well my lady fair – time is running out on you and it just could be in your interest to come clean in this matter for once in your life and settle up with me at once as per the terms of our agreement.

Faced by the bleak outlook for a sale and badgered by Harry, Andrée was persuaded by her former husband to turn to Leon Loucks, a friend of his second wife. Loucks described himself as a businessman and claimed at one point to have an import-export company in San Francisco, though he was a neighbour of Harry and Marjorie Hahn in Wichita Kansas. A large, hectoring man who was also capable of great charm, Loucks was yet another of the chameleon characters that seized upon the Hahn *La Belle*. He told his friends that he was an illegitimate child who had been abandoned by his shame-faced mother who 'sold' him to a medical research facility in Kansas City. There he had not been adopted, but used for the purposes of medical experimentation, until rescued by a prosperous and successful Dr Loucks, whose daughter, it turned out, was Leon's mother. Loucks also came to claim that he was the nephew of both Marjorie and Andrée Hahn – a member of the family – and, though it is possible that he was related to Harry's second wife, his claim to kinship with Andrée was spurious. Loucks, who had run a succession of businesses, lived with his business partner, Rex Reimer, and later the two men shared a house with two others, Chuck Shaver and Barry Ramsay, who worked for Loucks as his driver. In July 1975 Loucks signed an agreement with Andrée and Jacqueline giving him an option to sell for a fee of $500,000 (£208,000) payable on completion of the transaction. He had earlier also signed an agreement, unbeknownst to Andrée and Jacqueline, with Harry and Margery Hahn, promising to pay them a further $250,000 (£104,000) when the picture was sold. It is difficult not to see this arrangement as a collusive transaction designed to get Harry Hahn a larger share of the money when *La Belle* was sold than his entitlement under the agreement with Andrée. Certainly, it was a shock to Jacqueline Hahn when she learned in 2002 that her stepmother claimed to own a share of the painting.

The picture, meanwhile, had been languishing in the vault at Coutts in London. Helmut Ruhemann's son, Frank, who had been looking after his father's affairs, was contacted on 17 September 1975 by Loucks, who promised to pay him $50,000 (£20,800) once the picture was sold, in return for his father's work on the picture. The same day Loucks told Ruhemann he was shipping the picture back to the United States and paid Coutts £1,000 ($2,400) for the expenses associated with the removal of the painting. As Andrée explained to Kellerman when she gave permission for the release of the painting, she could not afford to exhibit the picture, ship it or insure it, and this was why she had consigned it to Leon Loucks.

Kellerman, who was by now over 80 years old, had forgotten to tell Andrée that Sol Rissen of the Madden Gallery in London still had an option on the picture that ran until the end of January 1976. Loucks was angry and tried to bluster his way out of difficulties, telling Frank Ruhemann that he would take no notice of Rissen. On 1 October 1975 he took matters into his own hands and put *La Belle* on a flight to Los Angeles where she was to be deposited in the Los Angeles County Museum.

As soon as he heard what had happened, Sol Rissen expressed public surprise and private anger. He had been told that *La Belle* had been moved for conservation reasons, which he rightly saw as a lame excuse to get the painting back to the United States. Over the next few months he and Loucks tussled with one another over who should sell the picture. At first Rissen claimed to have a buyer and wanted the picture brought back from Los Angeles, but Kellerman would have none of it and informed Andrée Dupas and Frank Ruhemann that he feared that Rissen was trying to steal the picture. He told them that on his last visit to London he had been shown a high-quality colour photograph of *La Belle*, and learned that the picture had been removed from Coutts, photographed in a studio and then deposited in Rissen's name in the Manhattan Bank. Kellerman had threatened to call the police before he got the picture back. Andrée was appalled; thereafter she wanted nothing more to do with Rissen and the Madden Gallery.

However, Rissen did not give up. He pestered Kellerman with calls, claiming to have a buyer who was offering $250,000 (£104,000) payable over three months. He then began calling Andrée in Los Angeles. His offer of $250,000 was countered by Jacqueline who said her mother would not take less than $300,000 (£125,000), would not see him if he came to Los Angeles and would not give him the permission he needed to show his mysterious client the picture at LACMA. She told him if he wanted to do business, he had to talk to Leon Loucks. However, Loucks told Rissen that he wanted $1 million (£417,000) for the picture; he then told Mrs Madden, Sol's sister, that the picture was not currently for sale. Rissen was incredulous. He told Kellerman that he did not believe Leon could find a buyer for $1 million, but that he had a buyer who would pay $400,000 (£167,000) and $25,000 (£10,400) for commission.

Soon, poor Frank Ruhemann was dragged into the negotiation, talking to Rex Reimer, Leon's partner in Wichita, who informed him that they wanted to carry out more research and to plan a publicity campaign before they put *La Belle* on the market. A few days after this conversation, Rissen called Kellerman and told him he had a cash buyer for $500,000 (£208,000), urged him to take the offer and pointed out that the Metropolitan Museum had already turned *La Belle* down. Then Loucks upped the ante. He had a buyer, he claimed, for $5 million (£2.1 million), someone who wanted to keep the picture for five years and do further work on it in the hope of making a greater profit. He was, he told Frank Ruhemann, angry with Rissen for 'muddying the waters'. Without the picture and faced with the hostility of Andrée, Rissen could only try to persuade Kellerman that Leon Loucks was 'a funny man' who was playing on the confidence of Mme Dupas. By April 1976, he had given up the chase. Loucks was now firmly in control of *La Belle* and was to remain so until his death in 2002.

At first Loucks was very active in the sale of *La Belle*, leading Andrée to believe that a deal was imminent. However, in a way that foreshadowed many subsequent incidents, a certain sale became suddenly transformed into a failure because of some unforeseen circumstance. Then, in 1976, while on a trip to Switzerland apparently in pursuit of a buyer, Loucks collapsed and was rushed off to hospital. Jack Chapman, a lawyer from Omaha, Nebraska, who was on vacation in Zurich, saw Loucks collapse and helped him get to hospital; he eventually arranged his return to the United States. Two years later, Loucks asked Chapman to help him sell the Hahn *La Belle*, and Chapman agreed to do so on a fee basis, where he would receive a percentage of the proceeds when *La Belle* was sold. For over twenty years the two men worked together on the project. They divided the labour: Loucks dealt with the two branches of the Hahn family and Chapman travelled both to New York and Europe to research the history of the picture and to pursue a buyer. The two men had frequent resort to 'agents', who offered to recruit buyers for a percentage of the sale price and they put together a so-called 'black book' which collated all the materials they had on the picture, as well as evaluations and expert opinions on the painting. For many years this remained their chief marketing tool for *La Belle*. However, the two men were having difficulties. They were not able to interest major museums such as the Metropolitan in New York, or the Getty and Norton Simon museums in Los Angeles, nor were they able to agree what they thought to be a fair reserve price at the New York auction houses of Sotheby's and Christie's, circumstances Chapman explains by claiming that the auction houses are still part of the 'Duveen machine' and the 'Berenson group'.

Though I cannot, for legal reasons, reveal the names of the experts in the so-called black book, Jack Chapman's deposition of January 2006 in the case of *Hahn versus Duveen*, and the figures interviewed in a BBC documentary *The Two Belles*, broadcast in 1993, show that the two men were unable to recruit experts whose credentials would pass muster in the museum world and Old Master art market. The one major Leonardo scholar who has examined the painting recently, Professor Martin Kemp, spent some time in Omaha, where Chapman and Loucks stored the painting, in 1993 and concluded that the painting, though very attractive and more 'seductive' than the Louvre *La Belle*, was probably a northern European copy of the first half of the seventeenth century, perhaps by the French academician, Laurent de La Hyre. This opinion, close to that of some of Duveen's experts in the 1920s, was rejected by Chapman, who complained that connoisseurship had not advanced beyond the days of Berenson and implied, in a letter to London's *Daily Telegraph*, that Kemp had been influenced by another Leonardo scholar, Carlo Pedretti, who was known not to accept the Hahn *La Belle*.

Gradually, the affairs of Leon Loucks and Jack Chapman became more and more involved. According to Chapman, they were in almost daily contact. Loucks, who was frequently short of money, was given cash advances by Chapman, who also paid off one of Loucks' creditors who for a while had been given custody of the picture because Loucks had defaulted on a loan of some $30,000 borrowed against the painting. The precise extent and value of the loans to Loucks and Chapman is very difficult to know. They borrowed money from a former business partner of Chapman's in Denver Colorado, from a group of investors from the same state, from a real estate broker in California and several creditors in and around Loucks' home of Wichita, Kansas. Sometimes, the money was secured on the painting; on other occasions the creditors were offered a lien that would have provided them with repayment with interest when *La Belle* was sold. About $500,000 in loans are clearly documented; the actual sums may have been much greater, though it is difficult to know because some of the transactions seem to have been notional. What is clear is that the two men had created a large web of credit and debt constructed around a debatable Leonardo as collateral. Soon they were to spin this web into a skein of immense complexity, involving more and more creditors and larger and larger sums of money. Something fantastic was being created.

During the 1980s Loucks and Chapman moved to take control of the painting. In 1982 Loucks signed a promissory note to his various creditors, agreeing to pay them a total of $5,285,295.88 (then approx. £3 million) within twenty-five years or at the date of the sale of *La Belle*. His first creditor, for the sum of $1,660,295.88 (£950,000), was J & A Enterprises, a company owned by Jack Chapman and his wife, Alice. The second lien holder was Claudine Olsen for $75,000 (£43,000), purportedly for monies advanced by her to Loucks. Andrée Dupas was described as the third lien holder for $500,000 (£286,000); Marjorie Hahn the fourth for $250,000 (£143,000). Rex Reimer, Loucks' business partner, was down for

$2,500,000 (£1,430,000), Barry Ramsay, one of Loucks' 'nephews' had a lien of $100,000 (£57,000) and Jane Bolton, the widow of a man who had lent money to Loucks was given a lien for $200,000 (£114,000). The promissory note stipulated that, in the event that *La Belle* was sold, all the money was to be paid to J & A Enterprises (i.e. Jack Chapman) which would satisfy its lien before using any additional monies to pay off the lien holders in the order that they were listed. At no point in this rather extraordinary document is it explicitly stated that Loucks is the owner of the Hahn *La Belle*, though this is implied throughout the text. This agreement changed the nature of Loucks' obligation to Chapman, which had originally been based on a contingency fee to be paid at sale of *La Belle*, into a debt incurred for services that Chapman had rendered his client. What is hard to fathom is how such a debt was incurred (it represented about 16,000 billable hours of legal work), just as it is difficult to understand how Loucks could have owed Rex Reimer $2.5 million, when his creditor lived with him in a modest house and worked at Boeing in Wichita.

It is unclear whether Andrée Dupas knew about this new arrangement, but in February 1984 she appears to have signed a Bill of Sale conveying what was described as her '50% interest' in *La Belle* to 'Leon L. Loucks and/or Jack F. Chapman' giving them the right to sell or convey the picture to anyone they saw fit, but recognizing that Chapman had 'an immediate but subordinate interest in said painting until such time as his current as well as future obligations past date hereof have been fully satisfied'. The circumstances surrounding this document are obscure. Certainly, the two witnesses to the document, Charles Shaver and Leon Loucks, were not present when Andrée signed it. They were not in California that February. Andrée's daughter's diary, which invariably records the telephone calls and contacts with Loucks, makes no reference to the document. Indeed, Jacqueline was virtually blind for much of the first couple of months of 1984 and was not able to assist her mother, by then well into her eighties, whom she described in several diary entries as 'confused'. The Hahns talked with Loucks on the phone on 17 February, 4, 18 and 25 March, and again on the 31 March when Jacqueline recorded 'good news – the painting might go into escrow soon'. In July Loucks called California to tell Andrée and Jacqueline that 'the picture should be funded next week'. There is no evidence that they had any idea that their relation to the painting had changed in any way. Gradually, the calls from Loucks dwindled away. According to Jacqueline's diary he telephoned on four occasions in 1985, chiefly to obtain documents about the picture. Before Andrée's death on 31 July 1986, he called once to tell them that 'Vincent P [perhaps the actor and collector Vincent Price who had seen the painting in Hollywood in 1947] doesn't want it.'

After Andrée's death Loucks and Chapman turned their attentions to Marjorie Hahn, who in January 1987 was persuaded to relinquish her supposed 50 per cent share in *La Belle* together with a number of other works of art, presumably collected by her late husband, Harry. Loucks purchased them all for a notional $1,312,000 (£875,000), but the money did not become due until 6 July 2006 (a date when, as it turned out, both parties to the agreement were dead). As part of the agreement, if Marjorie Hahn died before she was paid, her heirs inherited the promissory note, but not the artworks themselves. If Loucks died, then Jack Chapman, to whom it was now said that Loucks owed the sum of $5 million

(£3.3 million), would retain the art. To all intents and purposes it now appeared that Loucks owned the whole of *La Belle*, as well as a number of other works (including a putative Giambattista Tiepolo), though in practice Chapman had control of the art.

The truly parlous state of Loucks' affairs were revealed in 1990, when Hobbie Negaran who had lent money ($19,000/£12,000 in the first instance) to him, took him to court to secure repayment. In sworn testimony in August 1990, a bellicose Loucks confessed that 'I owe a lot of money,' that he had not been employed since 1983, that he had no income and no assets and relied for financial assistance upon his housemate and partner Rex Reimer. He did not even have a checking account in Wichita, though he did have one in Omaha. At that point he claimed that he owed Chapman about $10 million (£6.25 million).

The increasingly vertiginous (not to say absurd) sums of money promised against the Hahn *La Belle* reached new heights in 1996 when an 'Art Agreement' signed between Loucks and Chapman recognized and enumerated twenty-nine liens worth nearly $42 million (£28 million) on the picture. These included a lien for $21 million (£14 million) for J & A Enterprises, the company jointly owned by Chapman and his wife; $6 million (£4 million) to Loucks' partner, Rex Reimer; and an additional $1.5 million (£1 million) to Alice, Chapman's wife, on her own behalf. Jacqueline Hahn was to get $1 million (£667,000); Marjorie Hahn $1 million, and an additional sum of $350,000 (£233,000), after other liens were paid off. Some of the liens were for money advanced to help sell the picture – this was true of at least three of the creditors, Gary Marshik, Claudine Olson and Howard Farcus – though the sums of the liens were far in excess of the original loans. Other liens were rewards for working on the picture: van Dantzig's daughter was to receive $25,000 (£16,500); Frank Ruhemann $50,000 (£33,000); Patrick Bolan, a fingerprint expert, $100,000 (£67,000). However, many of the liens were for friends and family whose relation to the painting seems at best tangential, or to people who appear to have lent Loucks money. The entire proceeding seems to have been an exercise in *folie de grandeur*, in which a man with no assets at all, apart from a painting whose attribution was contentious and whose ownership was disputed, munificently dispensed a fortune among his creditors, friends and business partners, though the riches could only be disbursed if and when *La Belle* was finally sold.

The other effect of the Art Agreement was to increase the hold of Chapman on *La Belle*. This was enhanced in 2000 when Loucks conferred a 50 per cent ownership of the painting on Chapman, and finalized in June 2002 when Loucks, who was ill – he was to die of lung cancer in September of that year – consigned ownership to Chapman when the 'Leon L Loucks Irrevocable Trust' was set up to help him 'at time when GRANTOR [i.e. Loucks] is in dire health and financially unable to pay off medical and personal expenses and to increase [his] standard of living and remit payments to those who have assisted him over the many past years in making [his] life comfortable and enjoyable'. The sole listed asset of the trust was the Hahn *La Belle*. The trust also sketched out a new schedule of payments to be made on the sale of *La Belle* that added some new beneficiaries (including a number of members of the Chapman family) and reduced the amounts due to Loucks' creditors and those who had worked on the picture. When Loucks died, it must have seemed to Chapman that he had the Hahn painting well and truly locked up.

It is difficult to know how to interpret and understand the machinations that surrounded *La Belle* between the 1970s and the present. Loucks' involvement in the case seems to have come from either Harry or Marjorie, and to have been in part connected to the Wichita Hahns' desire to re-establish a claim on the picture that they had surrendered in the 1960s. Jacqueline Hahn and (according to her) her brother and mother repeatedly asked themselves why Harry had allowed himself to be 'taken in' by Loucks, who they came to see as deceptive if not plainly mendacious. Loucks himself was clearly not a man of either means or probity. He had a history of borrowing money and not repaying it. He had court judgements against him and at least one of his creditors believed him to be a fraudster. He was a fantasist who told people that he was about to inherit a fortune and that he was related to the Beech family, the rich and successful producers of light aircraft in Wichita. He repeatedly told Jacqueline Hahn that he was about to sell *La Belle*, producing excuse after excuse for why the deal fell through – the buyer died, got divorced, failed to turn up, lost the money and so on. He lied about his relationship with Andrée though, as Chapman has remarked, 'everyone was a relative to Leon'. But Loucks was useful to Harry Hahn because he served his purposes: he helped Hahn get back an interest, and he moved the centre of activity out of Europe, away from the West Coast and into the Midwest.

Loucks and then Chapman made repeated efforts to sell the picture, but seem to have been forced further and further down the art market food chain, dealing with wealthy but not knowledgeable collectors, quite a number of whom were not from the countries in which Old Master art was usually traded. As they made clear on the occasions when they borrowed money to sell the picture, they regarded them as 'investment opportunities' rather than loans, arguing that they had no obligation to return or repay their creditors until the investment was realized and *La Belle* sold. Given the problematic status of the picture in the eyes of the art world, these 'investments' began to look more and more of a lottery, a high-risk enterprise in which the probability of a return was extremely low, though, if it were to be realized, it would bring extremely large rewards. It is therefore not surprising that some of Chapman's clients looked a lot more like speculative investors than collectors of Old Master art.

However, even speculative investors want to guard against risk, and Loucks and Chapman's efforts to sell the painting were stymied by their inability to provide what many of their clients regarded as firm proof of the painting's attribution. Only one of Chapman's art experts, James Proctor, was prepared to give an unconditional statement about the painting, and he had no real power in the art market. As one buyer, who pulled out for lack of satisfactory evidence of ownership and attribution, commented, if the picture really was a Leonardo why weren't buyers and auction houses like Christie's and Sotheby's clamouring to handle a sale? The only way that first Loucks and then Chapman would secure a sale of *La Belle* as a legitimate Leonardo was by having it authenticated by experts whose judgement was trusted by museum directors and rich collectors. This they often refused to do. Certain institutions, like the Getty Museum, or individuals, like the Leonardo scholar, Carlo Pedretti, were repeatedly blacklisted as being 'against' the painting or as part of the art-world conspiracy that had begun with Joseph Duveen and Bernard Berenson. At the same time the liens that had been piled up on the picture meant that there was a positive disincentive for Loucks and Chapman to compromise their position and sell *La Belle* as what Professor Martin Kemp had described as a 'nice picture' but not a Leonardo.

For much of the time that Loucks and Chapman held *La Belle*, Andrée and Jacqueline watched passively as events unfolded, talking to Leon Loucks at regular intervals on the telephone. By the 1980s both women were in poor health and Andrée, in particular, was prone to anxiety attacks provoked by the changing news about the painting. She often talked about *La Belle* to her daughter and complained about its intrusion into her life. Every time a possible sale was mooted she had sleepless nights and then, when Loucks announced another aborted sale, she became ill, often with stomach complaints and vomiting. Neither woman was mobile: Andrée had crushed vertebra and Jacqueline continued to suffer from problems with her vision that plagued her for years. Harry Junior and his wife, who lived in the other half of a duplex the family owned in Ranco Park in West Los Angeles, wanted little to do with the painting and would not deal with Loucks, who Harry Junior believed to be fundamentally dishonest. The family lived out a singularly French existence made up of family meals (with lobster for special occasions to remind them of Dinard), a long list of ailments and regular visits to celebrate Mass. It is clear that Andrée now resented the painting and had little interest in it, but still hoped for a sale. The family took no action to secure their interest in the picture (they had no real knowledge of what was happening in Kansas) and, though they grew increasingly suspicious of Loucks, still looked upon him as their last chance.

In 2002, after Leon Loucks' death, Jacqueline Hahn tried to recover *La Belle* which she believed to be her property. She was met with promises of sales and money, and the repeated prevarications that had always characterized her dealings with Loucks and were now being repeated with Chapman. Running out of patience, in 2005 Jacqueline brought an action in the California courts against Chapman to secure the return of her painting. During the legal tussle that followed, and after Jacqueline's attorneys had taken a deposition and examined documents in Chapman's office in Omaha, a settlement was agreed between them and Chapman's lawyer, but Chapman, after much procrastination, reneged on the agreement. Hahn's lawyers then sought to get the court to enforce the settlement. Chapman responded by seeking to quash her initiative but his motion was denied by the court. On 30 September 2008 the case was settled under the terms of a confidential agreement mediated between the contending parties. The agreement has to be executed by March 2009.

The arrival of the Hahn version of *La Belle Ferronnière* in the United States in 1920 had been attended by a blaze of publicity and had triggered one of the great art trials of the twentieth century. The authenticity of *La Belle* may have been a matter of deep dispute, but at least the painting was in the public eye. In recent years she has lived a furtive existence – rarely seen, not publicly examined, the potential currency in a series of obscure financial transactions. It is a pity that such an important picture, the subject of so much debate, is no longer seen in the plain light of day. Disputes over her ownership and the continued belief of her current holder that the conspiratorial collusion of the major actors in the art world denies the painting its true status mean that she continues to be incarcerated. Let us hope that whatever the outcome, the case of *Hahn versus Chapman* will bring *La Belle* out into the open, where she can be examined and appreciated not just by art experts but also by a larger public.

Afterword

In June 2008 I arranged a meeting with Jack Chapman that I hoped would produce my first sighting of *La Belle Ferronnière*, the painting whose history had absorbed me so much and for so long. Flying into Omaha in the middle of one of those late afternoon electrical storms that punctuate the Midwestern summer did not seem like an auspicious beginning to my venture. The small plane bobbed and bounced in the fierce winds, tight-lipped passengers gripped the armrests of their seats as brilliant branches of forked lightning periodically illuminated the city in the distance. But I had other worries: this was not my first trip to see *La Belle* and Jack Chapman; he'd shown me bundles of documents about the history and provenance of the painting, but I had not succeeded in seeing the picture itself. Returning to Omaha seemed like a way to bring the story to an end – at least for me – though another part of me knew that any such expectation was not realistic.

I was apprehensive because I understood Chapman's reluctance to reveal the whereabouts of the painting. I knew that his claim of ownership was under dispute and that he was not winning his struggle with Jacqueline Hahn. With all this litigation, where was the picture? Was it really still in Omaha or had it been spirited away? Was it in Chapman's possession or was it being held, as it had been in the past, by someone else as security for a debt?

On each occasion when I have talked to Jack Chapman he had asked me the same question: 'Are you for it, or are you against it?' Did I think, he was asking, that 'his' painting was a genuine Leonardo or did I, like most experts in the official art world of university departments, museums and auction houses, take the view that it was a copy? Jacqueline Hahn had asked me the very same question. The proprietors, guardians and owners of this picture, I had discovered, inhabited a Manichean world of allies and enemies; they also tended to see those who did not support 'their' painting as part of a conspiracy or plot to exclude it from its rightful place in the oeuvre of Leonardo da Vinci.

This was a rather odd question, I reflected, as I headed for my Omaha hotel. Why should someone who is not an expert in Renaissance art, much less an expert on Leonardo, and who has never seen the picture in question, but only a rather poor repro-duction, be in any way competent to make a judgement about its authenticity? This made me think that the question was not so much about the painting and more about my attitude towards the art world: did I believe it to be populated by genteel con artists and tricksters – dealers, experts, curators and the like – who skil-fully manipulate opinion for profit and prestige, or did it perform the laudable function of identifying, preserving, displaying and sometimes selling objects which we value for their aesthetic power or as part of our cultural heritage? (Maybe, I ruefully thought, it does both.) When the holders of the painting put the issue like this, I realized, it had the advantage of making what a cynical observer would see as a privately advantageous but rather dubious act – passing off a copy (if such it is) as an original and thereby making a lot of money – into a much worthier accomplishment, using the painting in a civic-minded fashion to blow the whistle on the machinations of the art world. But, of course, I never pointed this out to Mr Chapman, who would probably have given me short shrift. Instead, I responded to his question by observing that I was neither for nor against the picture, but neutral, which I was bound to be until I saw it. I hoped that this comment would provoke him into showing me the painting.

Maybe it worked, maybe it didn't, but eventually, after some well-orchestrated delay and prevarication, Chapman drove me on the following afternoon into downtown Omaha to see the painting. The manager of the storage facility took us up to the space in which *La Belle* (along with a number of other paintings) is kept. As we entered a brightly lit room, he lingered nearby to ensure that nothing untoward occurred. In the centre of the windowless space was an easel covered by a red velvet cloth. As I glanced at it, Andy Warhol's images of the electric chair flashed through my mind. Chapman stepped forward to remove the velvet and then the wax-paper cover in which the picture is wrapped; it was like the moment in a magic show when the magician reveals his trick.

So here, at an address in Omaha that I am legally prevented from revealing, I finally see the Hahn *La Belle*. The picture is small, a little over twenty-one inches by sixteen, and seems very small when displayed, as it was there, without a frame. As I stared at it, I was reminded of what the art historian Martin Kemp said when he was in Omaha some fifteen years earlier: it's a seductive, 'nice' picture, its bright colours and rich hues largely unfaded. Certainly, it shines out when compared to the other works of art dotted round the room that had come from Harry Hahn via his second wife, Marjorie, and the late Leon Loucks. I thought about Joseph Duveen's testimony in the 1929 New York trial, about the way Lawrence Miller, the Hahns' lawyer, had goaded the English dealer into a splenetic denunciation of the painting. You could see that, to the untutored eye, it would be extraordinary (and apparently self-serving) to denounce something as 'ugly' and 'crude' with 'balloon-like' features that was superficially so pleasing.

I turned the painting over and could see not only the signature of Hacquin who had transferred the picture to canvas in 1777, but also the inscription of Georges Sortais, the French expert who had attributed *La Belle* to Leonardo when the painting was still in the possession of Louise de Montaut back in 1917. I noticed that the portrait has been on canvas more than once; you can see, as several experts have pointed out earlier, the edges of the old canvas beneath the new. Turning it back over, I also noticed that the jewel and band on the forehead of *La Belle* were painted rather poorly and had clearly been added after the rest of picture was completed – a sign for Duveen's experts that the picture was a palpable copy, though Harry Hahn always maintained that these details had been added much later by another artist. The most troubling and disconcerting part of the picture is the bottom where a great swath of off-white paint implies, but somehow does not form, a balustrade. Its imprecision seems counter to the painstaking technique of Leonardo's painting. But again, the Hahns maintained that this was a later addition, painted on when Hacquin removed the picture from wood to canvas. Then there are the eyes: as some of the earlier experts have commented, there is something peculiarly lifeless in one eye. I also felt that the left side of the profile of *La*

Belle has an oddly overworked boundary that seems crude and repetitious.

Jack Chapman grew a bit restless. He said that the eyes of *La Belle*, like those of the *Mona Lisa*, follow you as you move around the room; he reiterated his view that the picture we were examining was much more beautiful than the painting of *La Belle Ferronnière* in the Louvre. He seemed impatient to leave. I complimented the picture's beauty, but he was now more eager to tell me about the other works of art in the storage space, especially a large, damaged ceiling painting that he claims is by Tiepolo. The visit was over.

Looking back at it, I'm reminded of the question with which we started. 'When you look at a picture how do you know who painted it; how do you know that it is a great work of art?' The answer, of course, is that, as Helmut Ruhemann reminded the audiences on his American lecture tour, we (the general public who are not 'experts') do not know. This isn't to say that lay men and women can't appreciate and aren't moved by some masterpieces; they often are. But they are also inclined to like art that, in the eyes of experts, is neither original nor great. This is the source of the anxiety so many people feel about art. Art is supposed to have special properties that make it different from other images and commodities. An appreciation of that difference, of the values that art gives us – and this has been especially said in the twentieth century about Old Master art – is something that makes us, individually and collectively, better: more refined, more civilized, more cultured. It's this understanding (along with a lot of other stuff – pork bellies, railroads and steel – that we'll put aside for a moment) that prompted the foundation of public institutions like New York's

Metropolitan Museum and Kansas City's Nelson–Atkins Museum. It is this value that fuelled the Old Master art market. There's a strong sense that we ought to be able to appreciate art and that if we don't we lack something. In the corridors of the great art galleries and in the showrooms of the leading dealers, works of art have an aura that can seem intimidating and hard to understand. We know they are important – that's why they are there – but we don't always know why. We are forced, in a way that clearly makes many people uncomfortable, to place our trust in experts – museum curators, art historians, dealers – and depend on their skills to tell us why.

We, the non-specialist public, have a range of responses to this situation. The most common is passive trust. The throngs of tourists that make their pilgrimage to such shrines of culture as the Uffizi in Florence and the Prado in Madrid, or who push their way into the grossly overcrowded rooms in the Louvre where the paintings of Leonardo and his school are hung, willingly accept that what is placed before them are some of the finest artworks of western culture. Very few of these visitors can tell a Titian from a Giorgione or a Leonardo from a Boltraffio and many, frankly, don't care. They are aware of the huge apparatus called art history, but often cover their ignorance of it by claiming they know what they like and what they like is good. They are a bit like the apologists for Old Master art in 1930s Kansas City who took the populist view that somehow really great art will inevitably impress its greatness on the public. Almost always running in tandem with the public's need to trust because of its lack of expertise is the sense that art experts are not really necessary in a world where the great work of art shines through. To further complicate the picture, the extraordinarily high value placed on works of art – in 1999, for instance, the Hahn *La Belle* (if genuine) was appraised at $125 million (£78 million) – and the extraordinary iconic importance of certain works in national collections are sources of wonder, incredulity and sometimes scepticism.

The creators, guardians and beneficiaries of the art world inhabit a realm that most of us view from outside, like children pressing our noses to the window and peering in on a grown-up world, which is why we like it so much when the experts prove fallible. The public and the press love a good fake, a good forgery, the sight of an assured (not to say arrogant) expert being proved wrong and being forced, if briefly, to eat humble pie. It doesn't really matter that most fakes and errors are exposed by those from inside the art world, that, in some sense, their detection shows that the art system and its experts are doing the job they are supposed to do, discriminating good from bad, true from false. The focus is on the fallibility of the expert and therefore the apparent frailty of expertise. The famous museum director, Wilhelm von Bode, probably did more than anyone else to develop the great Old Master collections in Germany, but was always remembered for his supposed error over the Leonardo *Flora*.

When someone from outside the art world seems to challenge its experts successfully, or seeks to become part of the hallowed community of the owners of Old Master art, it is not uncommon to find many others from outside the art world cheering from the sidelines, just as so many in the press in the 1920s cheered on the ordinary Midwesterner and his pretty French bride. It is also to be expected that in such circumstances the art world tends to close ranks and to try to exclude the intruders. As I thought about the

Hahn case, I was struck by the uncanny parallels between the experiences of Harry and Andrée Hahn and those of Teri Horton, a retired truck driver with an eighth-grade education who in 1991 bought a painting she claims is a Jackson Pollock in a thrift store. If Harry Hahn was the 'Boy from the Corn Belt', Teri Horton was, according to the *New York Times*, 'One Feisty Woman' who 'takes on the art world'. As in the Hahn case, Horton's claim pits forensics against the connoisseurial eye. Peter Paul Biro, a Canadian restorer and forensics expert, claims to have matched a fingerprint on Horton's painting to one on a paint pot in Jackson Pollock's studio on Long Island. Pollock experts and Thomas Hoving, the former director of the Metropolitan Museum, dismiss the picture on aesthetic grounds and disregard the scientific evidence.

Horton is supported by Tod Volpe, a formerly successful art dealer who was imprisoned for raising money using works of art he did not own, and who has a syndicate that is trying to sell the painting. In his kiss-and-tell memoir, *Framed*, Volpe identifies Joseph Duveen as his hero and reveals some of the nefarious practices of the art world. Like the Hahn case, featured in the 1993 *The Two Belles* broadcast in the television series, *Every Picture tells a Story*, Horton's painting has been the subject of a documentary film, *Who the Fuck is Jackson Pollock?* It began, according to the *New York Times*, as a story 'about how forensics may be starting to nudge the entrenched tradition of connoisseurship from its perch in the world of art authentication', but ended up, according to its director Harry Moses, as 'a story about class in America . . . a story of the art world looking down its collective nose at this woman with an eighth-grade education'. The snobbery that Hahns' attorneys used so effectively against Duveen and his experts in 1929 is very much alive and well in Moses' film which skilfully pits cigarette-smoking, hard-drinking, sentimental but straight-taking Teri Horton against the preciousness, affectation and arrogance of Manhattan aesthetes.

Ordinary folk, common sense, science and objectivity: these are always the elements pitted against the privileged, wealthy, 'illusory world' as Volpe puts it in Moses' film, of galleries, museums, collectors and critics. The attack on the art world is usually democratic or populist. It takes the argument that has so often been made about great art in the age of mass society, that it is a duty to make it available to all, and turns it against an art world which is necessarily concerned with discrimination and distinction. It takes very seriously another fiction of the art world, that art somehow inhabits a realm of purity, and uses this as a critique of how art lives in that world, even while, in a quite contradictory fashion, it is fascinated by the money and publicity that surrounds it. And it calls on science and forensics, both because they seem to offer certainty and because they appear 'objective', not dependent on the singular skills of the expert, but on tests that can be replicated by anyone who follows the correct procedures. More often than not, when I've told people about the Hahn *La Belle*, they have responded with the ringing assertion that nowadays we must have the technical means to adjudicate its authenticity. I concede that techniques have got better but science can only have a negative effect, demonstrating conclusively that the painting is not a Leonardo, but it cannot alone prove that it is. We are impatient about uncertainty and ambiguity, the waywardness of much art, because we want it to follow the paths we have set for it. In almost every instance what is demanded is a sort of simplicity and clarity that many believe will be the gift of a technically superior future.

Of course, we all love good mysteries, but we prefer to know their endings.

As I ponder the role of the many characters affected by the Hahn *La Belle*, I'm struck by how oddly reluctant the Hahns, and even Loucks and Chapman, have been to relinquish their art. Like Teri Horton, who has apparently turned down several million dollars for her Pollock, they have often behaved in ways that seem at odds with the task of selling the picture: not asking the right experts, altering the painting's price, failing to provide documentation. The asking price of the Hahn *La Belle* has fluctuated enormously over the years, often reflecting the current financial state of its vendors, but it is surprising how often Harry or Andrée Hahn just stopped short of selling the painting. For its owners, art has functions beyond the financial and the aesthetic. Of course, from the point of view of the art world the work of art is supposed to do only a very limited number of things – create a special (aesthetic) experience in the viewer, possibly memorialize a lost age or set of values – and its efficacy in doing these is what makes it unique and also gives it market value, making it collectable. It is about transmuting transcendence into dollars and cents, a magic, as we have seen, often effected by the expert.

The Hahn *La Belle* purports to be such an object, but it also does much more. One of its most important effects is to enable its owners/vendors to mingle with an elite. It grants access to the art world from which most people, lacking adequate money or knowledge, are excluded. No one was going to be very interested in Harry Hahn (or, for that matter, Jack Chapman) once they no longer had the painting. *La Belle* put Andrée Hahn's (admittedly beautiful) face on the front pages of newspapers all over the

Western world. The painting took Harry and Frank Glenn to Hollywood, where they rubbed shoulders with famous producers and stars like Walt Disney and Edward G. Robinson. She introduced tycoon J.C. Nichols to Joseph Duveen. She focused the world's art press (albeit briefly) on Kansas City. And, of course, she did much more. She furnished new armour for Mau van Dantzig in his crusade against subjective art criticism, she helped Helmut Ruhemann propagate his view of connoisseurship. She even helped Leon Loucks borrow money and (sometimes) kept his creditors at bay. She made Loucks and Chapman business partners in a way that would never have happened had she not existed. Without the presence of *La Belle*, I doubt if I would ever have visited Omaha.

Not that the effect of the picture was always positive. Duveen suffered more than he gained because of his association with *La Belle*; Kenneth Clark found her embarrassing. The painting was often the subject of dispute between Harry and Andrée Hahn. Jacqueline Hahn's diaries attest to the pain the picture caused her mother, especially in her later years, and she herself believes that it blighted her mother's life by repeatedly raising expectations that could not be fulfilled. *La Belle*, we might conclude, has been a pretty unruly creature, ornery, errant, wilful and often badly behaved. Certainly, she has always been much more than an art object, whether as a copy or an original. And so an art-historical story that only dealt with the picture's authenticity would inevitably leave out much of *La Belle*'s effect on the world. Anthropomorphizing the Hahn painting is in some ways a conceit, though when I do so, I follow in the footsteps of many who became acquainted with the picture and, though they may have doubted her authenticity, never doubted her power.

As I ruminate on these issues in my overheated hotel room in Omaha, I'm struck by how difficult it has been to get away from her and how I have been frustrated by the impossibility of being able to resolve the story of *La Belle* to my satisfaction. Seeing the picture was in some respects an empty gesture. I learned certain things about the painting by standing before *La Belle*, but perhaps I learned more about my own absence of expertise. *La Belle* was looking at the wrong person if she ever wanted proper authentication. The features I examined were ones I had read about in the testimony for the trial, chiefly that of Duveen's experts. I was conscious that my view of the painting was strongly informed by what they had said. At the same time merely looking at *La Belle* revealed nothing to me about the properties of its pigments, the evidence that so strongly informed the decision of the majority of the New York jurors in 1929. I was just another of those people who stand before a portrait and ask themselves, 'Is it a masterpiece? Is it a Leonardo? How do I know?' – questions that are made all the more difficult because the Hahn *La Belle* is not surrounded by the people and institutions of the art world in which we normally place our trust.

What I wanted in that storage place in Omaha was skilled help. I felt that my entire experience with the Hahn *La Belle* had convinced me that what was needed – in this case and many others – was a better expertise. Not a more scientific one, as so many people hoped, but one that bore more than a passing resemblance to the vision of Helmut Ruhemann, in which the admittedly subjective talents of the trained and experienced eye worked together with the 'objective' expertise of science. Such cooperation cannot eliminate uncertainty but it can improve probability.

Afterword

As we have seen, there has been a long tradition of hostility between science and connoisseurship that continues to the present day. Duveen and Berenson were profoundly suspicious and sometimes arrogantly dismissive of the scientific investigation of paintings, fearful of their intrusion into the connoisseur's world. What they were concerned to protect was as much a culture as a technique, one that, for both commercial and aesthetic purposes, had to foreground unsullied notions of 'genius', 'spirit', 'taste', 'beauty' and 'civilization' and locate them in individual works of art. These, as Duveen and Berenson understood too well, were not values that could be presented to a wealthy client or collector by a man in a lab coat. But there was also the fear that the scientist might undermine the credibility of the connoisseur's judgement, not only by challenging his view of individual works of art but the very 'method', if such it was, by which his decisions were made.

The Duveen apparatus, the system of selling Old Master art that excited and excites the wrath of the likes of Harry Hahn and Jack Chapman, was designed to convince a small and extremely wealthy clientele of the authenticity and value of the paintings it offered for sale. In most respects the connoisseurship that sustained it was not so different from that which had been practised in earlier centuries. More systematic, more attentive to detail and in this sense more 'scientific', as Morelli had argued, but at bottom it remained a subjective technique dependent on the eye. This had been good enough for the great Italian, French, Spanish and English collectors from the age of Leonardo onwards, and remained so for the new American collectors of the nineteenth and twentieth centuries. However, the growth in public museum-going and art-historical education, together with the extensive vicarious participation in the art market through the newspaper press, created a different constituency of people who, like me before the Hahn *La Belle*, wanted to know if what they were seeing was a genuine masterpiece and great work of art. Most of the time, as I have said, the public takes the pronouncements of the art world on trust, but, when all is flung into doubt, people feel the need for an explanation that does not depend on individual judgement or intangible intuition. Ruhemann was right when he commented that the scientific investigation of pictures had been helped by court trials about the authenticity of art. Their notion of proof, one that the public understood, demanded a more rigorous, more objective expertise. Duveen thought he could use the court-room and the mass press to project the relatively enclosed art world and connoisseurship on to a much bigger screen. What he didn't understand was that the different venues and different audiences create different expectations.

The relationship between connoisseurship and science has, of course, changed since 1929. The place of scientific investigation is more prominent and accepted, despite the enduring scepticism of the likes of Thomas Hoving and the continuing rivalry between curators and conservators. It is increasingly common to have teams of scholars and experts, both art-historical and scientific, collaborating on the task of investigating an artist's *oeuvre*. Some of the social barriers to proper scholarly investigation have been removed as the art world has become more professionalized. But there is, in my own view, some way to go. Working on this book, I was often astonished at the cavalier (and, as far as I could see, largely groundless) judgements made by members of the art world, comments based more on fitting in with a consensus or on hearsay than any careful deliberation or consideration of evidence.

Repeatedly, I was told that the Hahn *La Belle* was a 'tainted picture' and that that opinion therefore made it next to worthless or, at least, unsellable. All of which is true, but was a tactic of expulsion rather than one that engaged with the issues the picture raised.

This is not, in any way, to take the side of those who have promoted the case of the Hahn *La Belle Ferronnière*, which has attracted more than its fair share of schemers and promoters who have been economical with the truth, and who have on many occasions obstructed a proper examination of the painting. What I hope for – and maybe I am being very naive about this – is a serious examination of the painting by experts of more than one persuasion. This has not happened since 1923 in Paris and there are no doubt many both 'for or against' *La Belle Ferronnière*, in Chapman's phrase, who would not think it worthwhile. However, it would make me feel that, even if it produced no decisive outcome, one of the most controversial paintings to appear on the twentieth-century Old Master art market had at least received its due.

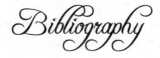

Introduction

The best writing on the Hahn affair is an excellent article, Andrew Decker, 'The Multimillion-Dollar Belle', *Art News*, summer 1985, pp 87–97. See also my two articles, 'The Lure of Leonardo', in *The Lure of the Object*, ed. Stephen Melville, Clark Studies in the Visual Arts, New Haven, 2005, pp 3–14 and 'Art and Science: A Da Vinci Detective Story', *Engineering and Science*, no. 1/1, 2005, pp 32–41.

Chapter 1

There is an abundance of excellent material on the late nineteenth- and early twentieth-century United States and the art scene. Quite apart from the novels of Henry James and Edith Wharton, there are excellent books on the art market, most notably Flaminia Genari Santori, *The Melancholy of Masterpieces: Old Master Paintings in America 1900–1914*, Milan, 2003. For prices and sales, see the classic Gerald Reitlinger, *The Economics of Taste*, 3 vols, London, 1961–70. Three books that in their different ways cover the American scene are Jonathan Freedman, *Professions of Taste: Henry James, British Aestheticism and Commodity Culture*, Pala Alto, CA, 1990; Remy Gilbert Saisselin, *The Bourgeois and the Bibelot*, New Brunswick, NJ, 1984; and Robert B. Stein, *John Ruskin and Aesthetic*

Thought in America, 1840–1900, Cambridge, MA, 1968. By far the best general work I have read on the period is Alan Trachtenberg, *The Incorporation of America: Culture and Society in the Gilded Age*, New York, 2007. There is no better introduction to the art demi-monde of the period than René Gimpel's waspish diaries, available in English as René Gimpel, *Diary of an Art Dealer*, trans. John Rosenberg, London, 1986.

Chapter 2

Probably the best general work on connoisseurship is Carol Gibson-Wood's *Studies in the Theory of Connoisseurship from Vasari to Morelli*, New York, 1988. The best English edition of Morelli's works is *Italian Painters: Critical Studies of their Works*, trans. Constance Ffoulkes, 2 vols, London, 1892–3. Cavalcaselle is the subject of Donata Levi's excellent, *Cavalcaselle: Il Pioniere Della Conservazione Dell'arte Italiana*, Turin, 1989. On Berenson, see the official two-volume biography, Ernest Samuels, *Bernard Berenson: The Making of a Connoisseur*, Cambridge, MA, 1979, *Bernard Berenson: The Making of a Legend*, in collaboration with Jayne Newcomer Samuels, Cambridge, MA, 1987. See also Meryle Secrest, *Being Bernard Berenson*, New York, 1979; Colin Simpson, *The Partnership: The Secret Association of Bernard Berenson and Joseph Duveen*, London, 1987; and David Alan Brown, *Berenson and the Connoisseurship of Italian Painting*, exh. cat., National Gallery of Art, Washington, DC, 1979. More generally, see Max J. Friedländer, *On Art and Connoisseurship*, trans. Tancred Borenius, London, 1942, and, amongst the large body of literature on connoisseurship, Carlo Ginzburg, 'Clues: Morelli, Freud and Sherlock Holmes', in *The Sign of the Three: Dupin, Holmes, Pierce*, ed. Umberto Eco and Thomas Sebeok, Bloomington, IN, 1988, and Karen Lang, 'Encountering the Object' in *The Lure of the Object*, ed. Stephen Melville, Clark Studies in the Visual Arts, New Haven, 2005.

Chapter 3

The reputation of Leonardo can be followed in two excellent books: Richard A. Turner, *Inventing Leonardo*, Berkeley, 1994, and Donald Sassoon, *Mona Lisa: The History of the World's Most Famous Painting*, London, 2001.

Chapter 4

Material on the Hahns comes from manuscripts and photographs in the private possession of Jacqueline Hahn. Material on Joseph Duveen and his firm comes chiefly from the enormous Duveen archive deposited in the library of the Getty Research Institute in Brentwood, California. When I began this project, six newspaper cutting books on the Hahn Leonardo were still in the possession of the Library of the Sterling and Francine Clark Art Institute in Williamstown, Massachusetts. These have now been acquired by the Getty. Joseph Duveen was the subject of a famous biography by S.N. Berman, originally published as a series of articles in the *New Yorker* and then published as *Duveen*, New York, 1952. The book was reissued as S.N. Behrman, *Duveen: The Most Spectacular Art Dealer of All Time*, New York, 2003. This wonderfully anecdotal but frequently inaccurate study has been superseded by Meryle Secrest, *Duveen: A Life in Art*, New York, 2004.

Chapter 5

The events of the 1920s are best followed through the very large body of material in the Duveen archive and through Harry Hahn's *The Rape of La Belle,* Kansas City, 1946. I was also able to consult the complete transcript of the trial in the possession of Jack Chapman of Omaha.

Chapter 6

Of the large body of work dealing with fakes, copies attribution and the art market I have found especially helpful Mark Jones (ed.), *Fake? The Art of Deception,* London, 1990; Thomas Hoving, *False Impressions,* New York, 1996; Frank Arnau, *Three Thousand Years of Deception,* London, 1961; and Denis Dutton, *The Forger's Art,* Berkeley, 1983. On the Wacker forgeries see Walter Feilchenfeldt, 'Van Gogh Fakes: The Wacker affair, with an Illustrated Catalogue of the Forgeries', *Simiolus,* vol. 19, no. 4, 1989, pp 289–316. The best book on van Meegeren is still John Godley, *The Master Forger: The Story of Han van Meegeren,* London, 1951. Frank Wynne, *I Was Vermeer,* London, 2006, is the most recent (and accessible) telling of his tale. P. Coremans, *Van Meegeren's Faked Vermeers and De Hooghs,* London, 1949, presents the scientific evidence of the court. Irving Wallace, 'The Man who Swindled Goering', *Saturday Evening Post,* no. 219, no. 28, 1947, is the article that made the case famous in the English speaking world.

Chapter 7

On Kansas City in this period see, amongst others, Harry Haskell, *Boss-Busters and Sin Hounds, Kansas City and Its Star,* Columbia, MO, 2007, Henry C. Haskell and Richard B. Fowler, *City of the Future: A Narrative History of KC 1850–1950,* Kansas City, MO, 1950. On J.C. Nichols see the rather hagiographic Robert Pearson and Brad Pearson, *The J.C. Nichols Chronicle: The Authorized Story of the Man, his Company, and his Legacy, 1880–1994*, Kansas City, MO, 1994. See also on the web www.umkc.edu/WHMCKC/publications/JCN/JCNintro.htm for materials on Nichols and his business. Kristie C. Wolferman, *The Nelson–Atkins Museum of Art: Culture Comes to Kansas City*, Columbia, MO, 1993, is an excellent study of a fine museum.

Chapter 8

Most of this chapter was made possible by access to the Frank Glenn archive in the possession of his widow, Ardis Glenn. I have to thank her for permission to use and cite material. As an ardent book-lover and collector, she has conserved the papers of her husband and of their book business with great care. Harry Hahn, *The Rape of La Belle*, Kansas City, MO, 1946, is, of course, essential reading. On Thomas Hart Benton see Henry Adams, *Thomas Hart Benton: An American Original*, New York, 1989, and Thomas Hart Benton, *An Artist in America*, Kansas City, MO, 1983.

Chapter 9

The bulk of the materials for the story of van Dantzig and Helmut Ruhemann comes from their respective family archives. The Van Dantzig archive is now deposited in the Netherlands Institute for Art History at the Hague. The Ruhemann archive is about to be deposited at the Hamilton Kerr Institute at Cambridge, UK. See also Helmut Ruhemann, *The Cleaning of Paintings: Problems and Potentialities*, London, 1968, and M.M. Van Dantzig, *Pictology: An Analytical Method for the Attribution and Evaluation of Pictures*, Leiden, 1973.

Chapter 10

The materials for this chapter come from the transcript of the deposition of Jack Chapman and accompanying exhibits, taken 20 January 2006 in the Case of *Hahn versus Chapman*, case number BC 33804, Superior Court of the State of California in the County of Los Angeles, and from the diaries and materials in the possession of Jacqueline Hahn.

Index

Index

Index